Here Comes China

Here Comes China

One American's Experiences in the People's Republic, 1979-2018

Dr. Melford A. Wilson, Jr.

Dedication

To my Chinese friends and colleagues

Contents

Introduction

T HE TIMING WAS EXTRAORDINARY. SO MANY PIECES
came together in the late 1970s: just as the Cultural Revolution ended and Deng Xiaoping and his like-minded, somewhat less ideological colleagues were allowed back from exile
in the vast Chinese countryside, I was becoming a tenured
professor of International Relations at Winthrop College—now
Winthrop University—in Rock Hill, South Carolina. Just as
this new Chinese leadership considered opening up the country to receive professional, expert assistance with their universities and industries, I was establishing myself as someone who
could be considered just such an expert. I had lived in or traveled through India, Pakistan, Afghanistan, Japan, Hong Kong,
and Taiwan on my journey toward becoming an Asian Studies
specialist, receiving State Department funding and a Fulbright
fellowship along the way.

Forty years have passed since those pieces all came together,
and I have traveled to the People's Republic of China more than

fifty times over the course of those decades. My travels never grew stale, because with each trip, I found the constantly and readily apparent changes, modernizations, urbanization, and development of infrastructure to be startling. I have seen these "Professional Years" of China's growth from their tentative beginnings, when people were still hesitant to believe that the Cultural Revolution was really over, to now, when the philosophy of granting experts with privileges is being reconsidered and challenged by China's current leadership. My career, and China's experiment with modernization via opening the country to foreign experts and educating their own impressive cohort of professionals, overlapped almost exactly.

———————

Before all that, though, China was my forbidden fruit, remaining just out of reach. My aunt, Mary O. Rice, had been a Methodist missionary in China in the 1930s and 1940s, and her stories of life in Shanghai, Suzhou, and even Mongolia were my first introduction to China. I was fascinated by her experiences during these tumultuous years for the country—characterized by battles with Japan for control from outside, and then from within between the Nationalists and the Communists. I remember my aunt recounting a tale of how once, when she was pregnant, she was chased across a field and into a stand of trees by a Japanese fighter plane that fired at her as she ran. Even that didn't deter her; she and my uncle Ed stayed in China as long as they could.

When I was in graduate school at American University, studying International Relations, I took courses under wonderful Chinese scholars and became good friends with the professor Michael Lindsay, Baron Lindsay of Birker, and his wife Hsiao

Li, both of whom lived and fought with Mao Zedong in Yan'an during the Revolution. Later, during my first year of teaching at Winthrop, I received a grant to found an institute on "Modern China." There, we hosted the top scholars in the country for a three-week seminar that included the first U.S. showing of the 1965 epic Chinese film The East Is Red, a dramatization of the history of the Chinese Revolution and its Communist Party under Mao Zedong.

Like everyone else, I watched with keen interest as Zhou Enlai, the first Premier of the People's Republic, and Richard Nixon's national security advisor Henry Kissinger made tentative gestures toward diplomatic relations that ultimately led to a meeting between Nixon and Mao. And yet the country itself remained closed off to foreigners like me. Once, during a trip to India, I hiked up to a Chinese border crossing, and later, when my wife, Janet, and I traveled to Hong Kong in 1970, I rode the local bus to the border and peered across, but those ventures were as close as I could get. I was an Asian Studies specialist who couldn't enter the largest country in Asia.

For those readers who might not be that familiar with China, the territory we now know as the People's Republic of China is about the same size as western Europe or the United States, but it has over two thousand years of history of having a centralized governmental system—with a few periods of division— based on a central belief system, a common ideology, and a common written language. This central government was divided into regional subsystems that paid deference to the central government. Although China was invaded several times, the invaders soon came to accept the prevailing set of organizational and belief systems.

When the Communists gained control of China in 1949, they brought with them a system based on the teaching of Mao Zedong. While might seem like a radical change, Mao's teachings in fact are a combination of all the basics listed above, but with different definitions of some of the points. Specifically, the ideology espoused by Mao is a blend of the traditional Chinese thoughts of Confucius and Daoism, combined with Marxism and a heavy dose of Maoism—Mao's own original thinking, of course. An example of this combined philosophy is Mao's view of history. The traditional Chinese view of history is that it is cyclical, while Marx's view is characterized by various periods with different classes that remain in conflict until there is a single classless society. Mao combined both, believing in the cyclical nature of history but also in class conflict. His classless society was a merging of the peasant class, the proletariat, and—in contrast to previous Communist theorists—the military.

During the three decades between 1949, when the People's Republic of China was established, to 1978-79, when Deng Xiaoping took control of the Party and, thus, the country, China's history was marked with stark changes and drastic, sometimes violent upheaval involving a series of campaigns—most notably, the Hundred Flowers Campaign, The Great Leap Forward, and The Cultural Revolution.

From 1966 to 1977, the extremist wing of the Communist Party, known as the Red Guard, tried to destroy every Western influence and every notion of what was traditionally "Chinese" during the horrific and chaotic Cultural Revolution. A good friend of mine watched the Red Guard beat his mother to death because she played classical music. Every one of my many Chinese friends has an equally gruesome tale. Universities were closed, books were burned, and professors were killed or sent to work in the countryside for "re-education." All schools taught the Little Red Book of Mao's sayings exclusively. China was so isolated during this time that the only nations it had diplomatic relations with were North Korea and Albania.

After Zhou Enlai and Mao Zedong died, in the same year, struggles developed as more rational leaders tried to gain power and punish the leaders of the Cultural Revolution. Order began to be restored under the pragmatic leadership of Deng Xiaoping, and China finally began to open to the outside world.

———————

Perhaps one of the most important themes of my experiences recounted here in this book is the traditional Chinese understanding of everything having a dual nature—yin and yang. In recent history, this idea of dual nature has frequently been a division between the ideological and the pragmatic. Thus, in each city, province, factory, university, or government business, two heads exist for every organization: one person is the Communist Party head, and the other is the management head—called "the expert" in China, but Westerners more often translate it as "the professional."

From the point when the Communists took over until the end of the Cultural Revolution, in 1977, the Party head was always the more powerful leader in organizations, dictating what should and what should not be done. The professional leader took direction from the Party leader, who in turn took his (and it was, more often than not, a "him") instruction from up the Party ladder all the way to the head of the Communist Party in Beijing.

In contrast, from 1979 until 2016, the person in control at each organization was the professional head. This book focuses

on the changes made in China during this time, which I call the
"Professional Years"—a time that happens to correspond with
my experiences in China. The years 1976 to 1978 were a period
of transition from Party control to professional control, and recently—from 2016 to 2019—the transition has been upended,
with the Party reasserting control more and more under China's
new "leader for life," Xi Jinping.

What follows in these pages is part memoir and part reflection on a unique moment in China's history. I am a professor
of international economic development and relations and I am
also a Southern storyteller; as such, I've included my memories,
lectures, adventures, and reflections in these chapters. I have
spent a career building an understanding between China and
the United States by teaching American students and professionals about China and Chinese students and professionals
about the U.S. This book is a continuation of that work.

Chapter 1
The Magnificent Transformation
Begins: China, 1979

Finally, I had my chance. The moment I heard that China was opening for educational groups, in 1979, I began plans to take a Winthrop group there in the summer of 1980. The plans involved a collaboration with Martin Driewitz, then the head of the education group desk for Northwest Orient Airlines. As our plans for the summer 1980 trip were ongoing, one day in May 1979, Martin called to tell me that an Oxford University professor who was visiting at the University of Kansas had signed up only thirteen people for a trip to China that was leaving in two weeks.

The call wasn't just informational: the low number was a problem, since China required sixteen participants to count as a group for purposes of a group visa. Martin told me that if I could get three people to sign up for the trip within in four days, I could go at half price. The full cost was $1,600, so I dropped everything, went over to the college credit union, and borrowed

$800. I got my friend and fellow professor Ed Lewandowski and three students to sign up and send in their money as well. The trip was on.

We all got our shots, piled in a car, and headed to the Atlanta airport for a flight to Minneapolis, where we joined the Kansas group. In addition to the organizing professor—who I'll refer to as "Oxford Man"—the group included one University of Kansas economics professor and two nurses who worked there. None of the three seemed to know anything about China or even be that interested in it. The rest of the group members weren't even affiliated with the university at all—they were just tourists who were excited to visit someplace new.

Indulge me in this chapter as I recall this trip to China, with all its firsts.

Hong Kong

We flew to first Anchorage and then on to Japan. The flight there was long, but fortunately, there were several empty seats, allowing us to take turns lying down. In Tokyo, we changed planes and continued on to Hong Kong. Landing in Hong Kong in those days was quite alarming: the runway was situated in the densely populated downtown, with buildings rising up on either side like the walls of a cavern. The runway ended right at the water's edge, necessitating a screeching halt.

I gazed out the plane's window and noticed what had been a beautiful, green hill during my 1970 Hong Kong visit was now covered by dozens of high-rise apartment towers—home to many of the people who had fled to Hong Kong during the Cultural Revolution.

Our group was staying on the Kowloon side of the city, at a YMCA on Waterloo Road. Oxford Man wanted to rest, so since I was the only one who had been there before, I took the group downtown, showed them the markets, and took them on the Star Ferry, which has run between Hong Kong and Kowloon since 1888. In those days, the lower part of the ferry was loaded with people traveling to and from the market with their pigs, chickens, and every odd sea creature you could imagine.

The next day, Oxford Man didn't know what to do, so I asked if he needed help. He declined, so I took my Winthrop group to the China Travel Service. There, I met up with Lilly, a woman Janet and I had met during our 1970 trip and to whom I'd written about my planned 1980 trip. Here I encountered my first lesson that, in China, who you knew was more important than what you knew. Lilly, it turned out, was a highly placed member of the Guangzhou Communist Party. We quickly got all of our paperwork done and picked up our train tickets to the border town of Shenzhen.

I was concerned that Oxford Man might think I was taking over the group, but he was a man of books, rather than travel, so he let me do as I pleased. He did not, however, make any preparations for his part of the group, so when we got to the train station the next day, his people had to stand in line for an eternity and fill out forms while we relaxed.

Shenzhen

There were no express trains in those days, so to get to Shenzhen, our first stop, we had to take the local train, which stopped every few blocks. After more than an hour, we arrived in Shenzhen.

We had a little more than two hours before our next train, to Guangzhou, was due to arrive, so I set out on my own to explore. Shenzhen was still more than a large village in 1979—it had just a single two-story hotel and only three paved blocks of road. One lonely cab was parked on the street, so I gently roused the driver, who was sleeping soundly, and asked him to take me to a local pagoda I'd spotted in my guidebook.

The pagoda stood at top of the only hill in the village, so I climbed it to get a better look at things. In all directions, the view was spectacular, surrounded by green rice fields still flooded from recent plantings. The water reflected the blue sky like a mirror, and the tall, green rice shoots gave the vista some texture. There wasn't a single soul in sight, in any direction. Clearly, Shenzhen's future as China's first "Special Economic Zone," with huge highways and scores of skyscrapers, was still years away.

The train to Guangzhou—known in the West as Canton—was a local as well. As the train stopped at each village, throngs of vendors descended on the train selling bananas, oranges, mangoes, bowls of various local foods, and carbonated orange drinks called *jiuzi shui*. What seemed like a chaotic mob to me was in fact a highly orchestrated event: one of the passengers told me that the same sellers met every train, day in and day out, and even had designated cars that they sold to. Guards prevented us from exiting, so all transactions were performed through the train's open windows. As the train pulled out of each station, I noted that the prices quickly dropped by half—another good lesson learned for the days and years to come.

Guangzhou

Once we arrived in Guangzhou, I felt like I was really in China. Millions of people filled the streets, most of them still wearing the blue uniforms everyone was required to wear during the Cultural Revolution. Giant swarms of bicycles came and went on every street, with lots of bells ringing, and at stoplights, the bikes would line up like they were ready for the start flag to drop at the Darlington 500. If pedestrians didn't quite make it across the street before the light changed, they were forced to run for their lives. As our bus moved forward, the bicycles parted like a boat slicing through a wave. The public buses were packed, but at every stop more people somehow crowded on.

Our guide was a woman in her late twenties who spoke perfect English. Each day, I'd do everything I could to sit in the front seat of our bus so I could see everything and pick the guide's brain during moments when she wasn't pointing out historic places. When I told her to stop me if I became a pest, she gave the perfect answer: "Most people want to just see the tourist sights, so it's nice to have someone who wants to learn about China."

One of my first questions had been troubling me since we'd arrived: Why did most citizens still wear the blue uniforms, when the rules had changed two years before?

The guide said, "People in China are very poor. They wear clothes until they wear them out. New Western clothes cost way too much, and many people are afraid that the Cultural Revolution will come back." She paused and then continued. "I have two Western outfits, both made for me by my mother so I would look better with the foreigners. CITS [the China International Travel Service] provided me with an official guide's uniform for when I am leading groups to busy spots like the Great Wall."

———————

All the Guangzhou restaurants served wonderful meals in dining rooms with large, round tables that seated eight. In the center of each table sat a lazy Susan loaded with twelve to fifteen different dishes, so everyone could easily help themselves. Despite all the choices we had, a few people in our group refused to try anything. Two large bottles of Chinese beer were positioned on every table, and just as with the food, we were to serve ourselves. The Chinese beer was great—Germans had built the breweries prior to the Revolution. Those who wanted soft drinks, bottled water, or more beer paid extra for the privilege.

I was told that after the Revolution, in 1949, every business was taken over by the government—except five internationally famous restaurants. In the two years that had elapsed since the end of the Revolution, thirty-eight restaurants had been allowed to privatize, many of which had been in the same family for over a hundred years. By the next year, when I brought a new Winthrop group back to Guangzhou, more than 2,000 private restaurants had opened—not including street vendors.

We stayed in a decrepit hotel in the oldest part of Guangzhou. The hotel's elevator, which would have been perfect for a BBC mystery series, could fit only two people and had old pull-style doors. Each room had two single beds and a balcony that looked out onto lots of buildings and the street below, packed with bikes and carts laden with everything from farm-fresh produce to boxes of what appeared to be electronics.

Every day, and often in the evenings after dinner, the guides took us to shops that sold carvings, jewelry, silk, and lots of tourist junk. I'd duck out of the excursions and walk the streets instead, making sure to take along a card with the hotel's name in Chinese should I have the luck to find an available cab (on one of my rides, I learned that most of the cabs were owned by Hong Kong residents who let their Guangzhou relatives drive them).

One day, I skipped the group's scheduled activity and instead went to the open-air market, which started by the canal and ran three very long blocks into the city. I encountered a remarkable sight even before I entered: a man walked by with a long pole balanced on his shoulder and a loaded bucket on each end. There's a Chinese saying: "For big load, use one stick; for light load, use two sticks."

The man dumped the buckets, brimming with fish guts, into the canal, setting off a war among throngs of birds that swooped about and made a tremendous ruckus. But the aerial assault was only half of the battle—fish of all sizes attacked the waste as well. The birds snatched what they could and tried to fly off with their spoils, but the fish were just as determined to swim away with at least some of the goodies. From time to time, a couple of fighting birds would drop a large morsel, and as it fell from the sky, the fish would leap to snatch it away before it hit the water. I was the only person who couldn't take my eyes off the action, as those who worked in the market saw it every day, but a crowd gathered to watch me as I stood transfixed by the battle.

The market itself had booths on each side and a very narrow lane down the middle crowded with people pushing their way through. The first twenty or so stalls were all fish, and some workers cleaned and gutted the merchandise while others haggled with shoppers. I noticed that the fish heads were intact, as in China, the cheek is considered the best part. The fish were weighed on makeshift scales: metal pans hanging from a T-shaped cross at the top of hand-held wooden sticks. Sellers weighed the fish so fast that only a skilled eye would know whether the count was accurate, and sales were completed within a few seconds. The purchases were either wrapped in sheets of newspaper or simply dropped into buyers' baskets, and the ritual would start over. Now and then, a buyer would cry "*tai guile*"—too expensive—and move to the next stall. Some shoppers held the fish about an inch from their faces and gazed into their eyes; I later learned it was the best way to determine freshness, as fish eyes cloud as they decay.

Beyond the fish stalls, people were selling all sorts of strange things. Some had croker sacks of spices, small seeds, and nuts. Poles that held holding up the awnings of some stalls were crowded with the claws of all sorts of birds (mostly birds of prey, like hawks or eagles) and next to them, bear paws and dried bats. A good fifty percent of what was for sale I had never seen before and hoped to never see again, including tusks that I feared had come from endangered animals.

The first block ended with the "egg ladies," old women who stacked their chickens' eggs into pyramids. There were probably thirty to forty of them seated around each of the four corners where the first market block ended and the second block began. Some also had eggs cooking in baths of dark tea in little pots on portable coal stoves. Shoppers ate these "tea eggs" as snacks as they strolled through the market.

A few of the egg ladies also offered very black eggs positioned on plates, and signs—the only signs in the entire market—sat next to the plates. These were called hundred-year-old eggs, a great delicacy in China (no, they're not really a hundred years old). Each seller had her own secret way of preserving the eggs, which were very expensive.

The second block of the market, the butchers' area, was filled with a clatter of "whack whack" as cleavers sliced through meat. Many foreigners skipped that part of the market, as dogs and cats were often sold there as meat. (There's a saying about

Guangzhou: "People here will eat anything with four legs except a table and everything that flies except an airplane.") A young boy who didn't want to pass up a chance to practice his English told me that dog and cat meat was prized for its high protein content, so it was mostly eaten by the old and the sick, and by the general population only during the winter months. He didn't know the English word "protein," but instead said the meat would "stop you from dying." (I figured out what he meant.)

Next in the market were stalls where rice and other grain products were sold. The government allocated a certain portion of wheat, rice, and other grains to each person—the "iron rice bowl"—but some didn't like the quality of the government-issued rice, so for special occasions, they'd spend a little money to buy a finer grade.

In the third block, countless varieties of vegetables and fruits lined the aisles. In those days in particular, Americans ate a limited selection of fruits and vegetables, so the sight was quite a shock to the system. As an example, I was amazed at how many different types of melon were available, and disputes raged about which types were the most delicious. One of the most prized was the Roosevelt melon. It was so named in honor of U.S. President Franklin Roosevelt, who once gifted China with seeds for what we now know as honeydew melons.

The next section of the block was dedicated to flowers, both cut and in pots. It was like being in a botanical garden. Given how little the Chinese earned—about nine dollars a month, on average, at that time—I was surprised to see how many made room in their budgets for flowers.

Completing the Guangzhou market were T-shirt stalls that lined the cross streets. One in particular sold tees emblazoned with "Become Rich" in English.

The sides of the market were flanked by textile mills, their windows yawning open to let in the fresh air. I peered into the windows to see women packed inside making clothes for export. They were very surprised when I stuck my head in, said "*ni hao*" (hello), and took a snapshot. The women, who for the most part appeared to range in age from sixteen to twenty-five, giggled and replied "*ni hao*" in a friendly way.

We were scheduled to visit a farming village during our stay in Guangzhou, but Oxford Man decided that he didn't want us to go. There was a problem with that: impromptu changes in schedule were not allowed yet. Opening up the country to educational groups was still a big deal, and almost every element of each tour was carefully choreographed to show China in the most positive light. We sat on the bus for an hour as he fruitlessly argued with the tour guides.

When we finally got to the village—a model one that had been approved for tourists—its nicely attired residents were waiting outside for us. Children began to dance, and firecrackers were set off; they were clearly even more excited to see us than we were to see them. Many of the girls grabbed the hands of their visitors and began to lead us around. Everything was very clean and prosperous looking, quite unlike the villages we'd seen from the windows of the trains and buses we'd ridden.

The one house I entered even had a small black and white TV that received three channels: one with variety-type shows featuring singing, dancing, and comedians; an educational one, like ETV or PBS in the U.S.; and a third that was really educational—like with information about how to treat animal and human diseases. The TV, clearly the family's most prized possession, was covered with an embroidered cloth to keep dust away; it was only one of two in the village (the other was in the home the other half of our group visited).

I asked the family a million questions about the TV, and one in particular stumped them: "How many hours of TV do you watch every day?"

The translator couldn't manage to help the family understand, so I decided to simplify things.

"When do you turn on the TV?"

"At 6:00."

"When do you turn it off?"

"9:00."

"And how many hours do they have TV?"

They looked at me like I was an idiot. "Three hours a day. From 6:00 to 9:00."

There were pictures of Mao on the walls of the home, but none of Deng. Curious, I asked why.

"Mao liked us to have his picture everywhere, and Deng does not like his picture hung up because he doesn't want us to think of him as another god." I suspect something was lost in this translation.

The village's primary cash crop was oranges, which they turned over to the government. In return, they received an allotment of grain for the village. Each family had its own private plot garden, and it was truly unbelievable how much they could raise on a plot that measured 120 feet by 100 feet.

During the Cultural Revolution, Deng had once been sent down to a village for a brief stay. He noticed that small private plots yielded ten times as much as the community farms, so he declared that every farmer had to have a private plot. Not surprisingly, production skyrocketed.

The presence of an older Chinese man who had joined our group began to concern me—especially once I learned that he was the former head of the Guangzhou Provincial Communist Party. I was afraid he was along to report back on us, or on the guide. He didn't join us on the trip to the village, so I seized the opportunity to ask the guide about him.

She was amused by the question. She told me that the man had lived in Guangzhou for his whole life, but since Chinese people were not permitted to tour around and see their own nation, he was taking this opportunity to see China. She added that he had likely visited Beijing a time or two for a Party meeting, but even then, travelers were not allowed to tour around.

"Besides," she continued, "our young people now have to study English in school, but even if was lucky enough to attend school in his day, he wouldn't have learned English. So it's safe to talk about anything in front of him." The truth of the matter was quite benign: he was a friend of her grandfather who had worked out a deal so he could join the tour.

On our way out of Guangzhou, we spotted a group of workmen on the bridge across the river hanging a long banner that promoted the Four Modernizations: agriculture, industry, defense, and science/technology. It proclaimed, "Each of these will require major financial investment and creation of a well-trained professional leadership and workforce."

We also saw many large road signs featuring a picture of a happy couple with a little girl between them. The sign had two not-so-subtle messages: first, the government was pushing the "One Child" policy, which was new that year, and, second, they were encouraging couples to celebrate baby girls. Traditionally, in China, the birth of a baby boy was considered a "big happiness," but girl babies were thought of as a "small happiness." Why? The boys stayed with the family, and the girls were married off into other families.

China was then in the midst of a major shortage of airplanes; the ones we flew in during the trip were Soviet built and purchased before 1959, when the countries broke off relations. Our next stop was Beijing, and our flight there was on a crowded old military plane that departed from Guangzhou's military airport. We were seated in the main cabin, and all our bags were piled up, from floor to ceiling, right behind us.

Beijing
Our flight landed at the main airport in Beijing. Both sides of the airport were lined with rows of fighter jets, an ominous sight. We taxied down to a building that looked like a warehouse, and in the building, we each underwent a clearance process, just as we did when we arrived in Shenzhen. It took forever for the Chinese officials there to match up our passports with the group visa list, so I made a mental note that for my next trip, I'd make lots of copies of the visa lists and line up the group members at airports and hotels in the same order that their names appeared on the list.

The baggage process there was quite strange: the military guys on the plane threw each piece of luggage out an open door for soldiers on the ground to catch. Some were heavy, missed the waiting men, and hit the ground hard. Thankfully, none popped open, because the conditions that day were cold and very windy (on my next trip, one lady's bag did open on impact, and dozens of Chinese troops ended up chasing her clothes all over the runways).

From the airport, we headed out on a three-hour drive to the Great Wall. The snaking road was two lanes and full of trucks, many of which were full of beehives—each truck appeared to have a hundred or more hives. I was interested in the reason why—bees were sent to the north in the spring to pollinate crops there and then taken south by truck or rail car, all the while pollinating crops along the way.

The trip up to the Wall was very slow, with no opportunity to pass, but at least the drive was interesting. Village after village looked as if it had from ten to thirty houses. Each house was walled off, and another wall surrounded the village. The road ran above the villages, so village life was in full view from our bus windows, with kids and chickens running around and people repairing or improving their houses. Most of the houses were single-story and constructed from big rocks and bricks.

We also passed a dozen or so walls and watchtowers that dated from even earlier dynasties and had not been restored. Each dynasty, we learned, had built a wall to protect it from northern tribes, and the Chen wall, constructed in 300 BC, was the first to connect all the walls into an early Great Wall. The watchtowers were used to spot invasions from the north; a guard would build a fire on top of his tower to signal trouble. The guard in the next tower would see it and do the same, so the message would pass quickly—knowledge of a coming invasion could pass a hundred miles in just an hour. (Our guide also noted that villagers often had stolen rocks and bricks from these older "great walls" over the centuries to build their own houses.)

When we finally reached the rebuilt part of the Ming dynasty's Great Wall—the wall so well known beyond China's borders—we drove through an impossibly small hole in it to reach the parking area on the other side. The space was so tight, with mere inches on either side, but the driver was clearly an expert. At that time, most of the professional drivers in China had been trained to drive in the military; being a driver was a high-status job.

Before venturing to climb the Wall, we all took a much-needed restroom break. There was a fee to go—the cost was equal to about five cents. The room itself was open, with a series of holes in the floor with footprints painted on each side so you knew where to stand or squat. The smell was ghastly and burned my nose; I tried to hold my breath.

Climbing the Wall was very hard and very steep. The stairs were obviously made for feet much smaller than my size four-teens, so I had to walk sideways. About halfway up, it began to snow and the wind began to howl, but I had no way of knowing whether I would ever have the chance to return. I fought on, all the way to the top; of my group, three Winthrop students and the two nurses all made it, but the rest turned back. The view from the top was well worth the climb. The fresh snow coated the tops of the Wall and made it seem so peaceful—in striking contrast to its true purpose, as a fortification to gain advantage over adversaries and keep out interlopers.

During our pre-Wall restroom stop, I'd noticed one Chinese man squatting over a hole and reading a book. Three hours later, after we'd completed our hike on the Wall, I took a deep breath, held my nose, and ran back into the same restroom. The same man was still squatting over the same hole, still reading his book. I thought fleetingly that perhaps the man had died mid-squat—because otherwise, how could he stand it?—but didn't pause to investigate. It was hard to believe, but I guess people got used to the smell.

It was late by the time we arrived back in Beijing, so we stopped for dinner at a restaurant in a public garden. There, we were served traditional northern Chinese food, with lots of steamed rolls and dumplings. Since they're steamed, these foods don't brown or develop a crust, and many of the people in our group refused to eat them because they thought they were raw.

That night, we stayed at an inn in a *hutong*, which is a narrow alley between walled courtyard residences (known as *siheyuans*). Our *hutong* had no lights, so we followed our guide down the alley to a door in a wall. Tucked inside, we found a dozen or more individual one-room brick buildings, each measuring about ten feet long by twenty feet wide. The inn was over 200 years old, and it showed—in front of each small building was a place to tie up horses.

My colleague Ed and I were assigned to one of the buildings. We each had a cot with a lumpy mattress along one wall. A single light hung from the ceiling in the center of the room, and at the one end of the room was what we'd come to expect, a hole in the floor with painted feet on either side. Opposite the hole, about four feet up the wall, was a spigot for washing up. There was enamel bowl for that purpose as well, but the water was unheated, so there was no way I intended to take a bath of any kind, sponge or not. A six-inch deep and six-inch wide trough was cut in the floor running from the spigot on one wall to the hole in the floor at the opposite end of the room, so to "flush," you just ran the spigot and the water would run along the trough to the toilet hole.

Despite the efforts of the room's small electric heater, it was quite cold, but there were lots of padded quilts. We both slept in our clothes, anyway, so we stayed warm. We discovered that the room's light had no switch, which set us into something of a panic, but the light turned off about 10 minutes into our stay (many in the group got caught in the dark before getting into bed). Electricity was still a scarcity in Chinese accommodations, so I made a note to bring lots of flashlights on our next trip. Just a year or two after our stay there, the entire block where our *hutong* inn had stood was flattened to construct a parking lot for the Forbidden City.

Since we were staying only a block away, the next morning, we walked over to Tiananmen Square and then on into the Forbidden City, home to emperors of the Ming and Qing dynasties. The guides there told us that there are 9,999 rooms in the Forbidden City, because it was believed that 10,000 would make the gods jealous. It is so large that it has no equal anywhere else in the world. I can guarantee that the gods must be pretty jealous, even if it is one room short of 10,000.

The big and beautiful main buildings were painted red, with gold-colored roofs, and they were lined up in rows, with massive paved courtyards between them. The rocks used as paving stones were enormous and so thick that no one could tunnel inside. The last building, the largest and grandest of them all, was where the emperor held court. Those who came to see the emperor had to bow down seven times, each time knocking their heads against the stone floor.

On this trip, of the thousands of rooms in the palace, only the women's quarters were open to the public. The compound featured many rooms arranged around a beautiful garden, and each room featured wonderful paintings.

To my surprise, artists were set up in the rooms busily making copies of the paintings. And then I thought about it—most of the paintings they were copying had to be copies themselves, because paintings made on silk or paper simply can't last for hundreds of years. I was told that an artist would spend a lifetime just learning to copy one of these masterpieces.

I decided to buy two of the copies right then and there, and I'm lucky to have them, because on my later trips, the women's quarters were sealed off. I have always preferred the more understated nature of the paintings in the women's quarters to the grand paintings in many of the other areas of the palace.

———————

Following the tour of the Forbidden City, we stopped for lunch and were served Peking duck. The city's name changed long ago to Beijing, but its native dish still bears its old name. Some of the people in the group were grossed out by the duck—neck, head, and all—being cut up at the table. That was fine with me, because I love Peking duck. I ate my portion and four others!

Tianjin

That afternoon, we drove to Tianjin, at that time China's fourth largest city. We had been scheduled to spend more time in Beijing, but there were no available hotel rooms—even our *hutong* was booked—so we traveled on. Tianjin lies just sixty miles from Beijing, but the main road was under construction. That left us bouncing along on bypass roads full of deep holes and mud puddles. To add to the mess, it rained all day long.

Tianjin, the port city for the capital, was largely built by the Soviets, and it served as China's link with the USSR during their eight years of friendly relations during the 1950s. To be honest, though, they couldn't stand each other. China thought the Soviets were in China simply to steal the fruits of the country's victory in World War II. They had long memories and remembered that the Soviets failed to support China in its wars against Japan and the Nationalists—but on the other hand, the Soviets could be useful in helping China build its industries. As for the Soviets, well, they thought that since China was Communist, they should consider that the Soviet Union was the leader of the Communist world, and that they should follow its lead. And the Soviet Union backed Vietnam, one of China's historic enemies, in its war against the West.

––––––––

Just six months prior to our visit, Tianjin had suffered an earthquake measuring 7.2 on the Richter scale, so much of it was still rubble. Ongoing aftershocks left residents afraid to return to their partially destroyed homes, so temporary living quarters—shacks, really—were constructed all along the middle of the city's wide main streets.

As a measure to restore order and rebuild Tianjin following the earthquake, the Party took control of everything, and I do mean everything. If, for example, one family lost its father and another lost its mother in the quake, the government intervened to force the surviving spouses to marry, even if they didn't know or like each other.

Like most of the buildings that had survived the quake, our hotel was a big, Soviet-built brick square with no decoration—just a plain brick building. The building had served as a hotel during the 1950s, so the rooms were well appointed, all things considered, with two single beds each and regular Western-style bathrooms. The dinner served in the hotel was plain Russian fare: heavy soup with ever-present steamed white buns. There were a few condiments: salted small fish, hot peppers, and lots of other peppers. As had been the case with all our other meals in China, each table received two big bottles of beer, but soft drinks—mostly fruit flavored—cost extra. Ed decided to get adventurous and tried mixing each one with the very cheap vodka on hand, to unpalatable results.

———————————

The next morning, many of the group asked to return to Beijing for more sightseeing. The thought of a three-hour-each-way trip turned me off, so five of us elected to stay for the planned Tianjin tour for that day of the Whampoa Military Academy, where Mao, Chang, Deng, and Zhou had all been students and, later, professors.

They were ready for us, to be sure: they had on hand a copy of The Meaning of the Constitution, a book I'd coauthored with a fellow Winthrop professor, Angela Holder, as well as—to my great surprise—a copy of my master's thesis on Kashmir! How they'd found it in the short time between my visa's approval and my arrival was beyond me. Three of the faculty members had even read it, so they asked lots of questions about Kashmir. They'd also found a copy of my dissertation, but they hadn't gotten government approval for students and faculty to read it because of its subject matter: Vietnam.

This was just about the last thing I thought would happen in China. Keep in mind that the universities had been closed by the Cultural Revolution for a full ten years. Thus, 1978 and 1979 became known as the "superclasses," because instead of one year of newly graduated high school students to pick from, the universities had ten or eleven years' worth. In fact, many of China's modern leaders have come from the superclasses.

The next day's plan was visit to one of China's many rug factories, and the manager who showed us around there was great at answering my questions. Each year, he told us, the government would send him forty to sixty new high school graduates, and he'd have to find work for all of them.

The workers, mostly women, made hand-tied silk and wool contoured rugs. They were divided into two groups: the best workers produced the traditional rugs, which featured about 200 to 300 knots per inch, and less skilled ones made flower rugs, which had only 75 knots per inch. (He told me that the flower rugs sold well throughout Southeast Asia, where bright colors are preferred.)

Of course, if you can't choose your employees, you'll eventually have an issue. Forced full employment, he told me, was a problem for all managers. At least ten of the workers he'd receive each year weren't good at anything. Some were put to work in the factory's nursery, taking care of the workers' children, and the rest were assigned cleaning and packing roles. The manager brightened as he told us that for the very first time that year, the government was considering a reform of the policy, and managers would be allowed to turn down up to 10 percent of their assigned new workforce each year.

We left that evening on a long, overnight train trip south, toward Nanjing. The trip was "hard seat," meaning that we all sat on benches with numbers painted on the seats. They were assigned seats, but not very comfortable ones, so we took turns either lying down on the seats (also not comfortable) or walking around on the train.

Word about our group of foreigners spread quickly throughout the train. Since China had been closed for twenty-five years, most citizens had never seen people from outside China. As adults walked past us, they'd pretend that they saw foreigners every day, but we noticed that they'd pass by multiple times. The kids, though, hid nothing: they pointed and stared and had lots to say. Some even began to cry. Everyone was curious, but very friendly, and the parents wanted to make sure their children got a good look—just in the most polite way possible. We greeted everyone with a smile and a Chinese hello.

Our seats took up only about a third of the car, and the rest of the passengers in our car were very amused by the gawkers who came to look at us. I noticed that as the looky-loos passed, our fellow passengers would laugh into their hands—my first lesson in how laughter is very different in China. Chinese people laugh when they feel awkward or embarrassed, and sometimes even when someone is hurt and they're unsure of what to do. The women in our car hid their laughs by covering their faces, while the men stared and then looked away, swallowing their laughs and biting their lips.

As the next day dawned, we enjoyed wonderful views of the countryside from north to south, with every stop bringing new surprises. At several of the stops, we paused next to cars loaded with hundreds of beehives headed north to pollinate fruit and vegetables. In other stations, neighboring trains were dedicated to moving farm machinery and workers for seasonal work in other, more verdant areas of the country. These early-morning stops reminded me of trains I'd ridden in India full of farmers bringing large containers of milk to market.

The north-to-south train trip was a great introduction to the significance of the change from wheat culture to rice culture. In the north, the very rich and yellow soil was ideal for wheat production, but there was very little water. The south was wet, with lots of water from monsoons, but the earth wasn't very rich. In north and south alike, huge amounts of human labor were set to work to produce enough grain to feed the giant nation.

Nanjing

Nanjing, China's old southern capital, had originally been a walled city, and much of the wall still stood, with a road running on top in some areas. In summer, the city is very hot, so shade trees line each side of every road. Our accommodations were in a nice, but not fancy, hotel, and our group went wild over its Western toilets.

On our first full day there, we trekked to the shore of the Yangtze River, which is up to three miles wide in some places in Nanjing. The first bridge over the river had been just finished a few years before, with train tracks on the lower level and cars and trucks on top. The bridge also featured a pedestrian walkway, so we ventured about a mile out to a point where we could hardly see either bank. The bridge was a source of great pride in Nanjing, and rightly so—prior to its construction, every train car or truck had to board a barge for transport across the river.

The Yangtze was crowded with all types of boats and ships, some of which were made of steel and concrete—a rather surprising material for shipbuilding. These were often filled with coal or bags of grain in front and a single-room home for the family living on the boat in the back. At the time, as many as a million Chinese people were living on boats, which represented a problem: the children didn't go to school, and school was required by the government.

Many of the boats were traditional Chinese junks, merchant vessels that have been used in China since the second century. Those traveling downriver coasted along with the flow of the river, but the upriver traffic unfurled their magnificent, colorful sails and rode the wind instead.

Our next stop was a city park, where construction was under way to remove part of the city's wall. I explored the site a good bit and scaled the rubble, turning over bricks, which were about four times the size of standard bricks in the U.S., as I encountered them and finding writing on each one. Curious, I carried a few over to our tour's translator, and with a stunned look, she told me that the writing was a record of the dynasty under which the brick was installed. I got my students to look around, too, and bring over what they uncovered. Every brick had a dynasty's name on it; in the end, we found bricks from seven different dynasties, the oldest being from the Han dynasty (about 300 AD). The discovery made the Chinese guides and workers just as excited as we were, as no one had noticed the writing before.

On the same tour, we visited a sacred memorial to the Nanjing Massacre (also known as the Rape of Nanjing). In the Second Sino-Japanese War, during a six-week period from December 1937 to January 1938, Imperial Japanese Army troops initiated a sustained campaign of mass murder, rape, and looting in which somewhere between 40,000 and 300,000 Chinese civilians and soldiers were killed (most Japanese military records were destroyed following Japan's surrender to the Allies in 1945, so the death toll remains in dispute). The site was solemn and moving, with many visitors there to honor dead relatives, and another reminder of the longstanding enmity between China and Japan.

On one of my later trips to China, I befriended Judge Zhang, one of the justices who presided over the Nanjing War Crimes Tribunal, which was established in 1946. He gave generously of his time with many of the groups of students who toured with me, relaying countless stories of living history and unflinchingly responding to their questions.

We then set off for Shanghai. Along the way, we spent a night in Wuxi, home to Lake Taihu, the third largest freshwater lake in China. When he didn't have to be in Beijing, Mao preferred to stay at his residence on the shores of Lake Taihu. The lake was lovely, but heavily polluted by the factories and farms that surrounded it.

Our hotel for that night was situated by the lake, and it featured a lovely garden. Several couples who had paired up during the trip decided to sit in the garden for the evening—and it was a quite romantic place, to be sure. Less romantic, however, was the constant scratching that bedeviled them at breakfast the next morning thanks to their uncountable mosquito bites.

The other memorable event during our stay in Wuxi was the menu for our dinner that night: small fried eels. Most of my fellow travelers wouldn't even try them, but to my delight, I found that they tasted like fried shrimp. I ended up eating the whole serving for the table of eight—have you noticed a trend here?—and when I returned home, I was diagnosed with hepatitis, likely from gorging myself on eels fished from that very polluted lake. It took me six months to feel normal again.

Shanghai

Shanghai, China's largest city and busiest port, was a sight to behold. Upon arrival we went straight to the Shanghai Mansions Hotel, a huge building completed in 1934—the golden age of Old Shanghai—and intended to cater to British tourists. This time around, I had a room all to myself, but there were significant drawbacks. The hotel was situated at a point on the Huangpu River where all the oceangoing ships docked and a steady traffic of smaller boats traveled downstream. Given all the river activity, the air was filled with blowing horns and ringing bells. My room was right on the corner, and while the view was exciting, it was so noisy that I could hardly sleep. Another complication: the roof over the hotel's entrance was right outside my window. Huge wooden barrels full of large eels sat just below my window, and they splashed around all night.

The next morning, we walked the length of the Bund. On this famous waterfront mile-long stretch along the bank of the Huangpu, hundreds of Chinese people congregated daily for their morning exercises. The river framed one side of the Bund, and a series of famous banks, trading houses, and hotels lined the other.

Before the Japanese and the Communist takeovers, Shanghai had been the largest port in the world. At the time we visited, 70 percent of all domestic and international commerce in China still took place there. The streets were filled with students eager to practice their English with us, and there was also a shop, The Friendship Store, that was open to foreign tourists only. At the time, China had two kinds of money: RMB or "people's money," which Chinese citizens used within the borders of the country but could not be used for imports or exports, and FEC (Foreign Exchange Currency), which foreigners could use to buy anything. Both currencies were valued equally by the Chinese government, but tourists who sold their FEC on the black market found that it could fetch up to 40 percent more than its official value. But since I was planning to return, it made no sense to me to risk doing anything illegal.

Massive Shanghai had been divided into zones before World War II, so some parts had an English flavor, other parts leaned German, and still others tended toward Japanese. Of course, the fashion district was French, and strangely, there was a Chinese district—Shanghai was the only city in China with a designated Chinese section. Americans and other foreigners tended to stay in what was known as the International District.

On a cruise along the river, I noticed that its west bank was cluttered with docks, international banks, and trading houses and the right featured nothing but naval yards and farms (we were warned not to take pictures of the hundreds of military ships we saw). Ferries across the Huangpu were the only option, as there were no bridges, and they were forced to dodge between the massive ships that were coming and going constantly.

While Beijing was a thoroughly bureaucratic city, Shanghai was all business and industry. Despite the Cultural Revolution, the port remained very much an international city, so it was far less unusual to spot people from all over the world. Outdoor advertising in other cities were all propaganda, and Shanghai had some too—we saw a few of the "One Child" policy billboards that we'd seen elsewhere—but there were also lots of ads for makeup and Chinese and Japanese electronics manufacturers.

Some shop windows even featured ads for Coca-Cola (most was sold in big bottles, but fancier stores and restaurants offered Coke in cans). We often remarked on how strange it was to have to buy water and soft drinks in restaurants, while beer was free.

––––––––––

Up to that point, all the guides who had worked with us had seemed to be on the same page about the major changes that were taking place in China. That came to an end with the city guide in Shanghai, an older man with nothing nice to say about any of it. He refused to answer our questions and instead recited his tour script from memory—a script from Mao's China, not Deng's—departing from it only to make disparaging remarks about everything foreign, especially the advertisements. He made it abundantly clear that he wasn't happy about our visit.

We found that for the most part, Chinese citizens fell into three groups. For the most part, the people we came into contact with were all for Deng's reforms. A member of our group asked our traveling guide once if she was a member of the Communist Party, and she replied, "No. They take up so much of your time in meetings, and I like to spend my spare time reading foreign novels. If any of you have some you don't want, I'll be glad to read them and pass them on to my friends!"

The second group, which I think was substantial, were concerned about the reforms because they feared a backlash, a return to the China of the Cultural Revolution or even the China of the Great Leap Forward, an economic and social campaign by the government that ran between 1958 to 1962 and ultimately led to the deaths of millions of people from starvation. Our city guide in Shanghai was firmly in the third group, who preferred the strict constraints of Mao's China and resented any change.

I fell in love with Shanghai, a forward-thinking city made up of immigrants from all over China. Few residents still wore the blue uniforms of the Revolution; most women and children wore brightly colored clothing that didn't really match—but after years of drab uniforms, who could blame them? When I'd observe something happening that I knew wouldn't be tolerated anywhere else in the country and asked about it, I'd always get some version of the same response: "Beijing is far, far away." Our stay in Shanghai, my favorite place in China, was much too short.

Hangzhou

From Shanghai, we took a bus to Hangzhou, the beautiful city Marco Polo claimed was larger than any ten cities in Europe. The trip was long, and there was only one gas station along the way. As the bus got filled up, we took a much-needed restroom break. (Some years later, on the same journey, I counted more than seventy-five gas stations.)

Everything we saw along the ride was the same—farms and rice fields. The rich land there yields three crops of rice per year, enough to feed a city the size of Shanghai. The traffic we shared the road with was all trucks full of produce and some strange carts; we learned that they were plows that had been converted into vehicles capable of towing trailers full of produce and people. (The guide added that peasants loved go to Shanghai, because life on the farm was boring.)

The city of Hangzhou lived up to Marco Polo's description. The center of the city featured a large manmade lake that was over a thousand years old. I was able to climb to the top of several very old and beautiful pagodas that surrounded the lake, and later, we visited a tea plantation at one end of the lake.

There, hundreds of women picked only most tender leaves, from the very tops of the bushes, to make green tea.

After touring the tea plantation, we traveled to a lavish and elaborate compound where Lin Biao, head of the military during Mao's last years, had made his home. Most believed that Mao's successor would be Lin, as he had authored the Little Red Book, which every Chinese citizen had been forced to carry and read throughout the Cultural Revolution. But he suddenly disappeared, and most of China and the rest of the world didn't know for sure what had happened to him.

We now know that Lin was killed in a fighter plane crash in Mongolia. The general consensus is that Lin had crossed Mao's wife, who feared he would try to take control, but the details are still hotly debated; I added my two cents on the topic when I published a paper on it in 1990.

———————————

Our route home had us flying from Hangzhou back to Guangzhou, on to Hong Kong by boat, and then flying back to the States through Seattle. The view on the river, crowded with Chinese junks, looked exactly like a centuries-old painting. During our one night in Hong Kong, everybody in the group ran to a nearby McDonald's. The chain was everywhere in Hong Kong—at one crossroads, you could see five of them from that one spot.

When we arrived in Seattle and went through customs, the police arrested a woman from the Kansas group and took her off to jail. One of the airport workers told us why: Chinese merchants who sold major purchases to Americans reported them all to U.S. Customs, and travelers who failed to report them and pay customs duties were arrested. I wondered aloud why merchants would turn in their own customers. The response surprised me: the sellers often had the item returned to them as a reward. In fact, some high-end jewelers in Hong Kong ended up selling the same item multiple times.

The one commonality among all the cities we visited in China were the children. Every time the bus stopped, no matter where we were, we attracted a throng of them. Everywhere we walked, dozens of laughing and playing children trailed behind us. Apparently, we were a great and very strange attraction.

At that time in history, and probably for long before, very young Chinese children wore *kaidangku*, pants with a split between the legs (when nature called, they'd simply squat wherever they were and do their business). They're still common in rural areas. Older kids in the cities wore blue outfits with white shirts, but in the countryside, the children's clothes were much more ragged and worn.

But whether the kids were in the cities or in the countryside, their enthusiasm about seeing outsiders remained the same. No matter how poor a village might have been, its children were well fed, happy, and playing as children should—something that was hard to believe, just a few decades after famine that killed millions and two years following the end of the Cultural Revolution, which turned the young and old alike into robots waving the Little Red Book.

On the long flight back home, I began thinking about how China compared to the other developing nations I'd worked in—India and Pakistan—and traveled to—Vietnam, Thailand, and Malaysia. China and India had better health care services. None of the countries had paved roads beyond the cities, and indoor running water and toilets were rare. The water wasn't safe to drink anywhere. While China's cities were crowded, there were fewer people living in their streets—mostly because the police cleared them out every night. All in all, I reflected, China seemed very much to be just another Third World nation.

This first trip to China fulfilled my dreams in every way imaginable. I could hardly wait to return with my Winthrop group the following year.

Chapter 2
The Early Years of
Magnificent Change

THE YEARS 1980 TO 1985 WERE A PERIOD OF MAJOR changes that mostly took place out of sight. In each of these years, I visited different areas of China in an effort to observe all of its many aspects—agriculture, manufacturing, trade, and so on. The government placed priority on reassuring its people that the country wouldn't just revert to the policies of years past. Many feared taking any risk at all for fear if the government would again change its policies, and that as a result of those risks, they'd end up punished, imprisoned, or killed—as had happened with previous changes in Party lines. As each year passed, these fears lessened.

The new stated objectives of the Chinese government were, for the most part, well received, but the strategy for achieving these ends unfolded slowly, over time. The strategy, and the changes they brought about, required buy-in from the population, as they represented a whole new way of thinking. These years were a preparatory stage that was necessary to achieve the objectives of Deng's Four Modernizations in the fields of agriculture, industry, defense, and science and technology.

To achieve these objectives, the government realized that the population must become fluent in English, the global language of modernity. Prior to the ten years of the Cultural Revolution, English had been taught in the schools for years. And even in the time of the Revolution, copies of Mao's Little Red Book were taught in English in Chinese high schools. At the same time, as China's doors closed, so too did common instruction in English.

English instruction was stressed in the schools from kindergarten through graduate school, and even those who majored in other foreign languages were also required to take English. Chinese leaders realized they needed native speakers of English to help the population learn, so the first "foreigners" who were welcomed into the country were English teachers—although truth be told, few were trained teachers. Most were simply people for whom English was their native tongue.

The other option was to send Chinese students to English-speaking countries, but it would be quite some time before China was willing to send its young people abroad—as there were significant fears they wouldn't return. It was less difficult for a student who was unmarried and didn't have a child to get permission to go abroad to study, as Chinese authorities felt that having a family back home would ensure the student's return.

These fears also prevailed about specialists who sought to travel abroad for short-term study. Everyone, it seemed, wanted to travel and see what the world beyond China's borders looked like. In many cases, permission for a trip would only be granted if the person's boss or representatives from the Party went along to be sure the person said only positive things about China.

In 1983, a Chinese woman visited Winthrop for a conference accompanied by her boss, the boss of her boss, and the local Party leader. I was told that she needed the chaperones because it wasn't considered proper for a woman to travel alone. When I remarked to a Chinese official that I thought this was a waste of money, he revealed the ulterior motive: Deng's people wanted the more conservative members of the Party to see the modern world so they would be less likely to oppose reforms upon their return. Even travelers who didn't speak a word of English quickly became converts to the new modernization program.

––––––––––

The first trips I made to China were only two to three weeks long each, but during each one, I visited different areas of China. In order to study and really understand China, I believed, it was important to go beyond the big cities and spend time in the smaller towns, ones with weekly or bi-weekly markets.

At the time I took these trips, the majority of Chinese villages were more than fifty miles from a paved road. The only times the villagers living in these places had contacts with markets was at harvest time, when the government would pick up its quota of the villagers' grain, or when a traveling peddler came through the village selling everything from cloth to needles to nails to plastic shoes.

China has an advantage over many underdeveloped nations in that so many of its regions, no matter how rural they might be, are connected to market towns and cities by water—its labyrinth of canals. Another advantage: villages in other developing nations lack the cohesive structure of Chinese villages, with all the houses clustered together. And yet a third advantage: Chinese people have been using money for exchange, rather than bartering or other systems so common to other underdeveloped nations, for centuries.

––––––––––––

The effects of the "One Child" policy were visible right away. Couples were told when it was time for them to have a child, and if the wife became pregnant before the couple's approved date for their allotted child, she had to have an abortion. By the time I arrived for my second visit, in 1980, abortion clinics were everywhere.

As soon as a woman who was not supposed to be pregnant missed her period, she was expected to report to an abortion clinic. Some apartment complexes went so far as to require the women who lived there to post their period schedule on their front doors, and older ladies were given the job of going door-to-door to make sure residents complied. Many of the Americans I traveled with found this hard to believe, but I reminded them: this is a modernization program, not a democratization program.

––––––––––––

Many of the changes during these first years of modernization were designed to encourage infusions of foreign capital and investment. Every major city held big trade fairs, and businesses from all over the world flooded in to get in on the ground floor of a billion-person market—and to access millions of low-wage workers.

For example, Toyota designed and built a car exclusively for the Chinese market. The Chinese were not allowed to have private cars, but businesses and taxi companies bought the Crown in droves, making it the most popular car in China for ten years straight. The car was intended as a sort of limousine, with a small front seat for a professional driver and a large back seat for passengers. While people weren't allowed to have cars, every park featured a fake car that people could sit in for pictures.

China Air, the state airline, began buying planes from Boeing, so fewer and fewer military and Russian planes were used commercially. Hotels began being built everywhere, as they brought in foreign dollars and made life easier for business travelers. Many of the new hotels were foreign chains, but provinces, cities, counties, universities, and military units got into the hotel business as well. They found hotels to be very useful, as they provided foreign currency exchanges and, as an extra benefit, provided jobs for relatives of the men in the air force.

In fact, the salaries paid to employees of hotels and private ventures were generally much higher than those of government workers, which ranged from forty to fifty dollars a month. During a 1983 visit, I rode in an elevator in a five-star hotel with the president of a major Chinese university. During the ride, he engaged the elevator operator in conversation. When we got off, he translated what he'd learned: the elevator operator earned twice his salary.

Despite all the changes, tips were still not allowed until 1986 (except in very few places, where a 10 percent service charge was allowed to be assessed). Tips were considered to be a totem of capitalism, which of course was verboten. Of course, so many of Deng's changes were inherently capitalist that I had a very hard time understanding what was and what wasn't. I asked around, and the general consensus was this: "It's capitalist if we say it is, and it's socialist if we say it isn't."

The Chinese government didn't have a monopoly on change. Entrepreneurs also began experimenting with all types of business ideas and systems during these years. Some, like the miniature theme parks that suddenly seemed to be everywhere during my early visits to China, quickly failed, but the entrepreneurs just moved on to something else.

In 1982, the government designated several Special Economic Zones (SEZ), areas that were allowed to have more free market-oriented activities, and Shenzhen found itself way out in front of the others because Hong Kong money had already been invested there. SEZs were envisioned as a giant experiment, a way to show the people of China what was possible with more free-market enterprises. Some SEZs fared worse than others; one in the province of Hainan was caught importing hundreds of vans, charging no duty on them, and then selling them on the open market—netting millions for the managers.

Few changes were visible in the villages, but farmers in towns close to cities began to grow more produce on their private plots and sell them at city markets (local governments responded positively to the trend by increasing the size of their private plots). Since the only people allowed to live in cities had to have residency permits, which were impossible to get, villagers trekked by bus or train every day and set up shop on the sidewalks selling produce and even custom-making dresses for women and suits for men right there on the side of the road. Foot-powered sewing machines were often the key to a good life, as most of the clothes manufactured in China were for export and the ready-made clothes at local markets were seconds or knockoffs.

At the same time, villages farther away from cities were getting left behind. One student from the far northeastern part of

China told me that because of the weather there, the people of his village worked six months a year and had nothing to do the other half of the year. He'd been tasked with trying to find some type of contract for handwork that his people could occupy their time with—and get paid for—during the long winters.

———————————

At first, only a few cities were open to foreign tourists. China wanted to show foreigners only their best, so they would go home and encourage more tourists and business travelers (and investors) to visit. Thus, cities were opened only when the government felt they were ready. As soon as each one opened, I made sure I'd be one of the first foreigners to visit.

On one of my early trips, I had intended to visit Hangzhou, but when the opportunity arose, I substituted Suzhou. Both are very old, historic, and beautiful cities, and Suzhou is famous for its canals, gardens, and old bridges crossing its waterways in the shape of a half circle and do not need supports. This construction system, which dates back more than a thousand years, made it possible for ships with masts and sails to pass through the canals.

Suzhou is the silk capital of China, and for a thousand years now, for the world. Silk, the main trading commodity of the Silk Road connecting China with the ancient kingdoms and empires of the Middle East and Europe, made the people of Suzhou very rich—mostly because the Chinese kept the method of making it a secret for more than a thousand years.

The secret is now out: Mulberry leaves are picked and fed to silkworms, which are the larvae of silkmoths, that are held in large round baskets—silk factories have hundreds of these. The silkworms eat the leaves, and you'd be surprised at how loud the sound of thousands of silkworms eating leaves is. The worms then enclose themselves for their pupal phase in cocoons made of raw silk produced by their salivary glands. The worms' cocoons are boiled, killing the larvae and making it easier to unravel the silk. Workers then pull the silk, thread by thread, off the cocoons and onto spindles. From there, it is spun into silk cloth, dyed, stitched into garments or made for other uses, and sold to consumers.

The wealthiest silk merchants used their wealth to build homes with glorious gardens. About a dozen still stand, each with its own unique character. They feature little ponds and pavilions and beautiful flowers all around, with the home centered in the garden plan to ensure beautiful views from every window, each of which with a different shape. Every garden also features some type of waterfall or fountain that fills the visitor's ears with the soothing sound of running water. Years ago, there were many of these garden homes, and now there's only a few, but frankly, it's a miracle any survived and prospered given all the wars and conflicts the region has suffered.

My desire to visit Suzhou had been quite personal, as my aunt and uncle, Mary O. and Ed Rice, had lived there in the 1930s. Mary O. founded a girls' school during their time there, and Uncle Ed founded a hospital. I spent some time on the trip trying to find each of institutions they'd founded, without success. But my search did lead me into parts of the city that were off the beaten (and tourist-sanctioned) path.

At that time, in China, school attendance was required for only six years for all citizens. If after those six years a person was unable to pass a battery of tests, he or she would be removed from school and condemned to a life of extremely hard manual labor. In Suzhou, I saw lots of people doing this manual labor in the scorching heat of the day, all without the aid of machines. None looked happy, and all looked like they were in pain.

Paving roads was an important part of modernizing China, and each new road required thousands of manual workers. In one place, I saw old women—or at least, they looked old—tasked with unloading barges full of tremendous stones intended for paving. The process was all manual labor: men or women positioned on the barge would lift a giant rock and place it on a woman's shoulders. She would stagger up the steep bank of the river, carry it down to a spot where a road was being built, drop the rock, and go back for another. Then, what looked to me to be teenage boys using sledgehammers broke the large rocks into small ones to create the base for the road.

Some years later, on another visit to Suzhou, I saw with my own eyes something I'd long known about China but had never witnessed before. A group of students and I were visiting one of Suzhou's very old pagodas. It was lunchtime, and we were taken to what looked like a snack stand to get food. But we bypassed the stand, entered a door, and then descended five floors of stairs to a deep underground space. There, we found a large dining room set up with a feast.

In the early period after the Communists took over, a constant fear of a nuclear attack from the U.S. or Russia prevailed. As a measure to protect Chinese citizens and sovereignty, workers started digging to build cities underneath cities. Mao's mandate was simple: another nation might attack China, but no nation on earth had enough people to control China.

After the Cultural Revolution started, many intellectuals and others that the leaders of the Revolution disliked or distrusted were sent to these caves and tunnels as forced labor to expand them or restore the ones that had collapsed. A graduate student once told me that her father, an English teacher by trade, had been viewed as an enemy of the Red Guard because of his job. He was forced to work and live underground for three years, and during that time, he didn't see the sun once. As a result, his back was permanently bent, like an old man's, and he was diagnosed with emphysema—at the age of forty-seven.

My student's father had been lucky: more than half of the men and women condemned to work underground died there. He was sick and disfigured by the work, but he was alive and able to work long hours each day teaching English to high school students and fill his evenings with tutoring sessions.

Guilin, an ancient summer capital for several of China's dynasties and the home of many significant battles during the Second World War, opened to tourism some years into Deng's reforms. Nestled in a scenic mountainous spot, Guilin took quite some time to restore and rebuild, but it became a shining example of the new China.

The Li Jung River runs through Guilin, and for forty miles downstream, it snakes through a range of oddly shaped mountains; the boat ride down the Li Jung is one of the most beautiful experiences on earth. As more and more tourists came to the area, Guilin became a must-see if only for the boat ride down the Li Jung.

I loved bringing my tour groups to the villages that surrounded Guilin. Each one, it seemed, was largely made up of a single extended family. The farms in the villages were very beautiful, and all the villagers always seemed excited to see us (they were not usually visited by foreign tourists). I tried to visit a different one on each trip.

Guilin isn't an easy place to get to. One trip I took involved a flight out of Xi'an. As we neared the mountains surrounding Guilin, the pilot was unable to lift the nose of the Russian-built plane enough to clear the mountains. Nonplussed, the flight attendant ordered the six rows of passengers who were sitting in front of the wings of the plane to the back. The shift in weight apparently raised the nose of the plane enough to allow it to clear the mountains. Many of the Chinese people on the flight were nonchalant about the whole thing, like it happened on every flight into Guilin.

As for me, I swore I'd never fly on a plane built in Russia again. Luckily, around that time China began to buy European- and American-made planes, but the Russian ones were still in service too. I quickly learned how to know whether a flight involved a Russian plane, though—in China, planes were numbered according to when they were put into service, and those with numbers below 490 were all Russian.

———

While most Chinese universities are fairly new, dating from the end of the Cultural Revolution, Guilin's excellent university is hundreds of years old. It lies in the middle of the city, its Ming-era buildings surrounding a large courtyard.

In more recent years, the university added a new campus outside of town. A friend of mine who was well connected there managed to get me invited to deliver lectures there several times. Whenever I had a schedule of delivering lectures for the State Department on understanding American foreign policy, I'd always make sure to include Guilin as a stop. The students and faculty there received me very warmly, as they often told me that visitors came to Guilin only to see its beauty and never interacted with or paid any attention to its people.

My first trip to Nanning, located in southern China, near Vietnam, was an accident. I had been visiting Guilin and was supposed to fly next to Shanghai, but as was often the case, the airport in Guilin became fogged in. In those early years, if the weather was bad, planes didn't fly. Once I learned that it would be two or three days before conditions would be clear enough to allow flights to resume, I hired a bus to make the trip to Nanning instead.

I'd imagined that a drive through the mountains would be beautiful, and it certainly was. On the other side of the range, rice fields covered the mountains and hills like stair steps. As we drove past the fields, they were full of families transplanting rice. One of the reasons why China has prospered for thousands of years is that both men and women alike work the fields. In China, everybody works—including some very old people and children. I once stopped an old man who was transplanting rice to ask why he continued to work at such an advanced age. He told me, "This [work] is a wonderful part of living. I plant the rice with care, and it has fed me all of my eighty years."

All was going well till until the road reached the main highway running from Nanning to Vietnam. In 1979, China and Vietnam engaged in a war that resulted in many thousands of casualties on each side. China's army was much larger, of course, but they were poorly trained and still used Korean War-era weapons. The Chinese troops were also quite green, having never been in battle. The Vietnamese, on the other hand, had just fought the Japanese, the French, and then the Americans in separate wars. Vietnamese troops were ready for war: they dug in, and their machine guns mowed down their Chinese counterparts. But China had a few tricks up its sleeves: new fighter planes and lots of bombs, which they rained down on the cities of Vietnam. The war ended in a draw, but for the next ten years, every few months battles would flare up again along the border.

On this day, on that highway, we encountered a major Chinese troop movement in preparation for the China–Vietnam war. For three and a half hours, we sat on our bus and watched as tanks, heavy weapons, and trucks full of thousands of troops headed for the border. As I gazed at the troops as they passed by, I noticed that none of them were armed and asked our bus driver why. The answer: no one in China can carry a gun, not even a soldier. The troops would be given rifles on the day of the battle, and those who made it out alive would turn them in after the battle.

Eventually, we all got off the bus and stood by the roadside to wave to the truckloads of troops. They were so surprised to see thirty-two Americans waving to them as they rode by that they soon started waving back.

I had read avidly about the 1974 discovery of thousands of terracotta warriors and horses buried in pits in Xi'an, one of China's oldest cities and the capital of the first dynasty. A farmer digging a well stumbled upon this great wonder, which catapulted Xi'an to its status as a sought-after tourist destination.

The site didn't officially open to visitors until 1984, but I was able to slip in during my first trip to China and stay in an old hospital that had been converted into a hotel. While there, I had the opportunity to walk around in the ruins and watch as archeologists labored to piece the ancient terracotta soldiers back together. Tomb raiders using torches had inadvertently ignited a fire in the wooden chamber the terracotta soldiers had been buried in, and the ensuing roof collapse had shattered the warriors into pieces. Each of the thousands of figures was different and had been broken in different ways, like a giant 3D puzzle. It's believed that the original sculptors of the figures made them as likenesses of real members of Emperor Chin's military; the emperor's tomb lies near the site.

Xi'an is interesting for other reasons. Unlike most other ancient cities, Xi'an's city wall and drum and bell towers still stood, as well as two very old pagodas which had been emptied of a cache of Buddhist texts but still offered great views of the countryside. It's also the only city in China with a very large Muslim minority area, including a mosque with writings in Chinese characters, rather than Arabic.

Perhaps the most interesting site in Xi'an—other than the terracotta warriors—is its Stele Forest. Steles (also known as stelas or stelae) are tall stone slabs that were erected in ancient cultures worldwide as monuments. Xi'an's Stele Forest is a former Confucian temple that has served as a museum for steles since 962 AD. Today, it is home to more than 3,000 steles—mostly from the Tang dynasty (618 AD–907 AD)—ranging from six to eight feet tall. Each stone is carved with proclamations or works of art, and in ancient times, scholars would rub them with ink to make hundreds of paper copies. The copies would then be sent like newspapers around the ancient kingdom, informing the Chinese people of important news and new laws and sharing the beautiful pictures and poems carved on the stones that still exist today. As each new dynasty began, the history of the preceding dynasty would be etched on steles, so Xi'an's Stele Forest offers 2,300 years of written history in one place. No other civilization in the world even comes close.

As the years passed and I brought more groups to China, changes in rules and regulations happened fast and always presented new opportunities and challenges alike. New air routes opened up constantly, and every year, new hotels rose into the skies of Chinese cities.

One hotel-related policy offered a great benefit for my groups: if a group booked a three-star hotel, which guaranteed little more than air conditioning and private bathrooms in each room, and a four- or even five-star hotel had availability at the time, the group would be automatically upgraded at no extra cost. While this might seem surprising, the Chinese government had sound reasoning for it: they wanted to keep the highest-end hotels at full occupancy because doing so would encourage private investors to build more of them. Higher-rated hotels were always in great locations and nicely appointed, so getting one or two five-star hotels for the price of three-star ones made my fellow travelers very happy.

I quickly discovered that my tour groups didn't like to stay in hotels owned by China's secret service or branches of the military, so I avoided those options. Yes, everybody and every institution built hotels, including universities, provinces, and city and county governments, because they were all vying for tourists' foreign exchange currency (FEC)— the only way they could purchase imported goods.

China's modernization was greatly facilitated by the introduction of many comparatively liberal laws. For example, the government could establish eminent domain and demolish any-thing that stood in the way of progress—with the provision that they would provide new housing for anyone who had been dis-placed. When I first heard of this, my American perspective got the better of me: I thought people would be upset about being forced from their homes. To my surprise, most I talked to were delighted—the new apartments had running water, bathrooms, and electricity. Residents I spoke to in Beijing didn't seem to mind that many of the more historic spots in the city had been turned into giant squares and parking lots in the name of progress.

Change was slower to come to other aspects of life in China. For example, the two-currency system was still in force, so if Chinese citizens didn't have FEC, they couldn't buy imported goods. Each month, workers received their pay from their em-ployers, known as *danweis* or work units, in the form of cou-pons and RMB (people's money) cash. Workers lined up out-side their *danwei's* finance office and were called in, one by one, each month to receive their pay in cash.

Banks were seldom used by Chinese people; most instead had lock boxes hidden away in their apartments. In theory, men were expected to turn their cash over to their wives or moth-ers, if unmarried, but most in practice held back at least some of it. Also in theory, men and women were paid the same, but in practice men usually got more—and when hiring decisions were made, men always had an advantage.

Coupons were required to buy almost any goods except fresh food. For example, there were two types of coupons for cigarettes: one for "good" brands that entitled holders to two packs per month, and one for what the Chinese called "trash" cigarettes, which entitled holders to six packs per month.

The sale of all cooking oil, meat, dozens of other necessities, and smoking products were all under a central government monopoly. Modern supermarkets didn't come on the scene until the mid-1990s. Gasoline was rationed, so if you were lucky enough to have a car, you could hardly use it. Only the government was able to import cars, and Chinese-built cars were terrible, with designs dating from the 1950s and very small engines. Schools and universities in cities were improving, but libraries had few books—the Chinese government remained deathly afraid of ideas from the outside world.

One law that remained in place until 1990 required *danweis* to provide coupons, healthcare, utilities, and even housing for their workers as a way to ensure against homelessness. It was typical to greet new acquaintances not by asking what their name was or where they lived but instead asking, "What's your work unit?"

But during the modernization period, as China switched from a planned to a privatized economy, children increasingly grew up, got married, and went to work for private ventures but still lived in their parents' *danwei* homes, presenting a flaw in the system. I once wrote a newspaper article about a family whose son and daughter stayed in their parents' *danwei*-supplied home after both married, and even after their parents died. The parents' *danwei* continued to provide housing, healthcare, utilities, and coupons for these two families, even though none of the family members worked for the *danwei*, because it was illegal to evict anyone. To make up for these kinds of expenses, *danweis* turned to developing privatized businesses—everything from hotels, restaurants, bookstores, auto repair shops, gas stations, and anything else you can imagine—to make money.

Despite their years hemmed in under Communist rule, the Chinese people embraced this entrepreneurial spirit. If one business didn't work, they'd quickly switch to selling something else—so fast, in some cases, that a store's signage and window displays might not have anything to do with what was actually sold there. I remember entering a Chinese medicine shop once to find that it sold nothing but men's white shirts. Where there had once been eight sightseeing boats on the Li Jung River, and there were soon more than a hundred.

Many of these new businesses were great at figuring out what other Chinese people wanted to buy but often misjudged the preferences of foreigners and tourists. For example, it was a good fifteen years before it was understood what foreigners would expect to buy in a grocery store—or even what a grocery store was. Chinese people were used to buying food in open markets like the one I described in Guangzhou. And for a housing development to be successful, it had to have a market. Some giant high-rise developments in China had no one living in them because the farmers in the area were used to selling at a particular market and refused to take a risk and move to another one. While cities were on the fast track when it came to change, the same could not be said for farmers or farm communities.

Finding and training employees in times of great change proved to be quite problematic. Foreign expats—other than those who taught English—were interested only in short stays. There was a saying that American expats in particular always had their return ticket when they arrived. When I advised American companies involved in contract negotiations in China, I reminded them that their local counterparts always had patience on their side if they knew when the Americans had scheduled their return flights. I recommended that they keep their planned departure dates secret and to talk as though they had long-term plans to stay.

But there were challenges that faced the Americans who did stay. It took years to build international schools for foreign children. Housing was a problem, as foreigners wanted things like heat and air conditioning—not to mention cars. Some companies, like IBM and Celanese, built little villages to house the families of their expat American employees working there.

During these years, Chinese leaders were afraid to send professionals abroad for fear they would not come back. They were also uncertain about what to do with the ones who went abroad and came back. Most were required to wait a year before returning to their jobs or classrooms to make sure they would not be disruptive to the systems already in place.

While China eagerly wished to modernize, doing so was a major adjustment for a billion people—and there were no models to follow. Eventually, most Chinese citizens overcame their fear of a return to the chaotic China of the past and committed themselves to modernization along with their leaders, but it took time to navigate these uncharted waters.

Our Adventures

I always referred to my China trips as "adventures" so the groups would expect the unexpected, and our visits to Guilin always seemed to be particularly adventurous. There's no question in my mind that Guilin is the prettiest spot on earth; I never tired of the beauty of the mountains that seemed to spring out of the river. On a boat ride on one trip there, I sat in the very front of the boat so my photos would be unobstructed. Just a few feet in front of me, an eagle soared down from the sky, hit the glassy water, and pulled out a foot-and-a-half-long trout. It all happened so close to me that water spattered my camera lens.

One year, my group stayed in a new five-story Guilin hotel called the Garden Hotel. After dinner one evening, several of us went to the hotel's rooftop garden for a 360-degree view of the city's jagged mountains. The moon was almost full, so we could clearly see the river's reflection of the mountains. Eventually, most of the group headed off to bed, as we were due to sail the river early the next morning, but I stayed behind with the last four people and the last five beers. When all the beer was gone, we decided to leave and found the door locked. We banged on the door and yelled as loud as we could, but all we got in return were echoes from the mountains.

At dinner that evening, I'd noticed that several of the windows in the dining room, which was positioned directly below the rooftop garden, were unlocked. I laid down on my stomach and peered over the edge of the roof, and in the moonlight, I could see that each floor was defined by a foot-wide ledge. My four companions held my arms as I slid down the wall and got my footing on the ledge outside the dining room windows. Hugging the ledge tight, I inched my way along the windows, rattling each to try to find an unlocked one. I was terrified, but I kept thinking of my boyhood in the Smoky Mountains spent hopping over streams on narrow logs. The fall from the ledge of the Garden Hotel, of course, would not be into a stream.

The first window was locked, but as luck would have it, the second window opened. I climbed through and to my great surprise nearly stepped on someone. The wait staff that had entertained us a few short hours before were sleeping on the dining room's floor, each with his or her own pillow and very colorful flower quilt. I carefully tiptoed through the flowers and bodies until I finally found the door.

As I exited the dining room, I found members of the hotel's cleaning staff sleeping in the hallway and on the stairs. As before, each had a pillow, but their quilts featured butterflies. It was hard to get up the stairs without waking someone; I have no idea how someone can sleep on a stair.

I finally reached the door to the rooftop garden and eased it open. In a whisper, I issued instructions to the group on how they would each have to sneak past sleeping bodies and then wait quietly at the elevator for the rest of us, as I was afraid the noise from the elevator would wake the sleepers up. We all made it back to our rooms without waking a single person.

On another trip, we left Guilin and flew to Chongqing, where we were to board a ship bound for the Yangtze River gorge. When we arrived at the Chongqing airport and were reunited with our luggage, we were overwhelmed with the odor of dead fish—it was terrible, and everyone was gagging.

I asked to see the head of the airport and told the rest of my group to guard the luggage so it wouldn't be put on a truck and sent on to the ship. The head of the airport refused to see me and sent word that the fish problem wasn't his problem. I sent back word that he'd have to find the person in charge of fish problems, as we were not leaving the airport until we saw him and would bring the fish bags to his office.

In the meantime, my brother, Dr. John Wilson, who'd joined me on this particular trip, and some fellow travelers had isolated the smell to six suitcases. (John is a Chinese historian himself.) Several airline officials showed up around that time, as well as the man who was to take us to our ship. After hours of negotiation, we came up with a solution: the good bags would go on to the ship in the same transport with us. Another truck would come for the smelly bags and take them to the ship's laundry, where the clothes inside them would be cleaned (yes, the fish smell had permeated the suitcases and infused the clothes inside).

The man from the airline said he'd give us $500 dollars in yuan to buy six new suitcases. I knew you couldn't get six decent suitcases for that, so once we got on the bus, I told the driver, "I'll match their $500, so take us to the number one department store." (The Chinese rank everything.)

I'd hoped to just take the six people with the smelly bags to the store's luggage department, but all thirty-two people on the tour wanted to see what a Chinese department store looked like, so we all got off the bus. The fish group and I headed for the luggage department and I told the rest to be back at the bus within an hour.

The store had a good luggage selection, so everyone was happy—so good, in fact, that five other people from the tour bought bags as well. Nearly everyone returned to the bus with armloads of packages and tales of great values.

Once we arrived at the boat, we found rather rudimentary boarding conditions. A plank not more than a foot wide ran from the shore for about two hundred feet to the ship. There was no way some of the people on the tour would make it, so six of the ship's crew had to help guide each person on to the ship. Two slipped off the plank and into the water, which was fortunately only waist deep. The crew then took care of the hardest part: loading all the new suitcases and a mountain of department store purchases up the plank and onto the boat.

On our trips, everyone was always looking for deals, and they were in the right place for it: negotiation is the Chinese way of doing business. Despite the fact that everyone had the same opportunities to negotiate, it always seemed that someone was upset because someone else had gotten a better deal than he or she had. So I set forth a rule: no one was allowed to lose their temper for less than $50.

Once, as we were checking out of the Green Garden Hotel in Beijing, a man was selling Olympic hats on a corner right by our bus. His asking price was a reasonable $5 per hat, and he sold several of them at that price. But as more people boarded the bus, they announced that they'd managed to get the price down to $4, and then on down to $3. Some of the people who'd paid the original asking price got mad and wanted to go after the man for "cheating them." I had the driver shut the bus's door and told the group: "You know you'd pay $15 or more for that hat in the U.S. You came to China to see China, not to save a few dollars on an Olympic hat."

People lose it over the pettiest things. For example, at one restaurant stop, an Army colonel in our group began yelling at a very young waitress who had charged him for nine additional beers (over the two the table received at no charge), while he insisted he'd had only eight. The cost for each one-liter bottle of beer: about $1. I intervened and gave the waitress $10. The colonel's wife led him away.

Sometimes our adventures began even before we left the United States. On the first leg of one trip, a USAir flight bound from Charlotte to Los Angeles, the door to the plane would not close.

As the crew pushed and pulled on the door, trying to close it, the door ended up breaking. We were informed that we'd have to wait for four hours for a new door.

I knew this would make us miss our connection to China, so I jumped out of my seat, pushed my way past the flight attendants (this was before 2001, so such action was still possible), and ran into the terminal headed for the United Airlines desk. At the desk, I explained my problem and asked if thirty-three seats were available on their next flight to LA, which was scheduled to leave in twenty minutes. If I could get these people across the airport in fifteen minutes, the representative told me, we could go.

I raced back on the plane, stood at the head of the aisle, and yelled, "All Winthrop people: get your carry-ons and quickly follow me. I will explain later." I didn't want to reveal my plan to the other passengers, as I feared they might try to beat us to the United flight. We ended up making it to the United plane just in time. Everyone in the group was amazed—especially Winthrop's president, Tony DeGiorgio, who'd come along on the tour that year. He asked how I'd known about the other flight, and I told him that whenever I take a group on a China tour, I always make sure I have a backup plan.

―――――――――――

The first stop of that same trip was Shanghai, and we were to spend four days there at Shanghai International Studies University (SISU), also known as Shangwai. When we arrived at the airport, SISU sent two modes of transport to meet us: a brand-new bus and an old, extra-long limousine—the type that was often used for diplomats, with Chinese red flags on the front (they were nicknamed Red Flags). The university hosts wanted me to ride in the limo, but I knew from previous trips how unreliable and smelly those cars always were. So I somewhat disingenuously insisted that Winthrop's president and vice president should have the honor, while I rode in the bus and delivered a lecture to the students.

My quick plane switch got us to Shanghai on time, but our luggage didn't catch up to us for a couple of days. On our first day, SISU held a welcoming event for us, but of course our good clothes were in the luggage we'd checked. I bought a terrible fifty-cent tie from a street vendor, and because Chinese stores at the time didn't sell dress shirts big enough for me, I wore it with the polo shirt I'd worn on the seventeen-hour flight the day before. I'd been told to dress formally for the event, so I borrowed a sport coat from a German professor I knew in Shanghai. It was too big, but it was my only available option.

To my surprise, the welcome ceremony was in my honor, with the university making me its first honorary full professor. I received a key to the city at the event (my key is number 223, and I was told that they had presented Rudy Giuliani, then the mayor of New York, with number 222, as Shanghai and New York were sister cities). The vice mayor of Shanghai then read a proclamation stating that my teaching had helped give China a more realistic view of the world, and that my books were being used for international relations and world-press courses in colleges all over China. I was floored—and also very embarrassed at the thought of the sad-sack get-up I'd be wearing in all the pictures of the event. It was a real eye-opener for Tony DeGiorgio, for sure, as I doubt he'd ever thought twice about me back at Winthrop.

The Taklamakan Desert is known for its burial caves. The dry air there preserves the bodies for thousands of years, and tourists can climb down into the caves to see them. I'd been to a couple of them before, and the one they picked for this trip was about a mile from the next village. As you might imagine, it's quite dark in a burial cave, so its lights were powered by a generator stationed in the center of the village. Dozens of extension cords extended across the desert floor and descended into the cave.

I am claustrophobic—I'd leave the door to an airplane wash-room open if they'd let me—so I decided to go down into the cave this time only because others on the tour were afraid to. In groups of eight, we followed a guide down a long ladder into one burial chamber, crawled through one four-foot-tall passage into a second one, and then went through another four-foot-tall passage into a third, which did indeed house a very well-pre-served body. But while we stood there in the third chamber, the lights blinked off and we were engulfed in the blackest black of my nightmares.

I panicked and tried to escape, hitting my head on the top of the passageways in each chamber. Bruised, breathless, and dazed when I finally emerged, I shouted to the tour guide at the mouth of the cave that the lights had gone out. Another man hopped on a motor bike and raced back across the desert to the village to restart the generator.

The tour guide told me that the lights often go out during tours. I suggested that the guide below should carry a flashlight.

"Oh, he has one."

"Why in the hell didn't he turn it on?"

"He knew we could get the generator going again. You should have been patient."

The Chinese are patient people, but this time, I think they were to a fault. That was the third and last desert tomb I ever visited. Mummies aren't my favorite people anyway.

I am cursed with a very bad back. It hurts pretty much all the time and often gets locked up. Over the years, I've tried both Western and Chinese medicine to solve the issues I have—with no luck. But on one trip, an acquaintance insisted that he knew a traditional Chinese doctor who could cure any back. So I gave him a try with the friend who recommended him to me in tow.

I stripped to my shorts, and he had me lie face down on a table. The doctor, who was very small, very short, and very old, suddenly jumped in the air and landed with both of his knees pressed onto my backbone. I was glad he was small, but he had superhuman strength—he placed one arm under my head and the other under my knees and began pulling inward, all the while pressing his knees into my back.

Before long, I was in so much pain I felt as though I was levitating above the table. I began to test my command of both Chinese and American curse words, and the friend who'd brought me whispered, "Please, Dr. Wilson, don't say 'turtle.'" I can't say that it had occurred to me at that point to say turtle, which is a terrible curse word in China. I'm told that it's because female turtles lay eggs on beaches and gangs of male turtles shoot their sperm on the eggs. The suggestion is that your mother isn't a discriminating person when it came to choosing sex partners.

My trips always seemed to have "interesting developments" that added excitement. Travelers to China never have all that much to say about the Great Wall once they get home, but a bus that breaks down in the middle of the Gobi Desert is a tale worth telling. When that misfortune occurred, we decided to venture outside for a bathroom break while we waited for help. As we dispersed to do our business, the women headed off to the right side of the bus and the men went to the left, and those who sought more privacy wandered off to find a desert plant or big rock to hide behind.

Now, the Gobi doesn't have sand dunes—just lots of rocks and miniature tornadoes called dust devils that quickly form and skip across the desert floor before disappearing. They're quite exciting to watch—out a bus window, and at a distance. To keep everyone's mind off the broken-down bus, I encouraged them to count how many dust devils they'd see as they walked around outside.

The words had no sooner left my lips when a dust devil appeared and headed right for us. We all raced back toward the bus and hid on its left side, as it was headed for the right side— the women's side. Luckily, it passed right over our heads, filling our ears with a "VAROOM" sound. As it skipped over the bus, I realized I should have warned them to hold their breath. Most of us ended up with a mouthful of dirt.

So what do you do in the desert with thirty-two stranded people? You send them out looking for the dinosaur eggs the desert is known for, of course. While the egg hunt was underway, the driver and I flagged down every vehicle that came our way.

"How many people can you take to town?" we'd ask.

The drivers of even the smallest cars would volunteer to take on four passengers for the forty-mile ride to the train station, and we managed to get most of the group on their way in this manner. Finally, a truck came to the rescue, so we piled all our luggage in the truck, placed the stragglers on top of the bags, and headed for the train station.

Once we arrived at the train, we couldn't believe our luck—our assigned train car was brand new, a sleeper with two bunks in each compartment. The only problem: a group of seven French tourists had gotten to it first and had spread their things over our bunks. Lots of arguments and shouting ensued as I insisted that our people should get their assigned berths. The French retorted that they'd gotten there first, so they had first choice, and they refused to let us or the poor railroad employee see their tickets—which were probably for another car that wasn't so nice and new.

Eventually, we managed to shuffle things around so we only had to give up part of one compartment to the Frenchmen. Our guide gallantly volunteered to sit in a separate, non-sleeper car, and I placed one of our travelers, a professor, in a compartment with three of the French tourists. What they didn't know was that this particular professor not only snored but also had a nasty case of sleep apnea that led him to leap out of bed yelling three or four times a night.

When we all got up the next morning, the Frenchmen were gone, and we never saw them again. That was lucky—but the unlucky part was that for the rest of the trip, each man tried and failed to room with the shouting professor. When it was my turn, I ended up sleeping in a chair in the lobby of our beautiful hotel in Beijing. A maid woke me up at 4:00 a.m. so she could vacuum under my feet. From then on, I dipped into my own pocket and rented an extra room to ensure peace and quiet.

The city of Qingdao was once a German trading post, and the German influence is still evident in its architecture. In the modern day, however, Qingdao advertises itself as the "garden city," a nod to the flowers that are found everywhere. Many Chinese couples travel there for their wedding ceremonies and honeymoons—or at the very least, for the photographs. All over Qingdao, professional photographers park trucks that serve as changing rooms, and the couples and their wedding parties spring in and out them in their finery to take photos at the most scenic sites in the city.

As Qingdao is a seaside city, there are many scenic spots along the water that are perfect for taking photos. I was told that there are thirty designated venues for photos, but most couples pick their favorite six. At the most popular ones, couples line up to wait their turn, sometimes for hours; in some cases, the lines are five to ten couples long, and the photographers constantly yell at each other to hurry up. The more expensive photographers have one person who sets up the lighting, another who does makeup, and a third who directs the couple to pose in just the right spots. All the pictures feature the city's flowers, and those who don't bring their own can buy or rent them at any location.

Qingdao is also the beer capital of China. Nine gigantic breweries there produce beer that tastes very German, and Qingdao's beers are exported around the world. Most of the breweries have tours but be aware when you first get to the greeting room. They will have you taste all the beers produced in that plant. The sample glasses are not small, and after four to six beers you're taken on the tour of the brewery.

Beware: the tour takes two hours, and as of my most recent visit, there were still no restrooms along the way. Go before the tour begins, or you may be dancing a German jig for the last half hour of it.

My friend Mel Goldstein joined us, as he often did, on a western China trip to Kashgar. As we toured a Shiite mosque in the town, Mel, who is Jewish, struck up a conversation with a man there. They talked on and on, and eventually, I signaled to Mel that we needed to go.

Mel tried to wrap it up, but the man responded that he wanted to continue the conversation over dinner at his home. I stepped in to thank him, saying that our group of thirty-two travelers already had reservations elsewhere for dinner. The man shrugged and told me that we were all welcome for dinner.

I asked my translator to explain the situation to the man. They spoke briefly, and she returned to tell me that she would cancel our previous arrangements and deliver us to the man's house at 7:00 p.m. I was flabbergasted—I couldn't imagine being able to host thirty-two foreign guests for dinner with a few hours of notice. On top of everything else, Joe, a graduate student on the trip, was celebrating his fiftieth birthday, and I'd arranged for a cake to be served after dinner. I implored the translator to intervene, but it was to no avail. She told me she'd make sure the cake was delivered to the man's home.

We arrived at the man's home at the appointed time and found a beautiful garden set up with lots of low tables and cushions on the floor. Two other tables, each with a dozen or so men seated at them, were arranged on the other side of the garden. Our host welcomed us with a long speech, and Mel responded with an equally long speech. Each of them celebrated the other as if they were brothers.

Then the food came: dish after dish of everything one could imagine, nonstop, for more than two hours. A band arrived and played both Eastern and Western music. The men on the other side of the garden got up and danced and sang along, and we eventually figured out that we were expected to join them.

Finally, a few of the bravest men from the other group came over to our table and asked the women in our group to dance. The rest of us men soon followed suit; the music was very fast, so we ended up really just jumping around. I even performed a mountain dance, which was received with much hollering and yelling.

The climax of the evening was the presentation of Joe's birthday cake. The band played the "Happy Birthday" song again and again, and everyone danced and sang. It was a wonderful night. Every time I see Joe, he reminds me that it was the happiest day of his life.

The best adventures are seldom planned.

Chapter 3
The Magnificent Road to Rich:
Higher Education in China

N O SINGLE THING BECAME MORE BROKEN DURING the Cultural Revolution than higher education, and it was entirely by design. All the country's colleges and universities were closed. If they weren't imprisoned and tortured or killed, the schools' faculty members were sent to the countryside to work in the mines and fields.

In some instances, distinguished professors were lined up on stages, made to assume the airplane pose—squatting and leaning forward, with their arms stretched out behind them, and beaten with bamboo poles until they lost consciousness and fell over. Guards would then pour water on the professors until they came to and the beating would begin all over again—all while hundreds of young members of the Red Guard cheered.

Other professors were sent to the countryside and ordered to dig deep holes in the ground. They were pushed into the holes and left there, sometimes for years. Once a day, guards would lower a bucket containing rice gruel down to them. After they ate, they had to scoop up their waste in the same bucket to be hauled up. Many of them died, but I came to know some who survived.

During the transition years, in the late 1970s, the surviving educators returned to their universities to start the hard work of reopening them. Their books had been burned, and colleagues who had sided with the Red Guard had taken over their apartments and, in some cases, even their clothes. Ten years after the fact, I asked a friend what the hardest part of his persecution had been. He responded, "Wearing rags every day and having meetings with other professors who were wearing my clothes."

When the universities finally reopened, the first year's class of students were outstanding—as they were the best students in the nation from the ten years during which the institutions had been closed. They were eager to learn, and the professors were eager to teach. A sign that hung over my office door at Winthrop read, "To teach is to touch a life forever." I wish I'd had another sign reading, "Teaching in China has changed my life forever." In 1985 and 1986, the years I had the pleasure of teaching twenty professors from all over China, I learned more about China from them than I did during my travels in any other year. I felt as if I was able to play a small role in China's transition.

China was in the process of modernizing, but it certainly had no intentions of democratizing. The government knew that education of the people was a cornerstone of modernization, but at the same time, there was great distrust and fear about what changes this education might bring. For this reason, I've used the real names of my Chinese friends and students only if they are dead or no longer living in China. All others are identified by pseudonyms.

In the spring of 1985, I visited Washington, D.C. to explore possible grant possibilities for Winthrop. As I'd previously worked with the Fulbright Program in India, I decided to stop in at the Fulbright Program offices to say hello. The woman I met with seemed very upset. I asked why, and she replied that for the first two years of the Fulbright Program in China, the organization had exclusively sent professors in "safe" disciplines that were unlikely to concern the Chinese government. Now that the program was in its third year, it finally had permission to explore new areas, but there simply weren't enough good applicants.

She looked me straight in the eye and said, "We need you to apply."

I reminded her that I'd already been granted a Fulbright in India. Undeterred, she said that was all the more reason to do it. It was three months after the application deadline, but she insisted that I fill out the forms right away. I did, and a week later I received an acceptance letter and assignment to Beijing University, considered by many to be the best university in China.

While I was impressed by Beijing University, I disliked the city itself. It has terrible winter weather, and in the spring, the level of dust in the air is so bad you can hardly see for months at a time. I went home to talk the matter over with my family, and everyone was positive—but they clearly had mixed feelings. Reluctantly, I accepted the offer.

A short time later, the woman who'd wooed me to join the Fulbright Program in China called to say that a professor set to go to Wuhan University had refused the appointment unless he could go to Beijing instead. I replied that I'd relinquish the Beijing position, but not for Wuhan. She called back within an hour and asked if I'd accept a position at Shanghai International

Studies University (SISU) instead. I'd recently read a report that ranked SISU as the top university in China in terms of efforts to modernize. I yelled out "Wonderful!" in the poor woman's ear—and it indeed turned out to be wonderful.

At Shanghai International Studies University, a key university in China—one of the best of the best—I would be teaching international relations courses to college professors from who came there from universities all over China. It took a while for me to realize that by teaching college professors from twenty universities, I would in turn be influencing not only them but also their students—and that they in turn would provide me with such a clear view of life and higher education in China.

At the time, English was the most popular major in China's colleges and universities, but nearly all classes were about language and literature. That year, however, China's Ministry of Education issued a list of twelve "practical" courses from which the English majors had to pick six, and the transition was to be immediate. This threw the universities into a panic, as most did not have professors to teach these courses, but all knew that these rules must be implemented. My courses—American Government, Third World Development, American Foreign Policy, and International Relations—fit right into their plans, and a fourth, World Press, would be taught by a fellow Fulbright professor. (Most of the other newly required courses were business or science related.)

In those days, higher education in China was extremely regimented: for any given course, students at all Chinese colleges and universities read the same chapter in the same book on the same day. Professors were required to write out their lectures; get them approved by their deans, Communist Party officials, and the Ministry of Education; and then read them word-for-world aloud to the class. Faculty members were ranked depending on how many courses they were approved to teach, rather than on their number of advanced degrees and publications or on the quality of their teaching skills. Conversational foreign language courses were somewhat less restricted, but their reading assignments were still uniform nationwide. It's not at all surprising that many Chinese students had trouble adjusting to the methods used by foreign faculty members.

My colleague Earl Rovit was assigned to teach American Culture and Literature at SISU as a Fulbright professor, and we shared a huge office—the size of a classroom—along with a young professor named Ge Pin, who had been assigned to translate for us. When Earl and I received our class rolls, we were very impressed with the group but puzzled as to why we were each assigned only eighteen students, when we'd been told we would have twenty. After scanning the rolls, we realized that neither of us had any students from SISU, and we'd been told by Fulbright that we'd have two each.

Politely, but firmly, we confronted the leadership at SISU about the issue, and were surprised at the reason given: they were "too busy to free up any professors." We pointed out that in exempting their faculty from the program, they were in violation of their agreement with Fulbright, which certainly would not have picked SISU to serve as a host if it were not participating. The next day, we each had two wonderful young SISU professors in our classes.

Later, we learned that some of the older professors at the university had prevented them from participating because they perceived it as a threat. Apparently, these professors believed that the young men would then have some sort of advantage over their elders, who took a more fundamentalist Communist approach to teaching and didn't care for the idea of changing the way they taught: memorizing and delivering propaganda-filled lectures.

The students, who came from schools all over China, ranged in age from 26 to 46, and the group was evenly divided by gender. I taught three subjects each semester for a total of eighteen graduate hours during the year—a very heavy load, but the government wanted change and it wanted it now. The days were full, as I taught two-hour-long morning and afternoon classes on Tuesdays and Thursdays and a third morning class on Mondays and Wednesdays. I hosted office hours for two hours, four days a week, and every day, students would line up to talk. They had great questions; some I could answer, and some we just discussed and researched together. All were surprised when I sometimes said, "Let's see what the class thinks about this." In China, the professor's word was law, and no student opinion was ever considered.

These students were extremely bright and hungry for knowledge, so staying ahead of them was quite a challenge. I saw them as colleagues and said as much. They protested, saying, "No, no, Dr. Wilson. Please, just call us students." I didn't feel that did them justice, so I responded, "Then I will call you comrades." At that, they were horrified, decrying the term as a tool of propaganda, so they finally allowed me to refer to them as colleagues. I was trying to show them that in a learning community, everyone's ideas are important. It took a while for this to sink in, but I did indeed learn a great deal from them.

The Books

I knew that almost no library facilities in China had survived the Cultural Revolution, so before I journeyed to SISU,

I collected books from all over Winthrop's campus and from friends at other universities—in all, a trove of 1,600 books. Fulbright agreed to ship them to China for me, but when the books arrived, they were stored in the garage of the American consulate, with boxes stacked on boxes. Just before our arrival, a typhoon had hit Shanghai and caused massive flooding, so the bottom row of boxes was underwater for a week. By the time I arrived, the books inside were covered in mold and ruined.

Sadly, I had to throw away about ten percent of the books due to the green slime that coated them, but I set up the rest in a library of my own in my office. About a month into the first semester, I assigned my class some readings out of a particular book and told them I was doing so early because there was only one copy—the other had been ruined in the flood. During my office hours that day, three of the students came in to tell me that they'd saved my ruined books.

The students had spotted the books in the trash and had made a herculean effort to restore them, soaking them—page by page—in bleach and then ironing them once they were dry. I cannot imagine the effort it took for them to do this for every page in more than one hundred books. I was greatly touched by their love of books and their desire for knowledge, so I insisted that if they loved books that much, they must keep them. Whenever I gave the classes reading assignments, I would borrow them so all the students could use them.

Fulbright had provided me with money for textbooks by Fulbright, but the funds were hardly sufficient given my teaching load. Since I was teaching three different courses each semester, I negotiated with a publisher to buy previous editions of texts so there was enough money to buy eight books for each student. They seemed thrilled; apparently, they'd heard that the

Fulbright professors who taught in other universities during the two preceding years hadn't provided any books. (There's a saying that if someone drops a feather in Beijing, everyone in China hears it land.)

In China, books were highly prized and guarded as closely as you might expect. That year, I was honored to be invited to give a talk at Fudan University, where I spoke from the same stage Kissinger and Nixon had occupied during Nixon's landmark 1972 trip to China. At Fudan, one of the few universities in China that offered a Ph.D. in political science, I was asked by the dean and the chair of the political science department if I would like to see their new building. The building was wonderful, but I was shocked by its collection of books—or rather, the lack thereof.

The library was a large room with many students, but the only books on the shelves were old magazines that had been scrubbed of any mention of China. When I asked where the books were, I was led behind a curtain and into a little room with a single six-foot-tall bookcase with books on both sides. Told that only graduate students could use them, I inspected the books carefully—textbooks, mostly, very basic undergraduate-level books and lots of dictionaries. Horrified, I asked (rather impolitely), "How can you give a doctorate if this is all that the students have?"

"Oh, there are more," the dean replied, "but neither of us has the right to hold the key." A young professor was sent to retrieve it, and he returned about fifteen minutes later with a key attached to a big chain. The dean pulled down a set of stairs ascending to an attic. We climbed the stairs, unlocked a door, and entered a space the size of the entire building covered with waist-high stacks of every new book in the field. Nothing was cataloged, and none of the books seemed to have ever been opened, as they all still had their dust jackets.

I was shocked. My hosts told me that throughout Chinese history, as regimes have changed, the first move is often to burn all the books. During the Cultural Revolution, in fact, all of Fudan University's books were burned. I like to think of my hosts' defensive maneuver with their collection as the Ming Philosophy of library science: hide the books, because someone may need them hundreds of years in the future. Unfortunately, I found that this was the rule, rather than the exception, in libraries across China.

This was the first time that the dean and the chair of the political science department at Fudan had been allowed in the room. Needless to say, they were excited—they were like little kids on Christmas morning, gingerly picking up book after book. It was thrilling for them, but I was saddened, imagining how hard it must be for them to teach without materials.

I thought about this for a while and pondered what I could do to make a change. Deciding to throw caution to the wind and break all the rules, I told the dean and chair that as payment for delivering the lecture that day, I wanted them to give me four books. I asked them to select the books. I took them, drew a pen from my pocket, and wrote a thank-you message in the inside cover of each book stating that I, in turn, was donating these books back to the library to be used by the faculty and graduate students. My hosts were thrilled, but sadly, they simply put them back on the shelves of the secret room. As we exited, the lock clicked shut on these and all the other books.

The Students

As their first writing assignment, I asked my students to tell me about themselves. I told them the purpose of the assignment was to gauge their command of English, but in truth, I was curious about their backgrounds.

In return, I received twenty stories, in perfect English, about the punishments they'd suffered during the Cultural Revolution, as well as information on their parents. Not one student mentioned being married or having children. I was surprised, and told them so, but they told me that talking about spouses or children was considered bragging. In fact, all but three were married, and ten had children. (I've found through the years that when asked about their children, most Chinese people say some version of the same thing: that the child "is very mischievous.")

––––––––––––––

A mystery about three of my students took a bit of time to sort out. I noticed that each Friday, two of them would check out three different books from my library, take them to Nanjing over the weekend, and then return them promptly on Monday morning of the next week. Curious, I looked into their backgrounds and found that they were identified as professors working at a school that I knew did not exist. It appeared that their university, and they, had been conjured into existence.

On one occasion, two of the mystery students visited me in my office. Since we were alone, I seized the opportunity to get to the bottom of things. I casually asked if they had to wear their uniforms when they taught. Without thinking, they responded in the affirmative.

I smiled and told them that I'd noticed they wore much nicer and newer clothes than the other students to class, and that I knew only the military could afford such finery. I added that I knew only the Military University in Nanjing could have so many books copied in such a short period of time, over a weekend. They laughed. The secret was out. I assured them that I wouldn't tell the other students, but they replied that everyone else already knew.

————————

My oldest student, Wang—who I referred to as my "super student"—was in her mid-forties. Like the mystery students, she wore nice clothes but paired them with army gray-green canvas shoes and matching socks. In our private chats in my office, Wang often set me straight on military matters, things like exactly how high a cruise missile can rise off the ground and still not be detected on radar.

One day, a fellow professor asked me how it felt to have a famous colonel in my class—in fact, Wang's parents had been on the Long March with Mao, and she and her husband were both colonels in the Chinese army. Wang taught at another military university and was the mother of two children, but she confided that if it had been up to her, she wouldn't have had any. But it wasn't up to her: Wang had to have one son for her parents to raise, and one for her husband's parents to raise.

We became great friends. Wang taught me so much about China that I told her she should be teaching me. Once, on a class trip, we were riding through a small town and she mentioned that her grandfather lived in the town. I told her that we could stop the bus so she could see him, but Wang bristled at the idea.

"We could never do that. He is rather poor and doesn't have the money to host a banquet for all of us. He would lose face if he could not feed us."

On the other extreme, I learned that a student known as Mei-mei—which means little sister—cried every night because she missed her three-month old daughter. She had been told by her university that she had to come to SISU to take my classes, which meant leaving her baby with her in-laws in a city three hundred miles away.

She assured me often that she was glad to be there, and that she was learning so much. But one day, I made the mistake of asking about her daughter. She ran out of my office in tears and returned about an hour later, still pink around the eyes. She apologized, but I quickly reassured her, telling her that it was okay and adding that I sometimes cried when I was away from my children.

In the middle of the semester, we had a brief holiday period. Meimei came to my office and asked to leave a day early, as she'd learned that no train tickets to her city were available for a full three days after our holiday period began. I told her it would be fine, and she was thrilled. Later, some of the other students told me that even with the rest of the class urging her on, it had taken Meimei a week to summon the nerve to ask me—and that Chinese professors wouldn't have allowed it.

Shu, a small, single woman, was about forty, which many Chinese considered too old to get married. Some even referred to single women of that age or older as "trash" or "throw away." That was hardly the case for Shu: she was the editor of China's second-largest economics journal, located right across the street from SISU at the Shanghai Financial Institute.

It took Shu about a month to start talking in class. I had assigned her a list of economic questions I had about China, and the material she'd produced was so good that I insisted that she share them with the class. None of the other professors had a background in economics, so her presentation was well received. From that day forward, she was a great asset to the class.

Shu always kept us up to date on the constantly changing economic climate of China in those days. For example, three Chinese cities—Shanghai, Beijing, and Tianjin—were granted the same status as provinces due to their size and economic power, and debating how much of the tax collected in those cities should go the central government was a consuming issue of the time. Chinese cities were the nation's most significant collector of taxes, and while the amount they collected was growing at a rapid rate, they received only 30 percent of it back—making it impossible for them to undertake much-needed infrastructure projects. Shu shared with us that a proposal had been made to increase this to amount to 70 percent, so we were unsurprised when it came to pass over the following few years. It was a good thing: Shanghai was able to build essential bridges and tunnels, as well as an elevated train system.

Our class loved hearing Shu's stories, but I'm not so sure about the truth behind all of them. She told us one about an electricity generating plant that China had sold to the Russians. It was taken apart and transported to a Russian city, but the Russians let the pieces sit out in the open for over a year. Once they finally got around to reassembling the plant, a cold Russian winter and subsequent hot summer had ruined it. The Russians refused to pay for it, and the Chinese replied that it wasn't their fault the Russians didn't put it together and allowed it to be ruined.

In China, Russians are often the butt of jokes, so while it's a good story, I'm not convinced.

All my students, except perhaps Shu, experienced at least some trouble getting along in Shanghai. The locals often felt a bit superior to Chinese people from other areas of the country. But some of my students figured out a way around this that they could have fun with: on shopping trips, they'd sometimes wear clothes like those that foreigners wore and pretend to be people of Chinese heritage who lived overseas by asking, in perfect English, if anyone at the shop spoke English.

Regardless, all was not well for many of my students. They received the equivalent of $1 a day for a food allowance, which meant a bowl of rice soup for breakfast, a bowl of rice with a few green vegetables on top for lunch, and the same for dinner. Sometimes they'd save up and visit a street vendor for rice with a bit of meat and vegetables.

One encountered lots of trouble, even though he was already a local. Li taught at another Shanghai university but was only released from half his responsibilities there, so he was taking my courses and teaching two courses of his own simultaneously. Each day after the classes he taught concluded, he'd jump on his motor scooter and rush right into our class. Then he'd have to hurry back to work, while the other students would stay at their desks studying until nine or ten in the evening.

One day, Li did not show up for class, and the head of the American Studies program at SISU called me in to explain his absence. Li's wife had expressed a wish to study in England, but the Chinese authorities feared she would not come back unless she had a baby and left it behind. So she had the baby, and her parents and husband were looking after the child while she was away. More or less as soon as she got there, she filed for divorce, and rather than writing her husband to tell him of his looming singlehood, she wrote to the head of his *danwei*.

So it was left to Li's supervisor at his university to tell him that his wife had left him and his child, and then the supervisor called the head of the American Studies program, who told me. Needless to say, Li dropped out of my classes.

I found the whole situation unbelievable—particularly the fact that poor Li's dirty laundry was aired by so many people—but the other students insisted that it was the Chinese way. There is little privacy in China, they told me. After all, when you meet acquaintances, rather than asking their names, you ask what their *danwei* and salary are.

───────────

All our classes were held in the same room. The students also ate all their meals there and stayed in the classroom until late at night, when they retired to their dorm rooms. My students' dorm rooms held four students (undergraduates were six to a room), so peace and quiet was a pipe dream. The classroom was like their home, and they enjoyed spending hours there discussing the day's classes.

In class each day, things were lively. The students asked questions that were always well thought out, even perhaps rehearsed. But one day, the class fell silent. I ignored it, but then it happened in the next class, and then in the classes the next day. Finally, I faced the class and announced that I wouldn't return to teach unless our classes were true give-and-take intellectual discussions: "This is a critical part of an American graduate education. If you want to just sit and listen to lectures, take some other class."

During my office hours that evening, about half the class came in, one by one, to explain that a Communist Party representative in the class had admonished them for their class participation, saying that China was paying to have me talk, not them. I'd been warned before coming to expect a Party spy in my classes, but since all the students were Party members, I figured they didn't need a spy. I was wrong.

The next day, I told the class that if they did not participate, they would fail, and if things didn't change, I would go to SISU's president about the matter. The next class, everyone began to talk again—all except for one student. That's how I knew for sure who the Party spy was.

My students told me that the Chinese viewed the rest of the world quite simplistically: there were First World nations, Second World nations, and Third World nations, and nations behaved like their ratings. I begged to differ with this outdated ideology, as it wasn't the way the world worked.

I told them that you might be able to run a state by an ideology, but you cannot run foreign policy by an ideology (actually, I don't believe you can run either by an ideology, but I figured it was best to save that for later). Instead, I instructed them on the practical approach to foreign policy followed by most nations: 1) self-preservation, 2) security, 3) well-being (in economic terms), 4) prestige, 5) ideology, and 6) religion. In the second semester, when we started the comparative foreign policy class, we studied how each major nation viewed each of these elements.

On the first test on this material, one student responded with the Communist Party line, and the others gave the Melford Wilson Party line. You could say that I had some trouble getting the Party spy to open his mind. When I learned of his identity, I'd been surprised, as he was one of the youngest students in the class and was from Tianjin, a very good university where both Mao and Deng had taught. But he certainly took his job seriously.

Speaking of tests, my students surprised me when they turned in their first test on material I'd taught. Each and every student's responses on the test questions were words from my own lectures, written from memory, word for word. Some of the students recorded my lectures, and I had no problem with it—I thought it would help them understand my Southern-inflected English accent—but clearly, they used the recordings to memorize every word. I adjusted my test questions and paper assignments so it didn't happen again, but my students simply adjusted, as memorization was the accepted Chinese way of learning.

In the same way, Chinese people tend to follow government policies even when they know they don't work. They know that challenging them will only cause trouble and could go on their record forever. A prime example is China's practices each Arbor Day during this time. During the Great Leap Forward, China lost millions of trees as the country built up infrastructure. So once a year, Chinese schoolchildren traveled to the countryside to plant trees. The tree plantings were a cause for great celebration and song ... but no one cared for the trees after planting, and most died in the heat of the summer. In winter, the dead trees were used as kindling, and the next spring, the same schoolchildren went to the same place to plant more trees, just like every other year.

I asked a friend once how long that had been going on.

"Twenty years, but no one would dare question the practice. If I said something about it to another Chinese person, I'd put myself and him in danger. That's why we like to have foreigners like you around, so we can talk to someone."

When the school year began, there was no heat in the classroom or my office. Once winter came, the students wore many layers of clothing to class, but their teeth still chattered as they sat. Earl and I nearly froze during one cold snap, so the administration agreed to provide our office with a small wrought-iron, coal-burning heater.

I watched as a gentleman came in one day to install it. The exhaust from the heater had to go somewhere, so a flue pipe rose from the heater to the ceiling and then ran along the ceiling toward the window. I wondered how that was all going to work, but I didn't have to wonder for long. The man took out a hammer and punched a pane out of the window. The exhaust now had a place to go, along with all the heat.

Somehow, the president of SISU found out about the curious installation of the heater. One evening, as we were having dinner, he apologized for it.

I smiled. "Don't worry. I know that the man who put in the furnace was a furnace man, not a window man."

He laughed. "You're more Chinese then I am."

The Collaborative Textbook

By the time the second semester began, my students expressed concerns about their ability to teach their students what they'd learned from me without the textbooks we'd used. I talked this over with SISU's international press, who convinced me to create a textbook that they would then publish. The book became the standard international relations text for all Chinese universities.

Shortly thereafter, the Fulbright professor who was teaching the World Press course at SISU asked if I could modify the textbook to also serve his students—so they would have a way to better understand what was going on outside China's borders.

At first, I thought it would be easy—more or less a cut-and-paste of the content of the book. Like most things that seem easy at first, it wasn't.

First of all, most journalism students in China were not as proficient in English as my students, so the book would have to be translated, with English on one page and Chinese on the opposite page (luckily, one of the students in my class had experience with translations and volunteered to do it).

Since all my students hoped to go to America to finish their doctorate, they were eager to participate. I wrote a few chapters, and each student wrote a case study as part of a book of articles on different world views. This became the third book. The bigger problem was getting the censors in Beijing at the Ministry of Education to approve the books. Eventually, key administrators at SISU had to get involved. After all, they had a big motivator to get the books published: they would have the prestige of having their own press publish a book in English that wasn't a language text. I ended up spending six more weeks in China to get the books finished and signed over all royalties to SISU, as the books were written at their behest. The books did very well, to say the least, as every college and university in China had to use them.

Most of the students in my classes planned to get doctorates, and if at all possible, they wanted to get them in the United States. Getting published is a huge benefit, of course, so I decided to make the textbook project a collaborative effort with my students. I wrote few introductory chapters and then assigned each comparative foreign policy student to write a chapter on the foreign policy of a different major nation.

The collaboration was not without its difficulties. Not surprisingly, some chapters were weak and some were super strong, so a good bit of effort went into revision and evening out the quality. On top of that, SISU's press instructed us to make sure each chapter ranged from eighteen to twenty pages. One great chapter came in at twenty-eight pages, so I told its author to cut eight of them. His revision was even better than the previous draft—but it was forty pages long.

One of the best student chapters was on Chinese foreign policy, but Beijing's Ministry of Education refused to approve it. I protested the denial to administrators at SISU, who affirmed that the chapter was correct at the current time but were more familiar with the realities of Chinese policy. They told me that the refusal was based on the idea that if policy changed, the Ministry knew they'd have to track down every copy of the book and destroy them.

Frustrated, I turned to a fellow professor at SISU to fix everything, and he did. He trimmed every chapter down to twenty pages and cut the China chapter altogether. I was upset, as the whole idea was to make sure all my students got published and enhanced their applications for doctoral studies.

"Don't worry," he responded. "I put the name of the student who wrote the China chapter on the African chapter."

The Four Famous Novels

I learned something about China every day I spent there, but my best lesson was that I still had so much to learn. At the time, Chinese people were only able to read a heavily censored list of new works, but all educated people read the same four ancient great novels. In his works, even Mao liberally quoted them. I always feel like a student when I am in China, and every day brings new lessons. I now know that you cannot understand Chinese culture without first reading these four novels. The nearest parallels in Western culture are Shakespeare and the Bible.

Dream of the Red Chamber, the story of an extended family, helps outsiders understand the hierarchy of Chinese social structure and how different family members interact. In the book, the various members of the family go through just about every life change you can imagine. Religion plays a relatively small role in Chinese culture, and some say that in China, family *is* religion. *Dream* is a glimpse into Chinese family dynamics.

Mao's favorite book, *Water Margins* (sometimes called *Outlaws of the Marsh*), is about a group of outlaws who try and try again to gain control of various areas of China—an epic tale of the art of conflict. Many of Mao's military tactics come from this book.

Journey to the West is the delightful tale of Buddhist monk Tan Sanzang's travels to India to collect the writings of Buddha. Every Chinese child wants to be like Sun Wukong, the powerful Monkey King who accompanies him to ensure a safe journey. Along the way, they meet all types of challenges—everything from evil spirits to wild animals. When the Monkey King cannot figure out how to overcome an obstacle, he uses his magic powers to travel to the island of Putuoshan, near Shanghai, and from there springs straight to heaven. In heaven, he gains new insight and wisdom from the Buddha and returns to either destroy the villain by tricks or convert him into a follower. By the end of volume twenty-three, they have a very large caravan, as you might imagine. The book is a fun action-adventure story to children, but adults read it more like Homer's *Odyssey*, as each test represents an obstacle one may face in life. While Sun Wukong sometimes uses violence, he usually uses his intellect to outsmart an enemy.

The last book, *Romance of Three Kingdoms*, is about a conflict among three kingdoms. Its central message is that weakness and strength are in truth the same thing, and that in a conflict, the individual who chooses the unpredictable path always wins.

Perhaps you see the common thread woven among each of these tales: cleverness always beats brute strength. This central idea of Chinese culture is at the heart of how China and the Chinese people approach the notion of "becoming rich."

In the first, a mighty army from northern China had conquered kingdom after kingdom across the country, encountering little resistance until it reached one particular southern city. Like all Chinese cities, this city had a giant wall, but walls hadn't prevented any of the army's other advances. The king of the city worried that his kingdom would fall, just like the others, so he called in a wise scholar to ask what to do.

The scholar told him that very soon, the army would send in spies to determine the city's weaknesses. Chinese cities traditionally closed their gates at night, but the scholar advised the king to take down all the gates, leaving the city wide open day and night. He also told the king to station musicians where each gate had stood to welcome strangers. These strangers, he said, should be offered food and friendship.

The king did as the wise man said. When the army's spies arrived, they were amazed. Never before had they seen such a thing: a wide-open city, with music, food, and celebration to welcome outsiders. They took this information back to Cao Cao, the general of the northern army. Cao Cao considered the situation and decided to pass the city by. The spies asked why.

He replied, "Any ruler who trusts his people enough to not have a gate or an army has too much support to conquer."

In the second story, Cao Cao reached the shores of the mighty Yangtze River on his way to conquer a city that lay on the other side. Peering across the expanse, he realized that it would take him nearly a year to build enough barges to get the army across. Meanwhile, the king of the city on the other side sent word to neighboring kings asking for troops and weapons to help fight Cao Cao's army.

All except one did; the holdout instead sent a wise sage and his companion instead. When the duo reached the city, their lone presence enraged the king, so much so that he ordered the men to be put to death.

Quietly, the sage replied, "You need arrows more than anything. I can get you 500,000 of the best arrows in three days."

The king laughed. "If you do not, I will kill you."

The sage asked the king to supply a hundred boats and lots of hay. With his companion, he filled most of the boats with hay and then soaked the hay with water. They tied the boats filled with wet hay together and filled the remaining boats with drummers, poised to signal their attack.

Early the next morning, before the sun rose, the Yangtze was covered in mist, and the sage declared that the time was right. The convoy of boats sailed across the river, and while they were still well out of the range of arrows, the sage ordered the drummers to begin.

The drumming awakened Cao Cao's army, who thought they were under attack. Hurriedly, they put on their armor and started shooting flaming arrows out toward the boats to sink them. As soon as they hit the wet hay, they were extinguished. For more than an hour, Cao Cao's men continued to shoot their arrows, but still the boats kept coming.

Finally, before the mist cleared off the river, the boats were brought to the bank on the other side. The city's troops retrieved the arrows of Cao Cao's army, and the king let the sage and his man go.

In China, the clever one is always the winner. Clever wins again—the key to understanding the populist approach to the new China.

———————————

The hardest thing about teaching in China, to me, has always been coming home. Chinese students don't just read their assignments—they truly study them. I'd say that on any given day, no more than half of the students in the classes I teach in the U.S. will have read the assignment, so when I lecture, I can't assume that the students have the background knowledge necessary to really know what's going on. I'll go even further: in general, about a fourth of an American class won't read the assignments or lessons until the day before they're supposed to be tested on them. During my office hours here in the States, unless I require students to come in, only a few show up. During office hours in China, every day, there was always a line outside my door.

So my Chinese students spoiled me. That 1985–1986 school year at SISU was so wonderful for me, and my students and I have continued our friendships. I am extremely proud of the fact that ten of my SISU students did in fact go on to get doctorates at major U.S. universities and today are working at universities and American think tanks (the downside, of course, is that the intent of their education was for them to return to China and change the way thousands of students learned about the world instead).

Fortunately, one of the books I wrote that year was well received and used throughout China, and thus it did affect the educations of many, many Chinese students. About eight years after the collaboration, I wanted to update the book. The chapter on international economics, for example, was way out of date—China wasn't even among the top ten countries in the world in trade at the time it was written. When I reached out about updating the book, the response from the Chinese government was surprising: they liked the international economics chapter as it was because it was an illustration to students of how far China has progressed.

———————

A last thought about my year at SISU: during my time there, I was asked to deliver a presentation about understanding U.S. foreign policy. The house was packed—about 2,000 students, all of whom I am sure were required to come. During the presentation, I mixed realism with humor and praise with criticism, hoping that my words would help the students better understand the U.S. and why my country would want to send me to China as a representative. During the question period that followed, I was asked if I would get in trouble for criticizing America. It was the question I'd hoped for.

I responded, "That is what free speech is all about."

Over the following years, I have delivered that same talk more than thirty times all over China, each time with the full backing of our government.

Chapter 4
Our Magnificent Family Year

THAT SAME SCHOOL YEAR, 1985 TO 1986, MY FAMILY accompanied me to Shanghai. My wife, Janet, had been an elementary school teacher back home, so she landed a position teaching at the international school connected to the American consulate. Janet thrived in her new role. Our daughter Marion and son Melford Jr. were both teenagers at the time, and John, our youngest, was in the fourth grade. Like their mother, they quickly acclimated to living abroad.

Janet made fast friends with the Consul General's wife, who served as the school's principal. One of their favorite pastimes was to shop together in off-the-beaten-track spots. If they showed up in the consul car, with the U.S. Government plates, the prices would double, but if they walked in with Janet pushing her bike, good deals ensued. Eventually, the vendors got to know them and offered even better prices, as they hoped they would send their friends. Since Janet taught their children, she knew many of the international families very well, and so her job also became a great source of contacts for me with the expat business community in Shanghai.

Our family was placed in a university-owned housing building specifically designated for international faculty. Our new home was located in what was then the edge of town, but now, given Shanghai's massive growth, the building is right downtown. Between our block and the block across the street, more than 100,000 people lived on our street, each in small apartments. An elementary school was located right next to our building. School started very early, so every morning we awoke to the sounds of music—first, for martial arts practice, and then for general exercise—as Chinese schoolchildren began their day with lots of exercise. Several school principals told me that they knew obesity would be the major problem to face this generation, and the exercise the children got at school would be all they received for the day. It seemed that unintended consequences had arisen with China's "One Child" policy: two parents and four grandparents rained sweets on those only children all day long.

All around us, new apartment buildings and other developments were going up. We loved to explore the new buildings on our bikes, and on one of our rides, we noticed a very large new apartment complex that was quite empty. Janet inquired about the curiously empty complex at the market and found out why: when planning the complex, the powers that be failed to include a market. Our street had two: The one run by the government had few customers except for the people there using their grain coupons for necessities. The free market where farmers brought their wares to town, on the other hand, was jammed: farmers sold out of their wares early in the day, so locals knew that they'd have to get up early in get fresh food for the day. Janet bought food from the farmers and vendors at our free market every day and shared their stories with us each night at dinner.

Janet's contacts at the international school also proved invaluable, as we were included in social activities with all the top expat businesspeople in Shanghai. We found it interesting in our relationships with these people that the Chinese notion of losing face extended to them as well. Most expats didn't share their future plans or present problems with fellow expats for fear of losing face, so Janet and I decided to become neutral listeners for our new friends. The first step was never talking about one foreign company when leaders of other companies were around.

We did the same with our Chinese friends, too, as they were hungry for sounding boards they could trust to keep things confidential. Once I established trust with these friends, they allowed me the follow-up questions I'd been dying to ask. My friends told me that confiding in other Chinese citizens placed them both in jeopardy even in the modernization period, because all feared a swing back to the days of the Cultural Revolution. After the Tiananmen Square crises, for example, all members of the Communist Party were called in for self-criticism—which means informing on others.

During such purges, people feel compelled to lie about others to save their own skins, so many found it easier to just avoid relationships altogether. In many large housing blocks, people did not even know their next-door neighbors. I once drove the wives of two of our friends home from an event. As we drove, they chatted and noted that they both felt they'd seen each other before. As it turned out, they lived next door to each other but had never met, even though their husbands had worked in the same department for years. When we parted that evening, they hugged like old friends.

Perhaps there was another reason why they'd never met: in Chinese society, men and women never bring their spouses to work functions, and most don't know whether their coworkers are married or have children. We were curious about changing the paradigm and seeing how couples interacted with each other in a social setting, so we made sure spouses were invited and encouraged to come to all of our parties At first, the men did all the talking, but slowly, Janet got the wives to speak up and participate in the conversations.

These contacts taught me a great deal about how China was modernizing and led to me being included in city planning. Back home in Rock Hill, I had served two terms on the city council and had been the first chair of the town's economic development corporation. The Chinese were hungry for information about city planning in other countries and had been frequently disappointed by attempts to gain some from expat businesspeople; most knew little about anything except their own businesses.

Foreign companies frequently had problems as employees and their families adjusted to life in China. Other than the U.S. government, IBM was the only company that held training sessions for every member of a family before being sent abroad. I'd never say that IBM's solution was the best one, but I often suggested that companies hold family orientations. Sometimes, Janet and I hosted sessions for groups of Americans going abroad. We'd always say, "It's not better. It's not worse. It's just different."

Our daughter Marion had little trouble adjusting. Always an independent girl, Marion approached every day in Shanghai as an adventure, whether it involved shopping, school, or having clothes custom made for her. She traveled the city on her bike as if she had lived there all her life, and her daily reports were wonderful.

Marion had always been very good at understanding people, and this gift was an asset in China. She quickly formed friendships with Chinese students her age and shared great lessons about Chinese families and the youth of China with us. Most young people there were extremely shy. Under great pressure to study all the time to excel in school, they were also particularly terrified of the five to seven nationwide tests given at the end of high school. The outcomes of these tests determined not only what university they would attend but also what major they'd be assigned, and thus what careers they would have. Before taking the tests, the students were required to list three top universities (called "key schools"), three provincial colleges, and three vocational schools that they wished to attend and the major they'd declare at each.

The process is quite a gamble: the schools pick the students, rather than the other way around. After the test results were ready, the deans of the key schools met for a week and selected the students they would take. Then the deans of the provincial colleges did the same, and finally the vocational schools selected their students.

Given the tremendous pressure to pick the right schools and do well on the tests, it's not surprising that in the last few years, private, for-profit schools have been founded all over China. This relieves pressure on students whose parents can pay and also opens up slots at the public schools for students whose parents can't. It's also a not-so-well-kept secret that deans at the most desirable schools keep a few slots open for students who barely miss the qualifications for admittance but have a different advantage: parents who can contribute a few thousand dollars to the school.

These days, these bribes even take place at the high-school level. The son of a friend of mine, who is a professor at a university, was just a few points shy of making it into a key high school. The school told him he'd have to pay $11,000 to get him in. In the end, he agreed to pay $5,000 and give special attention to the university admittance application of the principal's daughter the following year.

That year, our son Melford was in the ninth grade, and he took the entrepreneurial spirit of Shanghai to heart. Melford had always brimmed with moneymaking ideas, but in China, he made them a reality, first with a bread delivery business in Shanghai. In China, traditional breads were always quite sweet, and with only one Western bakery in Shanghai, expats had to travel all the way across town to get the bread, croissants, and other baked goods they missed from home. Melford saw an opportunity: each day, he'd ride his bike to the French bakery and fill dozens of orders from his clients. Then, he'd ride around the international community, bags hanging from his bike, and deliver the goods.

One of his deliveries met a most unpleasant end. Shanghai's streets were full of "yellowfish," three-wheel bikes that are unwieldy and hard to stop. As Melford biked across an intersection that day, a yellowfish ran a red light and hit him. Both cyclists suffered injuries and their bikes were damaged, but as a crowd gathered, Melford was shocked—they all stood around laughing and made no effort to help. In the end, an injured Melford had to walk home more than three miles pushing what was left of his bike. We all learned a major cultural lesson that day: Chinese people often laugh not because something is funny but instead because a situation is awkward and they're unsure of what to do.

Melford was enterprising in many ways. The women's basketball team at SISU needed a team to practice against, so Melford gathered a group of young foreign teachers and formed a team. He was a little bothered by the fact that our apartment building was surrounded by high-rise college dorms—with each room housing six students—and many of the students liked to ogle the foreigners across the way. So Melford being Melford, he decided to put on a show for them. He climbed onto the high, flat roof of our four-story building and juggled potatoes, much to the delight of hundreds of students who were hanging out of their dorm windows. This went on for several days, but after a while, the potatoes began to rot. So Melford took off his sneakers, got a few other pairs, and juggled them instead.

———————

It was the mid-eighties, but getting a phone call was still a much bigger challenge than you might think. No one had a phone, and that included us. Even our offices didn't have them. Instead, we'd go down the block to a convenience store equipped with a phone and pay to either make or receive a call. And if you were to receive a call, you'd have to carefully schedule the call and reserve the time with the convenience store in advance. Once the call began, a crowd would gather to listen in on your conversation (this wasn't considered impolite; other people's phone calls were a form of entertainment, and it's often said that there's no word for "privacy" in Chinese).

————————————

That fall, John was the only child in our household attending the same school where Janet taught in the spring. He had to travel by cab for forty minutes each way, every day, to the international school. The upside: his cab driver spoke Chinese to him during the long rides, and as a result, John mastered Chinese much better and faster than the rest of us.

That said, he deployed his knowledge of Chinese in unusual ways. Once, we visited a park on an island in the middle of Lake Wushi. When the trip was over and it was time for the boat to leave, John was nowhere to be found. As we all searched high and low for our lost boy, one of us noticed a crowd gathered by a small hill. At the center was John, pretending to cry and exclaiming, "*Woda iran shu!*"—in English, "My spouse is dead!" The puzzled crowd didn't know what to think, but we laughed. Our cleaning woman said this to us all the time in hopes of getting more money (eventually we found out that her husband was alive and well, and that she did this to everyone).

John's command of Chinese came in handy late one night. The whole family had joined me for a speaking tour, and our plane home was delayed in getting back to Shanghai. By the time we got out of the terminal, it was 2 a.m. There was nobody around; even the lights in the parking lot were turned off. John sprang into action. He disappeared into a parking lot and before long, a Red Flag limousine rolled up to us, with John in the back. He explained that he'd noticed on past trips to the airport that the limousine drivers tended to sleep in their cars. So he went to the VIP parking lot, looked in the parked cars until he found one with a sleeping driver, knocked on the window, and told him—in Chinese—what we needed. We all piled in and rode like heads of state back to our residence.

The Chinese adore children and think that all of them are cute, and blond children like John are considered so cute that they simply couldn't resist patting him on the head. At first, John didn't care for this, so we'd prepare him for it before going to crowded places. We'd form a circle, and each of us would pat each other on the head. We were all then ready for public pats.

———————

My family were all very welcoming to our Chinese friends, and their hospitality continued after we moved back to the States. Chinese friends have often joined us on vacations to the mountains or the beach. One even held his wedding in our living room, and his family stayed with us for three weeks. Another friend married near our mountain home, and all six of the bridesmaids stayed with us at our home.

Our Chinese friends responded in kind, and we found that even strangers could be very caring. Once, my sons and I were tossing a football on a soccer field, and I didn't know that the field was also used to play horseshoes (frankly, I had no idea that the Chinese played horseshoes at all). As I was going out for a pass, I tripped on one of the metal stakes, went flying through the air, and landed with a major wound on my leg.

A Chinese student who ran over to help didn't know how to ask, "Are you hurt?" so instead, he gave me the traditional Chinese greeting in English: "Have you eaten yet? Have you eaten yet?" We quickly determined that I needed medical help, so the young man helped my sons get me to a clinic.

Now, my boys would have rather died than go to the clinic. In China at the time, clinics were big rooms—almost as big as a basketball court. There was no privacy whatsoever, and the Chinese doctors required you to strip to your underwear to be examined. I protested, saying that other than the stab wound in my leg, nothing was wrong with me. No: I had to be completely examined, including my tongue, my eyes, and a check of my skin color from head to toe. Then they wrapped up my foot and leg.

A Day in the Life of the Wilson Family

6:00 a.m. A version of "Rock Around the Clock" sung by a Filipino singer blares over the loudspeaker of Shanghai Financial University (SFU), and our day in Shanghai has begun. The foreign teachers' residence of Shanghai International Studies University, better known as Shangwai, is located on the campus of SFU. During the Cultural Revolution, SFU was eliminated and its campus was given to Shangwai. Shangwai built its middle school and foreign teachers' residence on the campus. As part of the Four Modernizations program, SFU was reestablished and its campus restored, minus these two buildings.

6:05 a.m. The shower relay starts. Over the next half-hour, Janet, Marion, Melford, John, and I must shower and get ready for school all in a single, very small bathroom with a telephone-style shower that changes from boiling to freezing on its own accord.

6:10 a.m. Marion turns on the VCR to drown out the loudspeaker, which has moved on to Karen Carpenter, and pops in an American workout tape. I begin filtering and then boiling water for coffee on our little two-burner gas stove with no oven.

6:45 a.m. It's already a bad day. Xiao Liu is on duty in the apartment building's dining room. She is young and pretty and wishes she were a movie star. She is in fact, however, a terrible waitress. We will all surely be late for school. The other waitresses are so good and efficient; I hate Xiao Liu days! I place my order very loudly and in Chinese so Lao Rong, the cook, will hear. He will, I hope, cook what I ordered, rather than what Xiao Liu tells him I ordered.

6:55 a.m. Our breakfast conversation focuses on where we will visit on our next trip. Janet favors out-of-the-way places, like Peiling. John favors wherever his friends at the international school have been talking about. Marion longs to go somewhere strange and different. Melford would prefer to stay in Shanghai, where he can play basketball. My preference is to go anywhere that has a key university, because that means Fulbright will pay my way.

We reach a compromise: we will go to Xi'an. I am to try to buy tickets to this afternoon, but since I may have trouble, I'm to use the foolproof ticket scam. The scam is this: I bring John with me to buy the tickets at the CAAC Airlines office, and he wears his panda hand puppet and asks for the tickets in Chinese. Chinese people love children, so it never fails.

7:20 a.m. The cab arrives to take Janet and John on their hair-raising, forty-minute-long journey through Shanghai to the international school. The traveling music today is Pattie Page's "How Much Is That Doggie in the Window." John is delighted, and Janet turns a shade of green.

7:30 a.m. I pack up my books and lecture notes and ride my bike to school. I have two routes to choose from: through SFU's campus or through the free market and along Stinky Creek. Today, I pick the second way, and the lady who sells us eggs wishes me a big "*ni hao*" as I ride by.

7:50 a.m. At the office, my Fulbright officemate stops kidding my Chinese officemate long enough to tell me that the New York Mets won last night.

The dean drops by to ask for a letter of recommendation. He, like almost everyone else, wants to get to, or in his case, back to, the States to study. He also mentions that he, along with the vice president and the acting chairman (the chairman is in the currently studying in the U.S.), wants to meet with the three Fulbright professors, which includes me, for lunch.

Several students drop by to borrow books, ask questions, ask for recommendations, or just chat. The class monitor stops in to say that one of the students will miss class because her mother is ill and that the photocopies of the articles on Chinese foreign policy have not made it all the way around the room yet—one copy seems to be lost.

8:55 a.m. I make a big cup of coffee and go to class.

"Good morning, colleagues." I call them colleagues because they don't care for the use of "comrades," and "students" doesn't fit since they range in age from twenty-three to forty-six. All but two are university English professors. They have come from all over China to be trained to teach international relations at their universities, as China's Ministry of Education very wisely mandated that all English majors must take content courses in areas other than English as part of their graduation requirements. In theory, my colleagues will teach these courses, and the text we are writing together will be used in their courses.

I say "in theory" because my colleagues are very bright, and many of them hope to go to the U.S. for their Ph.D.s, rather than return to their universities.

Today's topic, "Parallel and Conflicting Interests of the U.S. and China in Southeast Asia," is a more than a little sensitive, so only the bravest will enter the discussion.

During the break, my desk is turned into a ping-pong table, the hall into a badminton court, and the outside courtyard into a volleyball game. Books serve as the ping-pong net, while imagination is required for the volleyball and badminton nets. I tease one of the students about his new hairstyle of curls and another about the spiritual pollution he gets taking tourists around each summer with the China International Travel Service. They kid me about not wearing enough clothes. They seem to enjoy my company, and I certainly enjoy theirs.

The second hour is less formal, and I signal the shift by sitting on my desk. The students try to convince me that China is a Third-World nation and that all Third-World nations are equal. Playing devil's advocate, I remark that must be why China considers the cultures of other Southeast Asian nations to be equal to theirs. This brings about a round of laughter and a very spirited discussion that had been missing during the first hour. No one is taking notes on the class discussion, which is too bad because it's really much better than my lecture. Earlier in the semester, I would have reminded them to take notes, but I've learned that a comment like that tends to end the discussion— so I hold my tongue.

11:12 a.m. Several students are getting out their rice bowls, so I know I've kept them too long again. I declare that it's *mei fan* (lunch) time, but they all wait in their seats until I leave the room. One colleague stops to tell me that she has received a full scholarship to a U.S. university but can't get a ticket to take the Test of English as a Foreign Language test until October. It's too bad, but I know that 9,000 students showed up the other day for the 2,000 available tickets (in fact other work units had gotten most of the tickets, so those 9,000 students were really vying for only 400 tickets).

11:45 a.m. My lunch with SISU leadership and the other Fulbright professors has far too many dishes, and half of the food isn't eaten. All the administrators are very nice, and they seem to really enjoy our company and each other's as well. And well they should—the vice president taught the dean, who taught the acting chairman. As at other key universities, nearly all faculty who are younger than sixty are graduates of their own universities. They insist that their own people would not be fairly treated at other key universities and that other institutions would never send their best professors to other places.

The arrival of the soup course signals that it's time to wrap things up, and we finally get to the reason for the lunch. The Ministry of Education and the Fulbright people have sent the curriculum vitae for next year's scholars. Not only are the scholars in the wrong field—history, rather than international relations and sociology—but horrors, they're all under forty. We Fulbright professors are concerned about the specialization problem, since the students are expected to teach in these areas, but the administrators are much more preoccupied about their ages. We point out that thirty-eight really isn't that young but lose the argument. Options are discussed, but we depart unsure of what they want us to do about the problem.

1:00 p.m. I retire to my apartment for a *xiuxi* (nap).

1:30 p.m. The *fuyuan* (maids) march into the apartment to wash the windows. Nap's over!

1:45 p.m. I bike downtown, a ride full of near-misses: almost killed by a bus, narrowly missed major injury from of a yellowfish full of ducks, and nearly smashed into an old man and his granddaughter struggling to carry a Japanese color TV set down the middle of Sichuan Lu, one of the busiest streets in Shanghai.

I walk my bike through a free clothing market, and the sellers all holler "HOOLLOO, HOOLLOO" at me. I hope to find some short-sleeved shirts in an extra-large size, but no luck. It's eighty degrees out and the vendors are all still selling—and wearing—long underwear.

2:20 p.m. The CAAC Airlines sign clearly states in English that they open at 2:00 p.m., but the man behind the counter tells me to come back at 3:00 p.m. I stop to buy a Royal Jelly chocolate bar, which has to rate among the best in the world, and walk through the mobs on Nanjing Lu, Shanghai's busiest street. Walking on Nanjing Lu is like trying to walk into a stadium when the football game has just ended and everyone else is coming out. I am bumped by people mumbling "change ya money" in a low enough monotone that they can't be heard by others. I'm stopped by several young students who wish to practice their English. From each, I beat a polite but hasty retreat.

3:00 p.m. Back at the CAAC office, I get a firm "*meiyou*" (no tickets), so I ride my bike over to the foreigners' food store, which we Wilsons refer to as the "funny food store." When you've been in China about six months, you learn that there's plenty of delicious food once you get past the sparrow meat and dried squid. I buy two *jin* of beef, one *jin* of bacon, a large can of tomato sauce, a big wedge of Mongolian cheese, some flour, and some onions. If the dining hall isn't hosting a wedding to-morrow night, as it often does, we'll borrow the oven to make pizza and show a movie from the American consulate's library of VCR tapes. One Western culture night a week helps keep the kids pacified.

4:00 p.m. It's rush hour, so Sichuan Road, the main shopping street, is impossible; instead, I take narrow back streets through what had been the old Japanese sections to get home. I weave past oldsters basking in the late afternoon sun and small children pointing with glee at the foreigners. One corner is so mobbed with kids surrounding an ice cream man that I have to get off my bike and walk it through the crowd.

I stop at my favorite basket store, and the man inside who speaks perfect English tells me about his education at a mission school and about his son, who now lives in Los Angeles. His son visited him last year, and he'd like to visit his son this year but must stay home to look after his sick wife.

On the corner of my street, I notice that the old man who makes caramel candies in the shape of mythical Chinese figures isn't there that day. A true artist, he once created forty-three different foot-tall figures (for only three cents each) for a Christmas party I threw for the students.

5:00 p.m. I arrive at our building just as the cab with Janet and John pulls up. Marion and Melford are still at their Chinese painting class at the middle school.

John tells me that the neighborhood children have gathered on top of the old Japanese pillbox (machine gun bunker) at the end of our street shooting homemade bows and arrows at another group of kids with toy machine guns, and that he couldn't tell who was winning. I try to think of a way I can use it as an example in a lecture.

5:30 p.m. All the foreign teachers and families gather for dinner. We share our tales about the day's adventures, solve the world's problems, and discuss the headlines in the China Daily. The big topic tonight is the local crackdown on gambling: 42,000 people turned themselves in to Shanghai officials yesterday, but the group of old men who play cards on the corner were out as usual today. There's always at least eight players and thirty others watching, so it's hard to believe that a game for fun could generate that much interest.

Tonight, a wedding banquet is being held in the dining room, too, so we're eating behind a folding screen. Little children peek around the screen to get a look at the funny foreigners. The bride is dressed in a red suit and wearing a red *cheongsam* (a traditional Chinese dress, also known as a *qipao*), and the two red tones almost match. The groom wears a gray suit with a purple-red tie and red carnation, so I'm sorry to say that his reds don't match. They are both very good looking and full of giggles. The groom puts a cigarette in the mouth of each male guest; the bride follows behind and lights each one.

6:30 p.m. Janet and I go upstairs to prepare for tomorrow's lectures, but the kids stay downstairs to play tabletop shuffleboard with bottle caps.

8:00 p.m. Construction starts on the building next door. I'm not sure why they only work at night. Tonight's effort is on the most important part of the building: the wall around it.

10:00 p.m. Lights out. Over the construction noise, I can hear the horn of a ship making its way up the Huangpu River. Another day in Shanghai ends.

———————

That year in China left a lasting impression on my family. In later years, Marion returned and ended up teaching English there for two years. John joined me on another of my trips, and later, after he married, he and his wife spent a year in China teaching English, leading tour groups, and acting in Chinese advertisements and movies. Seeing China transition over a period of fifteen years, he says, was amazing, but the one thing he's noticed that hasn't changed is the inordinate amount of stress that the Chinese share. Modernity has made their lives easier in many ways, but the intensity of their lives has only increased. China is in the midst of a race to modernity and a return to greatness, and the Chinese people pay the price in terms of their stress levels.

I am thankful to my family for not only giving me unique insights but also for putting up the fact that I spent so much time away from them

Chapter 5
Make It New (and Magnificent)

Ezra Pound was fascinated by Confucianism, and his famous exhortation, "make it new," stems from the story of Ch'eng T'ang, the first king of the Shang dynasty. Ch'eng had the characters reading "make it new, day by day, day by day, make it new" inscribed on his washbasin to serve as his own daily reminder of his charge. Some 3,700 years later, Deng set out to do the same in China with his Great Modernization.

I returned to China every year except 1989, the Tiananmen year (more about that in Chapter 10). Each time, it was like visiting a new nation. China was changing at a rate and scope faster than any nation ever has, not just in one area but in all areas of the lives of its citizens. The farms I visited in the first few years were clearly government showplaces (one woman even had a television set, albeit with only three channels). Soon enough, every apartment had a color TV, and most had satellite access to a hundred channels or more. When native son Yao

Ming played basketball in America, his games were projected ten stories high on one of the Pu Deng skyscrapers. Thousands of people, including me, stood on the Bund to watch.

The Chinese government struggled with this information revolution because they wanted to control the flow of information. Controlling print was easier, as the government owned all the newspapers and magazines. They could be counted on to print the Party line. But the internet, television, and mobile phones became a major headache for the Party. Consider, for example, the Chinese copy of the show "American Idol," "Mongolia Condensed Milk Idol." In its first year, each week, millions of people would text or call in to vote for their favorite contestant, and each week, the contestant with the wildest hair and music would win.

The government didn't know what to do, as all the "wrong" contestants kept winning. At first, government-owned newspapers took to criticizing the people's choices and praising the performers who focused on traditional Chinese songs. But nothing changed: each week, the people's favorite performer won. So the next year, the government took control of the contest. Every week, traditional Chinese singers won, and the show lost its audience and went off the air. I don't know a single person in China who watches Chinese official channels or listens to government radio.

In Hong Kong and Shenzhen, the most popular radio shows are call-in shows for lonely Chinese people, especially women. They have an immense following: young people listen in their rooms at night or with headphones during the day. The subject matter of the calls runs against the happy image China tries to project to the world: the callers are usually lonely and stressed out.

Early on in the Great Modernization, all farms were owned by the government, and villages were required to supply the produce to the government in what was known as an "allotment." The farms were instructed on what to plant based on national needs, rather than what would grow well in that particular farm's soil. Villagers worked collectively on the farms when and where the village leaders directed, and the production of the farm was first dedicated to paying the allotment. Anything left over was divided among the village's families through a monthly system, and they also received small plots of land to farm their own food under what was called the "responsibility system."

Deng quickly realized that the farmers produced nearly as much on these small, private plots as they did on the large areas under village control that were worked collectively. He saw to it that the private plot areas were expanded. Each family was given some amount of land—only 10 percent at the time of my first trip to China, but this was gradually increased until all land became allotted through the responsibility system. Today, everyone works their own land, from sun-up to sunset.

Under the responsibility system, a family contracts for land and pays the government a percentage of its production. (Some crops are still worked collectively, such as rubber and fruit trees.) Farmers began to use the profits they generated to buy fertilizer, which caused production to escalate further. While China produced massive amounts of food, in the year my family and I lived there full-time, 1985, many items were still rationed. Cooking oil, some meats, and cigarettes continued to be rationed until 1988.

The system continues to this day, but weaknesses have emerged. Many members of farm families have left the rural life behind and moved to cities for better opportunities. And it has left unchanged the fact that areas with poor soil or adverse weather conditions are impoverished, and residents often go hungry. The Party constantly publicizes its achievements in agriculture, but its attempts to make more land suitable for growing staples have not gone well. The best soils of China are producing at or near maximum levels, and as cities continue to grow, the need for more housing is overtaking existing farmlands. China has encouraged its cities to grow higher, rather than spreading out, but as its population continues to grow, dependence on imported foods has grown along with it. Recent American tariffs on Chinese steel and aluminum were countered by a refusal to buy soybeans and potatoes from the U.S., but nations surrounding China have stepped in to fill the gap.

The government stores are long gone now, but private farmers markets have expanded dramatically. Even though most homes have refrigerators now, Chinese people still prefer to buy their food every day. In the 2000s, for example, several big Japanese supermarket chains tried to infiltrate the vast Chinese market with suburban stores selling food, clothing, luxury items, and household wares. They performed poorly because the stores were designed the same way as their Japanese counterparts, with the luxury goods instead of necessities on the first floor. Since they shop daily, Chinese consumers want to get in and out quickly and don't consider shopping a recreational experience.

So Carrefour, a French chain, bought the stores, and once they changed things around, they hit the jackpot. A few years later, Walmart moved into the downtown areas of cities with similar stores catering to both city residents and suburban-dwelling city workers who stop in after work to buy food for dinner.

But I still prefer to go to the farmers markets, as do many Chinese citizens. They open very early; in many cities, wives get their children ready for school while the husbands venture out to buy the food for the day. In China, refrigerators are quite small, because while the Chinese pay very little for electricity, rates go up as you use more appliances. Thus, they tend to buy small units that use little electricity.

As China's economy has grown, more and more seasonal foods are imported and thus can be found year-round. Back in 1985, if we wanted to get sausage for a homemade pizza, we'd have to go to a single room over a garage to buy it. Fifteen years later, it seems like there's a Pizza Hut, McDonalds, or Kentucky Fried Chicken on every corner. The change in diet is quite evident among the youth of China, who are much taller and heavier than their parents.

The Chinese love to eat, and they eat well. No matter what part of China you come from, you'll say it has the best food, and you'll have criticisms for foods from other regions: Shanghai food is too greasy, Szechuan is too spicy, or Beijing is too doughy. The universal joke in China is that the Cantonese eat everything with four legs except the table and everything that flies except an airplane.

––––––––––

For years, China was dependent on other countries for natural gas and oil and forced to principally use domestic coal for energy, with disastrous effects to its air quality. To combat this, the nation constructed (and continues to construct) pipelines from oil-rich central Asian and Middle Eastern nations. Nuclear power plants have been built at a rate of one a year, and China is the number one nation in terms of solar and wind power. In the past, the Chinese government sought to show its visitors historic sites; now, it wants to show off factories and wind and solar farms.

While its efforts to move toward cleaner energy sources are impressive, China's transition from a nation with virtually no cars to becoming the largest consumer of autos in the world has added much more pollution. There is significant interest in moving toward electric cars, but for now, the grid is maxed out.

I once worked as a consultant to a carbon fiber company and suggested that it build its own power plant. Since the factory was located next to a major power plant, the company's leadership initially thought my suggestion was crazy. Soon, however, they realized that power plants often go offline—for example, when they run out of coal because another industry outbids them for coal shipments—so they followed my suggestion.

In 1979, at the time of my first visit, most people were still wearing the blue uniforms of the Cultural Revolution. But by the mid-1980s, Chinese textile plants were manufacturing top brands for export, so their seconds and knock-off clothes were must-haves for anyone under the age of forty. Some were so poorly made that Chinese called them three-generation clothes: the grandparents wore them first, and then after the first wash they fit the children. After the third wash, they fit the grandchildren. By 2000, every major city in China had a street dedicated to high fashion, with stores of all the international brands. These stores primarily catered to the newly rich, but even young people who were just getting by just had to have Nikes.

Older men still stuck to their drab suits, though, preferring to spend their money on their grandchildren. For some reason, though, neckties have never caught on in China except for formal pictures. Each time I visited a Chinese factory or business, the leadership would want to have a picture taken, and we'd all have to wait around while someone was sent off to find neckties for them. It happened so often that I started carrying around an extra black tie in my jacket pocket; if I was in a hurry, I'd pull it out and offer it to my host. Everyone would laugh; years later, they continued to tell the story.

That was in the days when Chinese textile factories were everywhere. These days, if you want to tour a Chinese-owned textile plant, you'll need to look in a southeast Asian, south Asian, or African nation, where land and labor are much cheaper. I recently bought a three-pack of underwear in a Walmart store, and while the package stated "made in China," the labels on each pair told a different story: one was made in Vietnam; another, in Bangladesh; and the third, in Sri Lanka.

———————————

Nowadays, the internet represents serious competition for traditional Chinese stores, just like it does here in the U.S. As millions of Chinese flock to the cities, retail businesses simply can't keep up, so young people in particular go online. Cyber Monday doesn't hold a candle to Girl's Day in the spring and Boy's Day in the fall; some of my friends say their children buy everything online, and they must keep a close eye on their credit card bills.

China is impressively forward-looking and focused on planning—perhaps most evident when it comes to housing. If feeding more than a billion people was China's first miracle, then housing them was surely second. When I first arrived in China, 70 percent of the population lived in rural areas. Today, only 20 percent live in the countryside, and the rest are concentrated into China's cities. In forty years, a billion people—nearly three times the population of the United States—have moved to Chinese cities.

The Chinese boast that their country has no unemployed or homeless people. While this is a bit of an exaggeration, it is amazing not only have they provided housing for so many, but also that the nature of housing in China has completely changed during the Great Modernization. As industries expanded into areas that had previously been farmland, the government was faced with providing both housing and jobs for people who had previously farmed the land. When I first arrived in China, city-dwellers lived in one of two types of housing: government provided or job related.

Most city-dwellers were housed by their *danweis*, or work units. The job-related housing units were generally set up in series of long, six-story complexes, and the monthly rent varied depended on the employee's wages. The units were small, and often, two or more generations shared an apartment.

The government-provided housing units were often old, historic homes that had been turned into apartments. Sometimes, the original owners still lived in the house, but their share would be reduced to just a room or two. In these facilities, kitchens and bathrooms were often shared by multiple families. *Danwei* housing was similar to government housing, but those who had more status, or who were veterans of the Long March, or who were in the army before the Communists came to power benefited from better arrangements in government housing. The rent was low, but the units were small.

In my opinion, *danwei* housing was a bit better than government units, as most of the *danwei* units I visited had a toilet and sink. On each government housing block in most cities, residents used a public bath house where they could sign up for a bath twice a week.

Danweis provided many services in addition to housing, such as clinics, subsidized food, and coupon books. Often, adult children who did not work for the *danwei* continued to live with their parents in their *danwei* housing even after they were married. Even if the children worked elsewhere, they got many of their parents' *danwei* services extended to them for free, and when their parents died, they would get the *danwei* apartment. It wasn't until the 1990s that *danweis* began to get out of the housing business, first by selling units to the workers who were already living in them; the price for each unit was dependent on how long the residents had worked for the *danwei*, and special considerations were also extended to veterans of military service.

As Chinese cities have dramatically expanded, many poor residents have been displaced, and the homes they lived in have been replaced with high-rise apartment buildings. When this happens, the previous residents automatically receive apartments in the new buildings. The housing is of course much more dense, but all newer units have private toilets—once a rarity in Chinese city apartments.

Rents in these apartments vary depending on the floor and the direction faced; most prefer apartments that face south, as the exposure to more sun provides more warmth in winter.

While higher floors are prized because they provide better access to crisp breezes, apartments that are near the tops of these buildings have a significant downside: power outages are frequent (in some areas, the electricity is shut off one day a week), and climbing twenty to thirty floors when the elevators don't work is a daunting challenge. Most of my friends who have had the opportunity to select an apartment have chosen units ranging from the twelfth to the sixth floor—up high, but not too high.

At the beginning of the Great Modernization, the philosophy was that if work could be done by hand, it was, as the nation placed a singular focus on making sure every citizen had a job. Each employer was assigned an allocation of workers, and in many cases, the assigned workers were incapable of filling the employer's open positions.

Managers complained about this on a constant basis. One of my friends who owned a pipe-making business figured out how to deal with his many unqualified assignees: he opened a chain of stores where people could get photocopies made twenty-four hours a day. Every copier he purchased provided jobs for ten people he didn't want working in his pipe manufacturing plants. Other employers opened restaurants or cab services to offload these unwanted employees. In 1988, the government stopped guaranteeing employment for all citizens, and some of the troubles in Tiananmen Square may have been caused by this.

Until the mid-1990s people still had to wait two to three years to get a telephone. The father of one of my students, who held a good job with the Bank of China, told me once that he'd been waiting for years for a phone. I sent him three packs of Salem cigarettes to use as a bribe, and he called me a week later on the phone he'd finally gotten.

Nowadays, if work can be done by machine, it is, and practically everyone in China has a cell phone. Times have certainly changed.

———————

When I first arrived in China, there were two state-owned tourist agencies: China International Travel Service (CITS), which handled international tourists, and China Travel Service (CTS), which handled domestic tourism. As for the travel itself, there was only one rail service, one airline, and one boat company, and all of them were government-owned as well. As China began to open its doors to foreign tourists, all of these government entities expanded rapidly, and soon, nearly every city had its own tourism service. As China became one of the world's most visited nations, these government agencies couldn't keep up with demand, so privately owned domestic companies and foreign businesses entered the market. China's national airline split into four different companies, and some of them became major international carriers. Perhaps no industry in China changed more during the Great Modernization than air transportation. Forty years ago, air travel consisted of some military planes and a handful of twenty- to thirty-year-old Russian planes, but now every city has a modern airport.

Of course, all those tourists coming into China had to stay somewhere, so the hotel industry boomed too. All at once, cities, provinces, universities, private companies, and joint ventures got into the hotel business; at one time, two of the largest five-star hotels in China were owned by the secret police and a third was owned by a company based in Atlanta, Georgia. One year, my Fulbright group stayed in a hotel owned by the Chinese air force and another owned by a university. Surprisingly, provinces and cities frequently invest in and own hotels in other provinces and cities. For example, in Shenzhen, every Chinese province owns either a four- or five-star hotel.

In general, Americans have a hard time understanding how governments and nonprofit entities can invest in private businesses. For example, the university where I taught in 1985, SISU, owns more than forty businesses, including hotels, restaurants, printing houses, bookstores, auto repair shops, and used car dealerships—and that's hardly a unique case. A Hong Kong-based shipping company, a county in Beijing, and an airline that jointly own a major hotel in Beijing and a group of hunting lodges in the far north of China once contacted me to work with them in a new tourism company they were starting. The idea was that the company would sell tourists packages that would involve traveling on the airline and staying in either the Beijing hotel or the hunting lodges.

The package was attractive: they offered me twice my Winthrop salary to lead four groups that they'd attract through advertisements in hunting and fishing magazines. There was a sweetener, too: they offered to let me bring as many groups as I wanted in the future to stay for free in their Beijing hotel, as well as a separate hotel owned by the shipping company, and the air travel would have been at half price. If I'd been thirty when the offer came to me, I would have jumped at the chance, but as much as I love China, I love my family more.

Shanghai's airport is accessed by a maglev train that travels 138 miles per hour. The government had planned to build similar trains all over the country, but the cost was daunting: they discovered that maglev track construction was four times more expensive than that of Japanese-style high-speed tracks. So now, Chinese cities are connected by high-speed trains traveling around ninety miles an hour. Construction is ongoing for similar lines to Germany and the Middle East, and one traveling through Pakistan into India is in the planning stages.

In 2012, I led a group of MBA students on a tour of Shanghai's city planning department. There, we marveled at a presentation on the routes of the high-speed trains and of plans for thousands of wind turbines and miles of solar panels. Clearly, China was focused on the future, a future with cleaner air and water.

The presenter told us that China was building rail systems all over the world. Impressed, the students asked what America should be doing in the same regard.

"Many of the lines are for transporting cargo, but even our passenger lines are making money everywhere in the world. Our system for building tracks and trains is far cheaper and far better than anyone else."

Then he rolled out a map of the United States. "We think you should use either an 'H' or a square design," he continued, pointing at the map. "The 'H' design would run a high-speed line up and down each coast and then on across the middle, connecting the two north-south lines. But some of our other planners think there should be two east-west lines."

The students and I were amazed that the Chinese were not only thinking of their future, but of ours as well. He added, "Of course we would design and build the lines and trains, but we would use American labor. We think our way would be half as expensive as anything America is considering. It would be good business for us, and maybe it would lead the U.S. to stop looking at China as an enemy and consider us a friend instead."

The prevailing wisdom in China these days is that the last century was the Atlantic Century, and that this is to be the Pacific Century. Given the current political climate, however, I believe that if the U.S. keeps swimming against the tide, this will become known as the Chinese or Asian Century.

Needless to say, this has immediate ramifications for our allies in the Pacific. America has long been the model, and this model has drawn thousands of professors and business and industrial leaders to China. China has long sent its children to America for college and graduate school. But in many areas, America is no longer the model. We have lost our way in the arena of international trade, insisting on going it alone and fighting the world instead of cooperating with other nations. The U.S. has lost the lead in new energy development due to its embroilment in fossil-fuel politics.

China has picked up the banner, and the solution to all of its problems lies in education. While the U.S.'s educational system is great, its politicians have successfully blunted popular support for it. In China, there is tremendous popular support for the educational system, but the relatively recent takeover of the administrations by Party bureaucrats, rather than the experts who led it out of darkness over the past forty years, represents a significant danger. Many people in China's leadership fear an educated population, and I'm sorry to say that this is true for America now as well.

Chapter 6
The Fulbright Groups

I N ADDITION TO SPONSORING INDIVIDUAL PROFESSORS, like me, in other countries, the U.S. government-funded Fulbright Program sponsors groups of American scholars to study overseas for extended periods of time. I was lucky enough to get funding to lead four of these groups. My first group, professors from Southern states ranging from Virginia through Georgia, studied education's role in the development of China. The second group consisted exclusively of professors from South Carolina universities and focused on China's many Special Economic Zones (SEZs), and the latter two were divided evenly between Winthrop faculty and area high-school teachers and explored the educational system in China, specializing in first in villages and then in cities.

China is very diverse from region to region. It's really more like a continent than a single country, and throughout its history, it has been divided much of the time. Long visits, like those that Fulbright groups benefit from, give observers a chance to really compare lifestyles. Perhaps the greatest advantage of these Fulbright groups is that they get to spend half of the five to seven weeks of the program at a single university location and the other half visiting other regions. During these "home" periods, we'd listen to guest speakers in the mornings and go on field trips in the afternoons. For example, our first group met with the head of an industrial pipe company one morning and then visited not only his factory in the afternoon but also a collection of the side businesses he ran (during his presentation in the morning, we learned that one of his ventures was a pipe factory in Atlanta, Georgia—a good lesson on the global nature of Chinese investment).

Our groups stayed at my former teaching home, SISU, for the first half of each program. SISU is a shining example of the diversity of Chinese businesses, as it has more than forty different side businesses of its own. In addition to the hotels, restaurants, printing houses, bookstores, auto repair shops, and used car dealerships I mentioned in the previous chapter, SISU also created a twelve-story building housing a for-profit university (using space on an athletic field) for students who lacked the test scores to get into SISU but who also benefited from rich parents. SISU's faculty had the opportunity to supplement their salaries by teaching courses at the for-profit entity. (After all, everyone wants to become rich!)

Several of my SISU colleagues hailed from nearby villages, and I was delighted when they invited my Fulbright groups to visit them—particularly since they weren't the government-approved villages tourists were usually sent to. Our groups spent the other half of their visits traveling to the "real" China to study it, rather than just hitting the tourist spots. You can learn a lot from visiting a single Chinese village once, but so much more if you go back several times and then visit six others.

Since the first group's purpose was to study education's role in the development of China, we spent a good bit of time visiting all kinds of schools and learning about the bold plans Shanghai had drawn up for developing the other side of the Huangpu River, which at the time was home to little more than ship repair facilities and some small vegetable farms. Today, those plans are a reality; the area is home to millions of people and boasts the largest number of very tall buildings in the world.

———————————

And we learned so much more as we explored city and village life. Perhaps the best part of the Fulbright time and money is that it enabled participants to observe everyday things and visit places we never would have seen otherwise.

For example, we took special interest in the childcare options of Chinese families. Most *danweis* provided their employees with housing, child care, health care, and even unions, but families who did not have *danwei* childcare had to place their babies and small children in nurseries that looked after them from Monday morning until Friday evening.

Chinese unions often work in a way opposite to those in the West: they do not represent workers against management. Instead, anyone working at a *danwei* can join its union, and they do lots of special things for their members. For example, during a visit to a *danwei* I made in the late 1980s, a truck bearing fifty apartment-sized refrigerators arrived. Refrigerators were very hard to get at that time, and these had been purchased in bulk by the union. The union's members met the truck, their fists full of cash, and carried the refrigerators home by any means you can imagine: taxi, bicycle, cart, or yellowfish bike (balancing a refrigerator on a bicycle requires a lot of talent—the husband on one side and the wife on the other, with the refrigerator cradled on the seat).

While it is habit for most Chinese people to shop for food every day and eat what they buy as fresh as possible, having a refrigerator clearly gives its owner the gift of time, trimming the number of shopping trips from two or more to one a day. Shopping habits vary from city to city, and the same can be said for cooking: in some areas of China, women do all the cooking, and in others, men do it all. In most cases, both usually participate in cooking meals unless there are grandparents in the home, in which case the grandmothers often cook for the family. There's even a Chinese saying recommending picking a wife from Suzhou, because even their arguments sound like sweet music, and a husband from Jian, because they make the best cooks.

Throughout China, in most households, women are saddled with two responsibilities almost always: washing clothes and cleaning house. The clothes washing is often done outside and requires vigorous beating of the clothes. Automatic clothes washing machines have become relatively commonplace only in the very recent past.

One secret to China's long run at a relatively high standard of living is that on farms, whole families work together in the fields. Family is sacred in China, and all life situations undergird this belief. In many less-developed and developing nations, only women do all the back-breaking agricultural work. Building dikes and terraces; maintaining the flow of water; and planting, replanting, and harvesting grain require lots of work, and in China, this work is a family affair. Older children look after the younger children while the family works in the fields, and everyone participates in and joins together for the evening meal.

The common practice of carrying children for most of the first year and well into the second as parents go through their daily activities has a price: by Western standards, Chinese children are late to walk. They are "potty trained," in a sense, at a very young age; traditionally, Chinese children have worn split pants rather than diapers and just squat by the side of the road or sidewalk when the time comes. Since 2000, however, disposable diapers have become popular among city-dwellers, and this has caused great problems. Previously, China never really had large amounts of non-biodegradable trash before. Now, they do, and the skyrocketing populations of cities are exacerbating the problem.

The growing plastic problem is also a major issue for fishermen, as the waterways crowded with trash cannot support life as they once did. As a result, the price of fish has skyrocketed. In the past, it was common for Chinese people to eat fish several times a week, but now they're lucky to have it even once a week.

———————

Yan'an, a village in the Shaanxi province, lies near the endpoint of the Red Army's Long March in 1935 and thus became the birthplace of the Chinese Communist revolution. I have always been fascinated by the Long March, and I've read every book I could get my hands on about it and Yan'an—and I've talked to every survivor of the March that I could find. Michael Lindsay, Baron Lindsay of Birker, was a representative of Reuters News Service in China and later worked in broadcast news at the New

China News Agency. Lindsay formed a close bond with Mao in the caves of Yan'an from 1938 to 1946. Later, he married a high officer in the Red Army, Hsiao Li, who was also a renowned horsewoman and national hero who led battles against the Japanese (the Japanese even had a bounty on her head). Later, after the Communists gained power, she turned against Mao, attacking him in her book Bold Plum.

I was fortunate to have Lord Lindsay as a professor for Chinese politics at American University. We became friends, and in the summer of 1968, I invited Lord and Lady Lindsay down to Winthrop for the Modern China Institute I ran with Dr. Nolan Jacobson, an expert on Buddhism from the University of Chicago. Jacobson had friends in the Communist Party of Canada, and through it we were able to put on the first American showing of The East Is Red, a film made by Mao's wife as a salute to the Cultural Revolution.

I so enjoyed hearing Lord and Lady Lindsay's personal stories about Mao. He told me that he saw Mao in Yan'an every day, but only got to talk with him about once a month, usually for a Reuters story or his radio show. That's because Mao was rather busy at the time, as during his Yan'an years he wrote a staggering forty-three books and nearly single-handedly directed the fight against the Nationalists and the Japanese.

In our conversations, Lindsay shared much about what he'd learned from Mao. Most of the troops in Yan'an in the early years of the Revolution were from south central China and had accompanied Mao and the other leaders on the Long March. The troops were mostly illiterate but, surprisingly, learned to read while on the March. They were required to march single file, and each day, a Chinese character was pinned to the back of each soldier, and the characters shifted down the line the next day—so every day, each soldier learned a character. By the time they reached Yan'an, they had a good start on literacy.

Lindsey was in a position to be honest with Mao in a way that others could not. For example, he once played a key role in the challenge of figuring out how to tell time. The traditional Chinese system divided the daylight hours into ten parts and the night into ten parts. Bells would ring to signal the start of each day and drums would announce the end of each day, so every Chinese town and city had a large drum tower and bell tower. In the south, where most of Mao's troops were from, sundials were used. And of course, there was also Western time, with 24 hours in a day.

Yan'an had very few watches or clocks, as the soldiers came from poor families, so since most were used to using sundials in the sunny south, Mao decided that sundials would be placed all around Yan'an. Unfortunately, Yan'an is in an area where, for much of the year, the sun is blocked by clouds of *loas* (yellow dust). The village lies in a deep, narrow canyon, and even on sunny days, the sun only reached the dials a few hours a day.

In Chinese society, being late is considered to be very disrespectful of fellow workers—and dangerously rude in the eyes of those of higher rank. Because of this, and the fact that the sundials were so unreliable, people would arrive for meetings or changes of shifts in the weapons and airplane factory at least an hour, and sometimes hours, early. The system simply wasn't working.

Lindsay knew that someone had to tell Mao that it wasn't working, but everyone viewed Mao as almost superhuman. Mao had said they were to use the sundial system, so they must.

Lindsay finally scheduled an appointment with Mao to let him know the sundials weren't working; Mao replied that no one had complained to him, but Lindsay eventually persuaded him to ask others. To everyone's great relief, they were finally able to honestly answer. Mao ordered that a few clocks would be placed in the village and in the factories so anyone could find the correct time by walking a short distance.

A similar issue came up with buildings and roofs, which were being built in Yan'an just as they were in south China. The climate was much different there, so the winter winds blew through the walls and the roofs leaked. Mao and the other leaders, who lived in caves, were completely unaware of the problem, so Lindsay again told Mao about the dilemma. He went on to suggest that they find some carpenters who knew the area well and have them show the southerners how to build for the climate. Mao agreed, and it was done.

When I asked Lindsay about his influence on Mao's political policy, he laughed at me. Mao was the expert on those issues, he replied, and no one—not even he—was ever consulted. Mao even planned battle strategies for his generals! According to historical records, many of the generals were often frustrated that Mao wouldn't let them finish off the enemy when they had the chance, but Mao's strategy was to show the enemy they could be beaten and quickly move his armies to new areas, where they could teach the same lesson. In the end, Mao's strategy was a sound one: he lost fewer troops and used fewer materials, but still managed to break the spirit of first the Japanese and then the Nationalists.

After the Japanese were defeated, the civil war with the Nationalists began, and Lord and Lady Lindsay each had a falling out with Mao. In her book Bold Plum, Lady Lindsay opposed the brutal acts of the Communist and even compared Mao to Hitler; in China and the Cold War, Lord Lindsay attacked Communist China's foreign policy and its failure to show appreciation for the help America and England had provided.

─────────

When I led a group of Fulbright professors to Xi'an in 1988, it occurred to me that I might have a chance to finally get to Yan'an and satisfy my obsession. I asked if any of the group wanted to go with me, and six hands shot up.

Unfortunately, I couldn't seem to find anyone who had ever been there or even knew how to get there. I hired a van and an interpreter, and we found out that a young lady who worked in the hotel kitchen had grown up in a village just thirty-five miles away from Yan'an. She was delighted to join us on our journey. We telexed ahead to Party headquarters to tell them we were coming—never ask for permission in China, just inform them and go—and left at 10:00 p.m. that evening.

After we'd traveled about twenty miles of paved blacktop, the road turned to dirt. About twenty miles later, it narrowed to a single-lane road with giant potholes everywhere —a road clearly used by few vehicles other than the occasional coal truck. It was very dark, but we could tell there were no guardrails or vegetation alongside the road.

At a dozen or so little villages, the road forked, so we'd knock on villagers' doors until we could wake someone to tell us which road to take to Yan'an. If the villager didn't know the way to Yan'an, we'd tell them the name of the young woman's village and see if they knew how to get there. And if they didn't know, we'd find someone else who did. This went on all night long.

Eventually, we arrived at the small village of Yan'an. It was breathtaking, with large cliffs on each side and a ragged river running through the middle. At the Party Guest House, we were given eggs and bread and shown to our rooms; exhausted, we got a couple of hours of sleep and then set off to explore. I told a few locals where I wanted to go—the caves, of course!— and they eagerly offered to take us to each place.

The cavern that surrounded Yan'an was littered with caves, and the three Mao had occupied were connected. He slept and ate in the first, his private cave, and in the second, he worked, writing books and creating battle strategies. The third was like a living room, with a sofa and a long table and chairs for meetings. Tucked away at the rear of each cave was a tunnel that led deep into the mountain, for hiding when the caves were under attack. The tunnels were small—you'd have to crawl through— but we were not allowed inside them. No glass was used in the cave windows, so all the light filtered in through waxed newspapers.

The caves were difficult to strike, but during a seven-year period, Japanese and Nationalist Chinese planes tried plenty of times. The Communists always withdrew into the mountain, however, and all the enemy could manage was to destroy a few caves. Few troops and none of the Communist leaders, including Zhou En Lai, Liu Shaoqi, and Ju Dai, that lived in the caves were ever hurt during these bombardments.

Zhou En Lai, the leader of the government, had two caves, but Zhou and his wife spent great stretches of time in villages and towns, helping them regain order and set up functional administrations (peoples' communes). If Mao was worshiped by the Chinese people, then Zhou was loved and respected like a wise grandfather.

Liu Shaoqi, who handled the day-to-day operations of the Party, lived and worked in the two caves right next to Mao's. This worked well in the early years, because Liu's wife, Wang Guangmei, and Mao's then-wife, He Zizhen, were best friends. But when He Zizhen traveled to Russia to serve as an ambassador, Mao took up with a B-movie star named Jiang Qing. Wang and Jiang were bitter enemies; during the Cultural Revolution, when Jiang and the extreme radicals gained control, one of her first efforts was to see to it that Liu was killed and Wang imprisoned.

The leaders' caves were located right next to each other. Each of the lower-ranking leaders had a single cave, and the rest of the army and the throngs of Chinese actors, intellectuals, and others who had fled the Japanese on the Long March cohabited in large group caves. We also got to see the caves where the Communists built airplanes, but we weren't allowed to visit the ones in which they built armaments because it was "too dangerous."

At the end of the day, we visited a hall in the middle of the valley where dances were held each Friday night. Mao loved to dance and sing songs, some of which were even in English. While we were there, a young girl in a traditional red dress came in and in the most beautiful, high-pitched voice sang "The East Is Red," the theme song of the Revolution. I was moved to shivers.

We clapped and clapped, and then she disappeared, just as if she had vanished. She reminded me of the Fox Fairy of Chinese mythology. I ran to try to catch her, but she was gone. I came upon an old lady and thought perhaps she knew where the girl had gone. I sang a few notes from "The East Is Red" and said to her, "*shao mai*" (small sister). The woman seemed to understand, so I tried to give her 100 yuan for the girl. She refused to accept, but my translator caught up with us and explained that I wanted the money to go the girl who'd sung to us so beautifully. She smiled and graciously accepted, telling us that the girl was her granddaughter and that she was honored to sing for foreigners.

In the dance hall, the closest approximation to a museum was a single glass cabinet that held a few items for sale. Most of the merchandise consisted of buttons with Mao's image, but a few Chinese knockoffs of Mickey Mouse and Minnie Mouse figurines were in there as well. I wondered how the hell had they gotten there.

At the dance hall, airplane factory, and hotel we each were asked to sign a guest book and I couldn't find a single name in any of them that wasn't Chinese. The hotel staff told me that the last foreigner who had come to Yan'an was a Dutch hiker who signed the register in 1966, but even he didn't stay there. Each year, seventy to a hundred Chinese people visited Yan'an—usually older people or students researching the Party—but a later article in the New York Times declared that we'd been the first foreigners to visit Yan'an since the Revolution.

Our hosts told us of plans to build a paved road and even a railroad link to Yan'an within the next five years. I know these have been completed now, but I don't know when they were finished. Recently, I learned that you can reach the city now by air, and that Yan'an today is practically a mini-Disneyland.

———————

Our ride back to Xi'an was in daylight hours, so we were able to fully appreciate just how dangerous our trip had been. The road ran along the crests of the mountains, with thousand-yard drop-offs on each side. Later, I learned that coal trucks often went over the cliffs, and that it was impossible to retrieve them.

Daylight also revealed that the little villages we'd stopped in for directions were located in high mountain meadows, with every inch planted for garden crops. Chickens, goats, and lots of children skittered around everywhere. One of the group members had brought balloons, so we decided to stop in each village to greet the kids. We gave each child a balloon and sticks of gum, and they went wild with excitement. I can't remember ever being welcomed more warmly than were in these villages.

To really understand any group of people, you must first understand what they fear most—not only in terms of security, but also in terms of basic survival. The Chinese were most afraid of the nomadic people that lived to the north, the Mongols, who controlled an area as large as that of the Roman Empire.

Dynasty after dynasty built great walls to insulate themselves from the Mongols, and again and again, invaders from the north managed to breach these fortifications. The Mongols figured out how to move their vast armies across barren plains and deserts, and they invented bridals and stirrups to help them control their horses during battles. Ironically, the Mongols served as a source of power for the empires of China. Weather and disease decimated the horse population in China, and records show that emperors purchased as many as a hundred thousand horses from Mongolia in some years.

I wanted to understand Mongolia, another place that was better to visit with a small group, so sixteen of us flew into Hohhot, the capital of Inner Mongolia. We stayed in a hotel in the city that night and then took off in a bus to see the real Mongolia.

The bus took us first over unpaved roads and then across open land. Along the way, we passed little clutches of houses that looked as though they'd popped up whole from the plains. Constructed of brick and sod on their northern and western sides to stop the winds that constantly blew across central Asia, the homes' southern exposures were left open to allow the sun's rays to heat the inside during daylight hours. Of course, the nights were cold: one resident told me that he slept with ten quilts—three underneath him and another seven on top of him, and little children slept snuggled up against the grownups to share each other's warmth.

After a while, there were no more little houses—just rolling hills. Everything looked the same at first glance, but if you looked carefully, you'd notice that the highest hills had large mounds of rock on top of them, and sometimes even prayer flags. The people who lived in the region navigated the land by climbing the highest hills and peering out to find the next highest hills with rocks and flags on top. For much of the year, the fine dust in the air is so thick that you can't use the sun or stars to find your way, so this method works well. I asked a Mongolian how long this navigation method had been in use, and he responded, "Forever."

———————

We finally arrived at our destination for the countryside stay, a large camp of yurts. Yurts are portable round tents made of skins or felt. I'd read that you could rent yurts for overnight stays, so I rented three and divided us up accordingly. We next went to a central yurt, where we were greeted warmly and told that the leader of our group—that would be me—was expected to drink some "ancient liquor." I was handed a large bowl full of this 130-proof firewater and did as I was told, and let me just say that it burned all the way down to my toes. We learned a lesson here and decided to rotate which of us would be the "leader" at each yurt we visited.

We'd been told that it hadn't rained in the previous three months, but that afternoon, when we set out exploring on camels and horseback, it started to rain. Then the most amazing thing happened: suddenly, the dry, brown hills turned green, and thousands of flowers appeared. We rode about, agape at the beauty of the scene.

Several hours later, we returned to our camp in darkness. Unfortunately, the yurt occupied by six of the women in our group had been left open, with the light on. This was unfortunate because the rain and the light had attracted thousands and thousands of bugs of all kinds. Literally everything was covered with the bugs. The women dragged their stuff out and desperately scraped off all the bugs, but the yurt was uninhabitable. They were forced to move into the other two accommodations, so we were all crammed in there, eight or nine to a yurt. To keep the insects, which were fighting to get in, at bay, we had to build small but smoky fires in the middle of each remaining yurt, thus making matters even worse.

Our dinner that evening was freshly killed goat, some porridge, and, of course, ancient liquor. They had no water, so I bought us twenty bottles of nasty orange drink—all they had—and we made do.

———————————

The next day's activities included races of brightly colored horse-drawn wagons and placing us on racing camels. I got them to let us climb a hill studded with navigation rocks, and it was indeed a great lookout. We could see many other hills with rocks and flags on top, even miles away, and of course the flowers, which were everywhere.

But along with the flowers, we got bees and all those many bugs. The locals told us that the flowers and bugs last for about two to three weeks following each rain, and then all goes brown again until the next rain—which could be anywhere from a month to six months away.

When we returned to camp, things were quite different: eight truckloads of Mongolian workers from Wool Factory #8 (all the stores and factories had numbers rather than names) had arrived for their annual outing. The group had quite a head start on the party, as they'd been drinking the whole ride there. Once we were there, they cut off the head of a goat, which apparently is a great honor.

That evening, a band showed up, the dancing began, and things really began to get wild. Several men grabbed women in our group and pulled them out to dance. After a while, some of the women wanted to stop, but a big and very drunk Mongol wouldn't let one of them go. I stepped in, pushed him away, and told our group to return to the yurts. The man I pushed got up to fight, but I was lucky: he was very drunk, and I was taller and had longer arms. I pushed him again, really hard this time, and he fell into the arms of his buddies. They all laughed, and I took that as my cue to get the hell out of there. I walked backward as fast as I could, afraid to turn my back, as there were dozens of them.

We all squeezed into our three yurts (one of which still had plenty of bugs), and outside, the factory workers built a large fire. They'd get a running start and try to jump over the fire, but many were so drunk that they fell in. Then there would be lots of yelling and rolling around to put the fire out, and everyone would laugh. Once that got old, they started running by our yurts and yelling at the top of their lungs. I asked our translator to find me something we could use to provide a little security, and she returned with a six-foot-long metal securer used to roast goats. Newly weaponized, I stood outside the yurts with a few others of our group to make sure no one got any ideas.

The second night, the factory workers had stopped running by our yurts, but they had plenty of partying left in them. To add to the fun, the camp had set a bug bomb off in the buggy yurt, which rendered it just as useless as it had been with the bugs. We all squeezed once again into two yurts and listened to the factory workers party until almost sunrise.

We had another overnight stay scheduled for our yurt camp out, but the next morning, I told the translator to get the bus: we were leaving. We tried to send a telex to our hotel in Hohhot, where we'd stayed before venturing out into the country and were expected to arrive the next day, to let them know we'd be coming earlier than expected, but the telex wasn't working. Our group slept for most of the ride back to Hohhot, and no one complained about leaving early.

But the people at the hotel weren't happy. There was a lot of arguing and back and forth, and I couldn't understand why. We knew we had been the only people staying there, and our group didn't take up even half of its rooms. Eventually, we figured out that the hotel simply hadn't cleaned the rooms since we'd left a few days before. I offered up a simple solution: everyone would return to the same room they'd left several nights before, and we'd pay for the extra night.

I learned a valuable lesson on that trip: Mongolia was not ready for prime time. But adventures like that are what stays with people. To this day, whenever I see folks that were on that trip, we love to sit around and tell stories of the yurts and of the workers of Wool Factory #8.

———————————

In the recap of my first trip to China, in 1980, I mentioned how much help my old friend Lilly, a highly placed member of the Guangzhou Communist Party and the head of Hong Kong's Chinese Travel Service office, had provided in expediting our tours. Well, ten years later, Lilly came to my rescue once again, and I learned a lot about the power of *guanxi* ("back door").

I was planning a 1990 Fulbright group tour. Lilly was able to work out a deal in which our group of sixteen could stay at a very nice hotel, the Miramar, for just two dollars a night more than we'd pay to stay at the YMCA. It's good to know people in high places.

Later, I needed Lilly to intervene on our behalf once more. While all had gone well with the planning session and the group's orientation, just one week before our departure, a Chinese American professor who had planned to go backed out. His concern: despite the fact that he'd been born in the United States, he was afraid that he would be captured. I pleaded with him to change his mind, telling him that his concern was absurd. I'd had several Chinese Americans participating in previous groups, and there had never been a problem.

He was resolute, though, and I had a big problem. Without the full complement of the original sixteen attendees, the trip would not be allowed to go forward. The group visa specifically included all of the people on the original list.

I went back to my list of applicants for the program and kept calling everyone on it until I finally found someone who was ready and willing to go (and who had a valid passport). Relieved, I called the Fulbright office about changing our visa, but they told me I couldn't. Next, I tried the Chinese Embassy in Washington. No luck. I even called the U.S. ambassador in Beijing and the councilor in Shanghai. At every turn, I was told no.

I finally sent a fax explaining my problem to Lilly, and she shot me back a very long fax full of solutions. I'll summarize it here:

- Enter China by going from Hong Kong to Guangzhou on a train.
- Have the others in the group go through Customs and Immigration as you normally would, and afterward have the bus driver take them to a restaurant to wait for you.
- You and the new person must wrap his passport, your original group visa, and a $100 bill in brown paper. When you're in the holding area for Customs and Immigration, you'll see a man on a bicycle by the fence. Hand him the parcel with the passport, visa, and money through the fence.
- Do not go through the Customs and Immigration line, no matter what the people there say. You are not in China until you go through.
- In an hour or so, the man on the bicycle will return with his passport and a new group visa. Then you can go through.
- A cab will be waiting for you once you're safely through the line, and it will take you to the restaurant to join your group.

So that's what we did. The fellow on the bicycle was there, just as Lilly said he would be. After about twenty minutes, everyone else had cleared the Customs and Immigration line, leaving just the two of us waiting by the fence. The people staffing Customs and Immigration, who were just over the line and thus were in China, kept calling out to us to come through. They even got a translator to yell at us in English, adding that the staff needed to have their lunch and *xiuxi* (nap) before the next train arrived. I responded, *"Deng yi deng!"* (wait a minute) and proceeded to ignore them. I knew we were safe—they couldn't step over the line and leave China. Eventually, everyone except a single agent and a military policeman left for lunch.

After about an hour and a half, the man on the bicycle returned and slipped the passport and a brand-new visa through the fence. I slipped him a $20 bill in return, and we strolled up to the Customs and Immigration counter as if none of this had transpired. We made it through with no issues, and a car, rather than a cab, was waiting for us as soon as we walked out the door. We were reunited with our group at the restaurant.

I learned to never underestimate what *guanxi* can do.

Chapter 7
The Magnificent Peaks:
Tibet and Nepal

Located high in the Himalayas, Tibet is a minority region of China where the Chinese government has long had trouble maintaining control. Its neighbor, Nepal, is not part of China but shares a long border with Tibet. China worries about both, as they share similar cultures and a religion, Buddhism. The Chinese government doesn't understand the people who live there and have not been able not control them, and anything the Chinese government does not understand or cannot control is feared.

All transportation from China to Tibet goes through Lhasa, the region's only large city. Dozens of high mountain passes permit travel into Nepal and on to the rest of the world. The Chinese government has been frustrated by its inability to maintain control over the movement of its people through these mountain passes. Groups of Tibetans travel this way every day on pilgrimages to Sarnath, the place in India where the Buddha received his enlightenment. If you want to have frank conversations with Tibetans about Tibet, Sarnath is the place to do it, as Tibetans are very careful about what they say in Tibet for fear of reprisals by Chinese authorities.

Tibet and Nepal are both mountain kingdoms in a pre-development stage, and few foreigners have been brought in to help in their modernization. Both areas share a harsh climate and few all-weather roads; they have seen little industrial development, and even schools are rare. The cultures there often stress their native languages and religions, and few modern books have been translated into the local languages. Tibet and Nepal are home to most of the tallest mountains in the world, and even the flat areas are at elevations above a mile high. The mountains serve as a barrier to all except the Nepalese and Tibetans.

Tibetans are largely dependent on agriculture and animal husbandry for their survival. Both Nepal and Tibet are heavily influenced by their own very unique branches of Buddhism and their people are very religious—something the Chinese government simply can't get a handle on.

A high-speed train line was recently established between Xi'an and Lhasa to make Tibet a little less isolated. In an attempt to gain more control over Tibetans, China has moved so many Han Chinese people into Lhasa that it really isn't a Tibetan city anymore; they have done the same in Urumqi, a city in the western part of China. These new Chinese immigrants work in tourism and in controlling the Tibetans, by and large. The Chinese transplants dislike the local food, the altitude, and the languages spoken there. China's attempts to transform Tibetans into Chinese people are failing, just as its attempts with other minority groups have failed. The government simply doesn't understand China's minority populations and how important their language, religions, and culture are to their existence.

Even though they represent a small percentage of the country's total population, China has problems with all of its minority groups. China considers them, though small in terms of population, to be a threat because they mostly live along the country's borders, and right on the other side, people with the same ethnic and cultural heritage live outside of Chinese rule. Like the Tibetans, they frequently cross China's borders using remote roads and footpaths, frustrating the government's attempts at control.

———————

Several years ago, I took the leap and traveled to the region with a group. I wanted us to experience the real Tibet in the region's villages and small cities, so I decided to enter through Nepal and then cross Tibet from one side to the other, ending up in Lhasa. To start, we took a Singapore Airlines flight from Singapore to Dhaka, Bangladesh and then on to Kathmandu. This first leg of the trip turned out to be a wonderful surprise.

The plane was full of Bangladeshi men headed home to see their families after working a year or longer in hotels in Singapore. They were very excited and had armloads of presents for their families, all wrapped in bright, crinkly paper. A doll's head stuck out here and there, and the men also had flowers (mostly artificial) for their wives (my seatmate told me there were plenty of real flowers at home, but these would last forever). The poor flight attendants kept having to tell them to sit down and buckle their seat belts, but they could only sit still a few seconds before getting up to talk to friends.

I enjoyed seeing how much fun they were having. The men joyfully took pictures of themselves and each other on the plane; my seatmate shared that none of them had ever been on a plane before. I asked him how they'd all gotten to Singapore, in that case.

He said, "When we left home, we had very little money, so we traveled by boat. Now we have made enough to fly back home."

I asked why they hadn't chosen to return home by boat.

He smiled. "It is a matter of status that we can fly home, and our families are so excited that we have enough money to fly. They will all be at the airport to meet us. Second, the boats are not safe once you have money. Someone on the boat will rob you, or pirates will attack the boat. None of us would dare take the boat back."

Upon our arrival in Dhaka, the flight attendant announced that the pilot would not land the plane until everyone was in his seat and buckled into it. She demonstrated how to buckle the seat belt over and over again. When the plane's wheels hit the runway, they all leaped into the air and yelled as if they'd scored the winning goal in the World Cup.

Visiting Dhaka then was like taking a step back in time. There were miles and miles of shanty housing, and all of the buildings that stood over two stories high were in a four-block cluster. Friends have told me that Dhaka has grown a great deal in the intervening year, but I'd never seen anything like it—a whole city made up of slums.

The flight on to Kathmandu was going to be our first chance to view Mount Everest, but it was fogged in. On my third day in Nepal, I booked a small plane to circle Everest, but we had to leave at 3 a.m. so we could reach the mountain at sunrise, before the clouds massed on the mountain. The five senior citizens on the tour were ready to go, but the students went out the night before and chose to sleep in instead.

When we got on the plane, the only other passengers were a multi-generation Indian family, everyone from the grandparents down to ten- and twelve-year-old grandchildren. It was dark until we neared Everest, and once we were there, the pilot circled the peak. To our surprise and delight, he invited each of us, one by one, to sit with him in the cockpit. The plane was not allowed to get closer than two miles from the peak, for fear of causing avalanches, but the view was amazing. The colors of the sunrise reflected off the top of Everest like a multicolored beacon. As big as Everest is, two miles seemed plenty close.

The oldest lady in our group, an eighty-seven-year old from Hilton Head, said, "I'm praying that we crash into Everest."

We all looked at her, stunned. "No!"

She grinned. "Then my grandchildren will have something to remember about their grandmother."

Only two members of the Indian family were interested in sitting in the cockpit, so the pilot let me sit up there for another round and then part of the way back to Kathmandu. As we flew, he pointed out many famous mountains and told me where they ranked among the top twenty-five tallest mountains in the world. Several of them had not yet been summited. He also showed me several of the high mountain passes Tibetans use to cross the border, and that explained a lot about why the Chinese government is unable to control their movement. It was a wonderful trip.

Kathmandu is a unique city. The King's Palace was a bit too colorful for me, as were some of the buildings and hotels (our hotel
was owned by a member of Nepal's royal family). But slowly
I realized that the colors of the city were largely driven by its
natural surroundings. Bright green foliage and vivid flowers
were everywhere, so it was only natural that the buildings and
clothes of the people fit into the same color palette.

Kathmandu's main market street was filled with hippies
who seemed to be stuck in a time warp and lots of Nepalese
and Tibetan antique stores. Wise shoppers know that many of
the items there are fakes. I learned a quick way to tell whether
an "antique" was authentic: lick your finger, rub it on the piece,
and sniff your finger. If it smells like tea, the item is new and has
been soaked in tea to make it look old. That's just a first test: if
you're considering an expensive item, you should reconsider if
the shop doesn't provide a letter of authenticity.

Just walking around at Kathmandu's altitude can make
you sick. Several of the people in my tour group had gotten
pills from their doctors to help with the altitude sickness, but
I found that it was better to simply spend a dollar a day on an
aerosol can of oxygen. There's a hole in one side of the top of the
can, and you place the large opening over your mouth and nose
and push down the spout. I found that ten puffs, ten times a day,
used up the can and kept me going just fine.

Kathmandu has a serious dog problem, as it's against Buddhist tenets to euthanize stray animals. During the day, feral
dogs take up nearly every shady spot, but at night they form
packs and are known to attack people. I told my group to try
to return to the hotel before sunset. Many of the students liked
to stay out after dark, attracted by the prevalence of marijuana
that likely was responsible for many of the visiting hippies as

well. I told them that if they did go out after dark, to do so in a group and carry the walking sticks the hotel provided to keep the dogs away.

———————————

The next day's agenda included a side trip to Swayambunath, a campus of temples and shrines I'd learned about as an under-graduate at Wofford College in an Asian art history class. It was a good distance from the city, so the ride there gave us a good opportunity to see the countryside and several villages. The road was terrible: much of the land, which had previously been jungle, had been cleared, so each monsoon season, nothing was left to keep the topsoil from washing down the mountain sides. The road suffered as a result.

Outside Swayambunath, a row of female beggars, some bearing signs of leprosy, lined the path. One elderly beggar was accompanied by her nine-year-old granddaughter, dressed in what looked like a school uniform. In perfect English, the child told us, "Do not worry. These women cannot come inside the temple grounds. This temple is special, as it is holy to Buddha. Do you need a guide?" We ignored her, so she made her pitch to us in German, French, and finally Spanish as well.

Impressed, I asked, "How many languages do you speak?"

"I am fluent in nine but can do the tour in thirteen."

We were amazed. Some of the people in our group tested her in German and then Spanish. Each said she spoke the lan-guages like a native, so I hired her.

She started the tour by telling us that Theravada, Mahayana, and Tantric Buddhists; followers of both the Hindu gods Shiva and Vishnu; and other Hindus considered the temple to be holy. That was straight from the guidebook, but she also knew who was buried in each tomb and stupa (a dome-like structure that encloses Buddhist relics). She instructed us to walk around the main stupa in a counter-clockwise direction and spin the prayer wheels outside of the stupa in a clockwise direction so our prayers would go straight to heaven.

We started each prayer as we began to circle the stupa, and we were advised that if we changed our prayer in the middle, we wouldn't have good luck. A hunched old woman wearing the maroon colors of the lamas (teachers) circled the stupa again and again. Our young guide told us that she did that every day, murmuring prayers for each of her relatives and then for world peace.

Most of the monks at the temple wore deep red robes, identifying them as Tantric, but a few wore saffron robes. Our guide told us that no Hindu monks were currently in residence, but they came up for holy days. I wondered aloud how to tell the difference among the monks, and she told me that they were easily differentiated by the white lines on their foreheads.

Our young guide was amazing. She told us that she couldn't go to school because she had to look after her grandmother, but that it didn't matter—the schools were closed most of the time anyway. Instead, she and her grandmother followed tour groups around, giving her lots of opportunities to speak to foreigners. She'd befriended many of the foreigners who lived in Nepal and came to the shrine often, which is how she learned so many languages and all the details of the temple. Our group bonded with her, and we all made sure to tip her well.

In 2015, a massive earthquake hit Nepal and destroyed nearly all of downtown Kathmandu. I saw pictures of Swayambunath on the news; all but the large stupa had been destroyed. Even it was damaged, but the famous eyes of Buddha painted on its top were still there, looking out over all the world. Ever since then, I've been trying to find out how our little guide fared—thousands of people died in the earthquake. So far, I haven't been able to find any information.

At a conference recently, I met the Dalai Lama. He was there to raise money for the survivors of the earthquake and for restoration of Nepal's holy places. Even he knew of our little guide, but sadly, he didn't know whether the quake had claimed her as a victim.

Nepal was torn by an off-and-on civil war for ten years, from 1996 to 2006; luckily, our visit coincided with a peaceful spell. In 2001, the king and most of the royal family was massacred by the crown prince, who then committed suicide (this according to witnesses, but it's commonly believed that another royal was behind the slaughter). Then there was the devastating earthquake, just fourteen years later—these wonderful people deserve better luck.

———————

I purchased tickets for our group to attend to a cultural arts show in a theater in the middle of town that night. The ninety-minute show was lively, with lots of singing and dancing and audience participation. When we got back to the hotel, a large group was checking in. One of the managers mentioned that they were tour operators.

We dined that evening at the hotel's restaurant, which had a stage at its center. The food was wonderful, and our tables were right by the stage. As we were finishing our meal, a troupe of singers and dancers took the stage. There was a flash of mutual recognition among us, and we all began to laugh: it was the same group we'd just seen at the theater.

The tour operators were amazed that we foreigners knew them. I turned to them and said, "They're good friends of ours!" That only confused them more.

As the show went on, various members of our group were called onstage to participate. One of the dancers announced, "Since most of you know our songs and dances, we'll add a few new ones!" We all laughed and applauded.

Afterward, the hotel manager thanked us profusely. He said that our enthusiastic presence at the dinner left quite an impression on the tour owners and that many had expressed a desire to bring their tourists there in the future.

The next morning, we set out for Tibet on a beautiful drive through high mountain passes—some more than four miles high. By this time, everyone in the group except one lady had gotten wise to the practice of using oxygen cans, so we were all adjusting well to the altitude. The highest pass of all was barren of trees and featured a brightly colored pole on top. Ropes spread out from the top of the pole, making it seem more like a tent or a maypole. From each rope hung hundreds of prayer messages that made a flapping sound in the wind as the prayers were sent to heaven.

Along the way, we stayed overnight in a lovely château with what had been billed as a great view of Everest. The bus couldn't make it all the way to the door, so we had quite a climb up—but porters carried our bags. We saw a beautiful sunset over snow-capped mountains, but Everest's summit hid away in the clouds.

The next day, after more mountain roads and high passes, we reached the border. On the opposite side of a long bridge lay

Tibet, and the bus was not allowed to cross the bridge. I told everyone to stay on the bus, as dozens of porters were banging on its sides, wanting to carry our bags across. I'd been told not to trust them, so I wanted to be sure everyone and everything stayed on the bus.

Everyone seemed to have a gun, and in that way, it reminded me of Afghanistan. The area was dangerous, but it was under the control of a local strongman. In my pocket, I carried a letter I'd had stashed away two years, waiting just for this crossing, with the strongman's name written on the outside in both Chinese and English. It was a letter of introduction asking for safe passage.

I stepped outside the bus and walked a few paces toward the bridge. A man emerged from a compound behind a high, barbed-wire fence on the Tibet side, crossed the bridge, and approached me. I handed the man my letter and two hundred dollars and told him we had twenty-one people and their luggage to transport across the border. The man replied that he'd need more money to pay the porters for our luggage, so I gave him another hundred.

The man looked at me and said, "Do not go with anyone except the ones my men say are okay. Your people should only carry a small bag each and should hide their passports well. My men will carry all of your bags to a bus on the other side. Do not even talk to anyone along the way."

The man and I returned to our bus. He spoke briefly with our driver and shooed away all the other would-be porters except his own men. I coaxed all of the passengers off the bus, and we began our journey across the bridge silently. When we got to the other side, there was no bus waiting. I was panicking a bit inside but kept my cool.

We were then greeted by a new guide, who seemed surprised to see us. She told me that they hadn't expected us to arrive until the next day, so she went into the customs office and made a call. She came out and told us to proceed through customs, and since I had visas for everyone, we passed through quickly.

And then we stood there, for two long hours. Just as I was really beginning to panic, a long, white van with exactly twenty-one seats pulled up. The bus belonged to the guide's brother (she was Nepalese, and he was Tibetan). Since there was just enough room for us on the bus, our luggage had to be tied on top. I must have looked worried, because the guide turned to me and said reassuringly, "Don't worry. It never rains this time of year."

The single-lane, dirt road that lay before us was cut into the mountainside, high in the air. Every time another car—or worse yet, a truck—approached, there would be lots of yelling and we'd have to back up to allow enough room for the vehicle to pass. Speaking of that—passing a slower vehicle was absolutely terrifying. In some spots, the road was a narrow cavern whacked out of the side of the mountain, and the guide had to get out of the bus to make sure our luggage didn't hit the cliff above it as we passed through.

The worst of all was when we reached a point where a landslide had occurred, completely covering the road. Because it was so treacherous, the guide had us all get out of the bus and walk across. The drop off on the side of the road was so far down that we couldn't see the bottom of the ravine, but we did see a number of wrecked trucks and vans down below.

In the quiet, the guide said softly, "If you run off the road here … that is it. There's no way anyone could survive that."

With that, the driver backed up the bus to get a running start and went up and over the earth covering the road.

After we'd been on the road for a while, I mentioned to the guide that we hadn't had any lunch. Since we'd arrived a day early, that was a problem, but at the third stop, they brought out hard rolls for each of us and paper cups full of tea.

We went on and on for the rest of the day without seeing a house or a person—well, except the drivers of the trucks, and thankfully there were few of those. Shortly after we left the craggy mountainside and reached level ground, we arrived at a lodge. They were ready for us, with a delicious dinner served by the light of kerosene lamps. After dinner, we each received a lamp of our own to take to our rooms and a box of matches, in case the lamp went out.

My room was spacious, with a single bed and a bathroom with a sink and toilet. A can of oxygen rested next to the bed. The room had no heat, and as soon as the sun went down, the temperature plummeted. My bed had a quilt, but I slept in my clothes because it was freezing. In the morning, we were served hard-boiled eggs, bread, and tea for breakfast.

While we ate our breakfast, I took note of the clothes of the Tibetans working at the lodge. Their dress was unusual, with one shoulder uncovered, and a heavy robe that could be flipped from one side to the other. The guide told me the reason: because of the altitude, the sun is very hot, and the shade was very cold. The sun is so hot, in fact, that Tibetans use it for cooking: large mirrors direct the sun's heat toward a black pot full of water to make tea or a loaf of dough to bake bread.

On the next day's ride, we were able to see Everest for over an hour. We didn't see anyone for almost the whole day, but then a couple of Sherpas showed up. There was lots of bottled water on the bus, because high altitudes take their toll and the air was very dry. Since there was plenty of water, there were also plenty of bathroom breaks, with ladies on the right and gentlemen on the left. We made a stop for lunch—hard-boiled eggs and bread again, but this time with jam on the inside. After lunch, our driver took a nap—an hourlong nap right after lunch is a must for all Chinese people.

During our drive that day, the air was so clear you could see for miles and miles. The road was mostly made of dirt and very bumpy, but every twenty miles or so, we'd encounter a mile of smooth, paved road. I wondered out loud why, and the guide told us that the Chinese government paved a mile of road here and there to use as airstrips for faster movement of troops during incursions with Tibetan separatist groups.

From time to time, the road would span a high mountain pass, and the top of each one was home to one or more poles with hundreds of prayer flags attached—the thought being, the higher the prayer flag was, the more likely the prayer was to be read in heaven. We didn't see anyone at all on the road the entire day except two trucks, but Tibetans randomly showed up at each stop, as if by magic. At the first, we met two men who were hunting a mountain lion—"a very big cat," they said—that had been attacking their flock of sheep and goats. At lunch, we saw four men who were looking for lost sheep. At our last stop, a group of hungry men were looking for a broken-down car that was supposed to be carrying supplies; we gave them the last of our lunch.

We drove for days on that long, dusty road until we reached the rivers that wind through Tibet, cut through the mountains, and then continue on through southeast Asia. In each of the areas we entered, the women there wore aprons that identified their native tribe. Along the riverbanks, we saw many houses and yurts, people working in their gardens, and children placing toy boats in the river and then chasing them along the banks. Every now and then, a child would wade in to catch his boat, yelping because the water was so cold, and the other children would laugh. Some joys in life are universal.

We turned off onto a sandy road to see a monastery famous for its age and size, but also because the Chinese government considered it to be the center of the Tibetan independence movement. Each day, monks rolled large tapestries of Tibetan religious designs down its high walls that could be seen for miles. Some of these were viewed by the Chinese as treasonous, but our guide said that only Tibetans can understand them and that they usually convey religious messages.

Finally, we reached Lhasa, a busy city with many hotels and lots of little lanes with big walls on either side—most of which were too narrow for a car to go through. I figured the group needed a break from all the touring, so we went straight to our hotel. Everyone, and everything, in the hotel was Chinese—we got the message loud and clear that we were in China.

After a little rest, we went to a market area with a Tibetan Buddhist temple, with worshipers lying flat on the ground with their heads pointed toward the statue of the Buddha, and many ladies wearing brightly colored aprons. Bells jangled constantly, and little colorful pieces of prayer papers hung on trees, bushes and even on electrical guide wires; every time the wind blew, the prayers would go straight to heaven. We climbed to the top of the temple, which afforded the most wonderful view: lots of children flying kites in courtyards surrounded by walls and people crowding in the market below. In the distance, we could see the Potala Palace, the winter residence of all Dalai Lamas from 1649 to 1959; the mountains; and a gorgeous sunset. Afterward, we headed back to the hotel for a delicious twelve-course Chinese meal and a good rest.

We'd need it, because the next day we headed to Potala Palace. Perched high on a mountain, it is a full seventy-seven stories tall. It had been on my wish list for years, but I was nervous about all the stairs because I'd had a knee operation just two weeks before leaving the U.S. Our bus made it to about forty stories below the top; I was relieved, as I thought we'd have to climb the whole way.

On the top floor was the Dalai Lama's former residence, a small but beautifully kept apartment with a lovely arbor of flowers in a small garden. The Dalai Lama was exiled to Dharamshala, India, in 1959, and in 1961, I visited a Tibetan school in Mouseri, India, in hopes of meeting him—to no avail. (I've since had the pleasure of meeting him at several Asian conferences in the U.S., and he always talks about how sad he is that he cannot return to Tibet.

About a third of the floors in the Potala Palace were open to the public; those that were closed were monks' residences. The rooms we could enter were lined with nine-foot-tall bookcases full of Buddhist texts. The first shelf was about three feet above the floor, and Buddhist monks and followers walked in a reverent crouch below them—a practice intended for special blessings. (There was no way I could walk around like that, but the Tibetans seemed to have no problem.) It seemed that every open space in the rooms was crowded with crouched worshipers, chanting as they moved along.

A single set of dark stairs led from floor to floor throughout the palace, but every Tibetan there carried a lit candle. The stairs bore a thousand years' worth of dripped wax that collected the dirt from visitors' feet and shoes. After about ten flights of stairs, my newly repaired knee gave out, so I had to sit on the stairs and slide from step to step on my bottom for over fifty flights. By the time I reached the bottom, I had an inch of black wax on my butt and could hardly walk.

I thought a moment about what was worse—a blackened bottom or no pants at all. It wasn't a contest: hundreds of Tibetans looked on in amusement as I took off my khakis and threw them in a trash bin. For the sake of modesty, I tied my windbreaker around my waist to walk across the parking lot to the bus. The bus driver noted that there was plenty of wax still on me, so he covered my seat with newspaper. We had another stop planned that day, but we went to the hotel first so I could change.

That afternoon, we visited Drigung, a Tibetan monastery built right into a mountain. It was primarily a school for monks, but its other purpose was thankfully not in use the day we visited. People bring their dead relatives to the monastery to prepare them for the next life—by cutting them to pieces and having their bones split. The pieces of the body are then wrapped in the dark red cloth worn by Buddhist monks and taken up to the top of the mountain behind the monastery for a "sky burial": birds of prey quickly devour them. A monk explained that this was better than burying bodies and letting them rot, because then they're not good for anything.

"When you die, within a day you become part of another living creature," he said. "We believe in reincarnation. At death, the spirit immediately transfers to a newborn baby."

At each of the Buddhist sites we visited in Tibet—even the Potala Palace—few mentioned the name of the Dalai Lama for fear of being turned into to the Chinese government. China wants Tibetans to forget about the Dalai Lama and instead follow the man they named as the Panchen Lama, or the second holiest man in Buddhism (the young boy identified by the Dalai Lama as the Panchen Lama back in 1995 disappeared shortly thereafter and hasn't been seen since). You could feel the tension everywhere: the Tibetans are afraid that China will send in the military to kill and imprison Tibetans who continue to follow the Dalai Lama, as they have many times before, and they resent the many Han Chinese people who have been moved into Tibet.

These days, most Tibetans consider going to Lhasa akin to visiting a foreign land—namely, China. For others, it is a tourist destination, not a place to live. World tourism has discovered Lhasa; planeloads of tourists from all over the world arrive daily, and a high-speed rail line brings visitors from China as well. Much of what I saw on this visit—the monasteries, specifically—are now closed to visitors. The Tibetans who live there now are prisoners in their own city.

Chapter 8
Become Rich

IN THE FIRST MARKET I VISITED IN CHINA, I NOTED WITH amusement a T-shirt emblazoned with the slogan "BECOME RICH." I'd wanted one as a keepsake for my first trip, but the sizes ranged from extra small to medium—certainly at that time, no one was thinking of extra-large foreigners like me.

You can still find these shirts in Chinese markets, but now it's Americans who are buying them. If you wanted to sum up what China's Four Modernizations have meant to the lives of the common Chinese people, "become rich" just about does it. In 2017, a Shanghai newspaper boasted that a new millionaire was minted in the city every day—and they even wrote about it in terms of the U.S. dollar.

That is, after all, the main reason why country people continue to stream into China's cities. Throughout the 1980s, villagers who visited the cities were mockingly called "10,000-yuan peasants." They'd come to the city for one day and one night and wouldn't know what to do with their new wealth and all the modern conveniences they encountered. They'd walk up twenty-three flights to their hotel room because they didn't know how to use the elevator (or that there was one). They'd order every dish on the menu in a restaurant, enough for an army, and sit there eating for hours until it was all gone and the waiter had to help them up. The 10,000 yuan would be gone, but they'd come home with something to brag about.

Nowadays, those 10,000-yuan peasants drive into the city in Audis. One villager I know cut an opening in his living room wall so he can drive his luxury car into the house, right alongside his seventy-inch TV. When I asked why, he gave me lots of answers. He first said he didn't want to show off to the neighbors. I replied that I was quite sure the whole village knew about his car.

He smiled. "Yes, but isn't it beautiful? I like to look at it as much as I like to look at my TV. Plus, it might get injured outside."

Many Chinese people have made their fortunes at home, but plenty more have made them abroad. There are colonies of Chinese-born people working all over the world, including large ones in the Baltic states—Latvia, Lithuania, and Estonia.

One young millionaire—we'll call him Chao—told me his own get-rich-quick story in Estonia. Some of Chao's friends were performing in the symphony in the country's capital, Tallinn. He decided to visit and brought along two very large suitcases full of a dozen or so items he'd picked up in Shanghai that he thought would sell well there.

Once there, Chao opened his suitcases on the main square and began his business, keeping close watch on what items sold best and which had the biggest profit margins. He returned to Shanghai to stock up again, and the next time Chao returned to Tallinn, he brought four suitcases full of his hottest-selling items, leather jackets for men.

You see, Chao's business enterprise faced a challenge: he couldn't get a wholesaler to ship jackets to him in Tallinn unless there was a business address. Standing in the square and selling goods out of suitcases certainly didn't represent a fixed address, so Chao needed a way to get more goods into this new market quickly. It didn't take long for him to figure out how.

Chao searched Tallinn's main square for a business that seemed to be doing poorly and found one quickly: a shop run by an elderly owner and his son, who were having a hard time attracting business. Chao asked the owner if he could keep his suitcases stored inside the business while he stood in front of the shop and hawked the leather jackets. In return, he'd give the owner 15 percent of each sale. (Chao added that if he'd done the same thing with a Chinese merchant, the merchant would have demanded half of every sale and within days would have become a competitor.)

The men agreed, and within an hour, the first suitcase was empty and Chao had moved on to the second. An hour later, Chao went back into the shop to get the third suitcase. Before long, all four suitcases had been emptied. The owners were amazed—some of Chao's buyers had even ventured into their shop and made purchases there after buying jackets. The shop owners quickly agreed to Chao's request to have the jackets shipped there. He sold 300 jackets in the first month and 500 more the second month.

Impressed, I asked Chao what his current role in the business was. He only had to do two things, he said—change the

window display every few weeks and count the money that continuously rolled in. He opened a second shop in the same way
in St. Petersburg, but it didn't do as well, so Chao was on the
search for the next gold mine in other Balkan cities.

It was always hard to get a translator to work with my Fulbright
groups, which ran five to seven weeks in length, with half of it
spent on the road. On one of my planning trips, the dean at SISU
told me he had the perfect person all lined up for me for the next
group. I'll refer to her here as Qing. Qing was an honors college
graduate student who stood barely five feet tall. She was shabbily
dressed and very thin, but she was perky and pleasant, and her
English was great. I hired Qing on the spot and gave her some
money to buy clothes and a suitcase for the road.

By the end of that trip, Qing had made such a great impression that three of the women in the group took her to downtown
Shanghai and bought her Nikes and some nice casual clothes.
Qing then told me of her desire to get an MBA at a university
in the U.S., so I did some maneuvering and arranged for her to
attend Winthrop University.

Some time later, everything fell into place and Qing was due
to arrive to begin her studies. I met her at the airport to pick her
up, and since Chinese students usually don't have any American money upon arrival, I handed her $200. She thanked me,
declined, and pulled a fat roll of cash out of her pocket.

To my surprise, Qing had arrived in the U.S. early and arranged to stay with a friend in Chicago. The little market on the
first floor of her friend's building had a help wanted sign in the
window. Qing got the job, an opening for a stocker, on the spot
and worked a full eight hours on the first day she arrived from

China. A couple of days later, she noticed the sign was back in the window, so she asked the owner what position was open.

"I need someone to run the cash register."

Qing told him she could do it if he showed her how to work the register. He demurred, saying that she didn't know the prices of the items for sale. Qing smiled and challenged him to test her. Sure enough, Qing knew the price of every item in the store. She'd memorized them as she stocked the shelves.

By her fourteenth day in the U.S., Qing had amassed nearly a thousand dollars.

After she graduated from Winthrop, I lost touch with Qing for a time. One day she called to say she'd be visiting South Carolina, so I invited her to stay at our house.

Qing was there on a business trip, as she was the cargo manager for a large American shipping line. She had come to Charleston to complain that they couldn't seem to get her ships unloaded and distributed fast enough.

"Trucks. You Americans are stuck on trucks. I need a port with good rail connections." Qing's next stop was Jacksonville, to see if their rail routes were up to snuff.

I asked about Qing about her family. She told me that she'd bought a house in Los Angeles and brought her parents over to live with her. That didn't work out so well: her parents wanted to boss her around, so she bought another house for them to live in and was negotiating for a third.

Qing laughed. "This is America, and I am only thirty-three. In America, you can wait until you're forty to get married and have a family. It's not like China." She paused. "One of the reasons I had to get away from my parents was that they kept telling me I was too old to marry. They just don't know the American way."

Gambling is a huge pastime in China. In every area of every park, you'll find a group of old men playing various games for little bits of money. Many Chinese people raise crickets and say they do it because they're good luck, or because they like to hear them chirp, but you can bet that the man of the house is taking the meanest one to work with him. In every mill on every payday, a group will set up in a corner to watch crickets fight and bet on one to win.

Stock markets are little more than an organized (and legal) system of gambling, so they were welcomed in modernized China. In 1990, the Shanghai stock exchange opened with much fanfare and excitement. Like exchanges elsewhere in the world, its crowded, bustling trading floor surrounded by boards that kept the shouting traders up to date with markets around the world.

Soon after the exchange opened, nearly every block in Shanghai was home to a brokerage house. They were busy all the time, with customers lined up at computer kiosks to buy and sell. If someone spent too much time at a terminal, then pushing and shoving might ensue. Today, almost all of the houses are gone, and people buy and sell stock on their own computers and phones. The exchange's floor is radically different, with a few dozen traders milling around where there used to be hundreds. The exchange building used to be alive with all types of people, but now you can stroll right up to the observation balcony and not run into a soul.

Nonetheless, plenty of activity is going on. The stock ticker reveals all. China has two grades of stock: one is open to the world for trading, and on the other, only Chinese people can trade. From time to time, the government tries to speed the market up or slow it down, but everyone knows what's going on.

People find ways to "play the government," as the Chinese like to say. It's said that the Chinese investors know more about the market than anyone in Beijing. Still, many Chinese small investors have lost everything by chasing stocks for far too long. When they crash, they take small investors down first. As the Chinese like to say, "Gamblers get too greedy."

One of my Chinese friends came to teach at Winthrop for a year and brought along his wife. She was an accomplished woman who worked as an accountant, but she didn't know much English. To improve her mastery of the language, his wife watched financial channels on TV all day long and into the night; her husband complained that he had to go to his building's lobby to watch anything else.

When the couple returned to China, the wife quickly put together a new business with eleven other accountants/stock market addicts. The model for the business was VectorVest, an American stock analysis and portfolio management company. The new company sold subscriptions to people looking for advice on stocks. The wife and her eleven partners became rich.

———————

Some years ago, the entrepreneurship spirit spread to forty workers at Lu Xun Park, a beautiful refuge spanning four large city blocks in Shanghai. Every morning and evening, the park is filled with people taking their daily exercise. It costs just a few cents to enter the park, and students and old people pay a reduced rate.

The park workers' *danwei* housing was concealed behind Lu Xun's trees and bushes. It occurred to the workers that very few people were using the park's four corners, since they were located on very busy roads. They saw an opportunity and decided to build high-rise condominiums on each corner. Once built, the buildings featured four units on each floor, each with sweeping vistas of the park, the SISU campus, or the river and skyscrapers of Pu Deng.

In Shanghai, most of the residential space is jammed together and few apartments offer views of nature, so these new apartments were very desirable. A friend of mine encouraged me to buy a unit for its pre-construction price—$50,000—but I declined. He was right. By the time the buildings were finished, the units were selling for triple the original price. This was several years ago, so I'm sure they sell for much more now.

And the park workers? They tore down their old *danwei* housing, moved into their choice of the new condos, sold the other units, and split the profits.

A very exclusive kindergarten located in a high-priced neighborhood near Shanghai's Bund was struggling financially. Although the tuition was expensive, the school simply couldn't afford to stay in business. So its leaders talked a hotel developer into building on the school's land and reserving the building's top floor for the school, with a playground and athletic area on the roof. In China, it's not that unusual to put a school on top of a building—they do it in Hong Kong all the time. But this instance was unique in that the school made the gamble; in Hong Kong, the government does it.

Chinese people never brag about money, but they often buy expensive, showy items that prove to the world they've become rich. Ask about it, and they'll refer to it as an "investment." And if you comment on their business acumen, they'll never say that they—or others—are smart. Most of the time, they just say they were "lucky," or the greatest compliment of all, "clever."

While many people are putting on a good show, all is not well. The Chinese government has long encouraged its people to invest in stocks, but China has no equivalent to the U.S.'s Securities and Exchange Commission, a regulatory body intended to protect investors from fraud. In 2015, many Chinese investors chased the price of a stock up and then it—and they—went broke. A farmer who had invested in the company said he didn't know what his family would do. He'd invested all of his savings in the stock, which zoomed from $35 per share to more than $200 per share—and then dropped to zero the next week. When China transitioned to a market economy, the Chinese people lost much of the nation's safety net. Not everyone is becoming rich.

Government-owned industries now compete against for-profit industries. The government industries maintain some advantage, as their raw materials are secured at below-market prices. But in the supply chain, private companies get what they need first, and what they get is of better quality. Government firms get their raw materials by their due date, but never before. Private industries pay higher salaries, and therefore their talent is better skilled. The government industry provides more services for its employees in return for their lower pay, but every year, the costs of providing those services go up.

Since the Chinese government doesn't have an army of economic experts advising it, it's done very well in good times but often does exactly the wrong thing during economic crises. President Trump's ongoing trade war has hurt some of America's most profitable industries, such as soybeans, automobiles, and airplanes. China's retaliatory tariffs and maneuvers were equally economically unwise, as they led to increased food prices for the common man. Certainly China can turn to other countries to supply food, but it takes a long time for farmers elsewhere to increase their production enough to make up the difference. It also hurts American farmers, as they are saddled with too much inventory. My point is that politicians are not suited for making economic warfare. To stabilize the Chinese economy and prevent a recession during this trade war, the government has had to infuse billions into the system. And to stay on the good side of the United States, China continues to buy a lot of our debt.

The Chinese are great savers, but they also like to spend on expensive items. Just as in the U.S., housing is the number one expense, but cars are a close second. Twenty-four million new cars were sold in China in the last year. If a particular city seems full of Volvos, that's likely where they are made; in some big cities, several brands have plants. The Chinese are also building their own makes of cars and are trending toward building more and more electric vehicles.

Of course, there's no place in China's crowded cities for dealerships, so groups of manufacturers rent out soccer fields for a weekend and fill them with cars, lined up bumper to bumper. Once those cars are sold, there's nowhere to park them (a few high-end condos have parking garages, but they're rare). Traffic is terrible in Chinese cities, so it's almost always a slower go to drive instead of public transportation, no matter how many belt or ring roads are built.

The youth of China today find phones and computers to be the most valuable status symbols. Those with iPhones or Samsungs take them out at Starbucks or McDonalds to make sure everyone notices what a high-end phone they have. Clothes and shoes are also important, with an emphasis on imported brands. I once overheard one person say to another, "I like your shoes. How much did they cost?"

It's not rude to ask how much things cost or how much a person makes. The training materials we were given as Fulbright professors advised us to tell inquisitors who were curious about our salaries to reply, "About the same as a foreign expert." Apparently, everyone knows what a foreign expert makes, and many nations pay their experts a salary plus a separate foreign expert salary from the Chinese government. Fulbright doesn't allow its professors to take money from China, so we can't be told what to teach, or what not to teach.

In 1999, Jack Ma founded Alibaba, which is now the largest online shopping site in the world. The site debuted at the perfect time, as by that point, most Chinese people either owned a computer or had access to one. China was breaking ground on new megacities and expanding its existing megacities. Retail was slow to catch up. City property values and salaries were growing so fast that there simply wasn't room for major retail stores to get established. Ma filled this gap with Alibaba, which sells just about everything.

For example, Ma realized that there were millions of single Chinese women with good jobs and money to spend, so he created a holiday of his own, "Girls' Day," when everything for women was on sale for 25 percent off. It was tremendously successful, with young women planning what they'd buy as much as a month ahead of time. Today, Alibaba's Girls' Day outperforms

Black Friday and Cyber Monday sales in the U.S. by more than double. And now there's a Boys' Day.

Starbucks plays a similar role in China to what it long has done in America: it's now regarded as a nice place for single professionals to meet. Even carrying around a Starbucks cup of coffee is a show of success and status.

Suburban housing is another true status symbol, and in China, it usually involves very large houses on very small lots. When I was interviewing for a job in China once, I toured three homes that were very nicely appointed and at least 3,500 square feet in size, and also no more than ten feet away from a very similar house. In an obvious attempt to attract foreigners, one of the developments even included a small church. The salesman said, "Don't worry! The community fees will pay the minister's salary."

Those with really big money join golf clubs. There aren't many of them, as land values in China are sky high. They're generally located in places where it's difficult or unlikely that houses and businesses would be sited. An example: one near Beijing is positioned right by the Ming Tombs.

All large multinational corporations (MNCs) that seek to do business in China face the same dilemma: the challenge of securing government permits. The Chinese government wants MNCs to locate their China headquarters in Beijing, but few foreign companies have interest in doing business there. The weather isn't great, given its propensity for smog, cold winters, and *loas*, the fine red-yellow dust storms that cloud the skies of north China periodically from January to April. Many

companies claim that Beijing's workers tend to think like bureaucrats, with an unwillingness to work a minute beyond 5:00
p.m.

Some MNCs decided to set up showy offices in Beijing
high-rises and staff them for show, but they chose to do their
real business elsewhere, perhaps in rural counties near big cities. Often these counties will give the companies the land on
which they build or lease it for a long term at a low cost, allowing the MNCs to avoid paying the high property costs of the cities but still allowing them to do business near big-city airports,
sea, and rail connections.

The Great Modernization always had a consequence: opening
China's doors to the world. Now that the country is open, China
is liberally flexing its status as a global power—and taking advantage of the U.S's trend toward turning inward. China's large
population must be fed and put to work, so its government must
think globally, for everything from sourcing raw materials and
to finding markets for Chinese goods.

While the growth of China's economy has been wonderful,
problems remain. The major decision makers in Beijing now
are Party leaders, rather than businessmen and economists.
The moves they make to solve problems or encourage growth
are often uninformed and can backfire. For example, the entrepreneurial spirit is strong in China. While many Chinese
people wish to set up their own small businesses, banks are often unwilling to extend them the loans they need to make it
happen. The government wants to encourage small businesses
and controls the Bank of China, so they use that power to force
lenders to make the loans. But the Chinese government is also

beholden to the big MNCs it attracts, and those companies tend to stifle or suffocate small businesses.

The government of China moves very slowly on monetary policy, and by the time it finally gets around to doing something, the economic situation may be too far gone. It is hard to control a rapidly changing economy, and slow-moving Beijing generally makes matters worse. This is universally true among developing nations, but some others benefit from having economic experts as their top decision makers.

On the other hand, the government has been very responsive when it comes to long-term decision making. It has invested heavily in infrastructure and new energy sources, and it is actively engaging and investing in projects worldwide to ensure that China will always have access to raw materials and a foothold in emerging economies everywhere. In my travels to other countries, one of the first questions I ask of government officials is, "How are the Chinese investing in your economy?" In many cases, the answer is in building railroads.

The secret of much of China's economic success has been its flexibility. For example, in the 1980s, China bought textile equipment from almost every mill in the textile-heavy areas of the Carolinas. There was a concerted effort to develop a textile industry in China until about 1990, when the only textile mills I could find were printing and finishing mills and those making high-end finished clothing. I asked a mill operator where all the textile machines had gone. His answer: Vietnam and Bangladesh.

"So you sold them?"

He laughed. "No, we still own them. But land and labor are just too expensive in China. We moved them to countries where land and labor are still cheap."

Likewise, Chinese manufacturers have closely watched the retail market there, noting which imported products sold the best domestically and then copying the product outright. Other products are modified to better suit the Chinese market: for example, Chinese manufacturers focus on wall-mounted air conditioning units that insert below apartment windows. When it comes to clothing, Chinese manufacturers have modified their designs to better suit Chinese silhouettes, rather than considerably larger Western ones. On my first visit to China, the men's belts for sale in the markets would fit around the small waists of most Chinese men twice. By 2000, every man was able to buy a belt that actually fit.

On one of my visits, our group toured a factory that made leather jackets. The leather came from Argentinian cattle and was tanned on the ship on the way over. At the end of the factory's line, seamstresses sewed labels into the jackets. All the jackets were identical, but the four seamstresses had four different labels in their machines: one was Lord & Taylor, another was London Fog, and the latter two were private labels for Walmart and France's Carrefour department store.

Once the jackets were inspected, all that were deemed second quality had the label sliced in half but still clearly visible. I asked our guide where the seconds ended up.

"Everywhere from Thailand to Russia to Hong Kong to right here in China," he replied.

In the 1960s, the factories of Hong Kong developed an innovative production system that is still used today throughout China. When an order comes in for anything from a child's toy to a mink coat, the factory produces an order that exceeds the requested total by 10 to 15 percent, so if a reorder comes in, it can be quickly filled without having to reset the machines, as that is the most time-consuming and expensive part of the production process. If the reorders don't come in as expected, the overage is sold on the wholesale and retail markets in Hong Kong or China at a quarter of the retail price. This was the reason for the legendary draw of Hong Kong's Stanley Market: it was loaded with first-quality goods—the "real thing." Second-quality goods and knockoffs can be found at Hong Kong's Temple Street Market or similar markets in any Chinese city, but then again, you get what you pay for.

China's manufacturing industry has long been plagued by quality issues, particularly in the realm of toys. When foreign companies place orders with Chinese factories, the manufacturers typically outsource most of the small parts necessary for the products to as many as a dozen workshops in villages around the country, making quality control challenging. A recent problem with red lead-based paint being used in toys happened because a single village ran out of its usual supply of red paint. Instead of going through the time-consuming process of reordering their usual brand of red paint, they purchased paint from the local farmer's supply that was intended for use on barns. The villagers had no idea that the paint made the toy dangerous.

Once, on a flight from Hong Kong to Shanghai, I sat next to a man who worked for Coca-Cola. He told me that his job was to tour and quality check in six can manufacturing plants all over China. In the past, he said, he'd only had to make an unannounced visit to each plant once a month, but in order to maintain standards, he'd had to increase the frequency of his visits to every two weeks—in some cases, visiting the same plant three days in a row.

My Chinese friends often tell me that I never should have signed over the royalties for my International Relations text-books. (What they really mean is that I was a fool.) I've tried to explain that my motivation was never money. Instead, I was trying to get China to stop looking at the world through the distortion field of their ideology and look at it realistically. Becoming rich has never been something that I desire, because it seems to me that getting rich just sets off an insatiable lust for more. You never feel like you have reached your goal.

Chapter 9
Life in Magnificent China,
1979-1990

From 1979 to 1989, most Chinese citizens could be categorized into three groups: those who were married and lived in cities with or without children, single city dwellers, and people who lived in villages. Most city workers were employed by a *danwei* that provided their job, housing, medical services, and compensation. Their compensation was paid in cash every other week—always a base amount plus "add-ons," or additional pay, for some things, like previous military service or holding an office in the Communist Party, and big additions for military service or Party membership prior to the Communist victory of 1949. There were never any deductions.

Teachers and professors got add-ons for moving up a rank; for example, after preparing two advanced courses, professors were reviewed by a board and promoted from instructor to lecturer. Those who were invited to join the Communist Party or who had a job or office in the Party would also get add-ons. Before students heard a lecture or took an exam, the professors who wrote them had to have them approved by both the university and the Party. A professor might get a one-time add-on for bringing in a new business and teaching contract for courses. Of course, none of this is big money: a lecturer might earn the equivalent of $30 a month and perhaps $5 to $8 in add-ons.

Spouses sometimes didn't mention their add-ons to one another. In those days, most husbands turned their money over to their wives, who pooled the money and paid the bills with them. In some parts of China, such as Shanghai and Tianjin, husbands would often go to the market each morning to buy the day's groceries, so they would get more of the monthly share anyway. Otherwise, if a husband needed money, he had to ask his wife for it, so holding back the add-ons gave a husband a little more spare change—it was often referred to as "cigarette money."

Chinese couples of the time often argued, and at times actually fought, over money. The next most common reasons for family arguments were smoking and gambling. Pretty much all Chinese men, and plenty of the women, smoked before marriage, but most women would quit once they said "I do." And the men … well, many of them would claim that they had when in fact, they hadn't. Part of the reason was for social purposes, as among men, sharing cigarettes was an opening to a conversation. Offering up an imported cigarette was a reliably good way to butter someone up if you were after something.

In most housing complexes in cities, older women were assigned to track the menstrual cycles of younger women as part of the "One Child" policy. In some cases, charts were posted in hallways with each woman's period schedule. If a woman missed a period, she was sent to a nearby abortion clinic—and they were always nearby. During that time, China had its own version of the Pill, but it was dangerous and failed often. If women got pregnant while on this form of birth control, they faced high risks of fetal abnormalities and future infertility.

On the same topic—no one in China at that time was allowed to have sex before marriage. A few weeks before her wedding day, a bride was taken aside and filled in on what sex was like and given careful instructions about how to avoid pregnancy.

Single men were often just as ignorant. Once, I walked in on a very quiet conversation between my office mate and one of his students, who was to be married the next week. After the student left, I asked what that had all been about. The student had asked him what a woman "looked like" and what he should do on their wedding night, so my office mate had helpfully drawn him some pictures. He laughed and told me, "They didn't cover this part of the job during the Fulbright orientation." As soon as Star TV began broadcasting in China, with all of its French movies, a lot of Chinese people got a broader base of sex education.

Since premarital sex was against the law, single people had no access to birth control. On one occasion, a heavyset German exchange professor was headed to Hong Kong for a little vacation, and several of his single friends asked him to pick up condoms for them. The professor stopped at a 7/11 store to buy a six-pack of beer and a gross (that would be 144) of condoms. The woman at the check-out counter said, "Sir, don't you have your order reversed? Shouldn't that be a six-pack of condoms and a gross of beer?"

Getting married in Chinese cities wasn't easy. There was a very small window for city-dwelling women: they were expected to stay single until age twenty-four but were considered old maids at thirty. The men had a little more time—they weren't expected to be married until the age of thirty-five—but if they dated someone for "too long" and then married someone else, they could be sued by the first girlfriend for breach of confidence.

At colleges, the genders were separated with strict rules (but nowadays, that's where most people meet their spouses). Dating *danwei* coworkers was ill advised, because if it didn't work out (or even if it did), everyone would be talking. Discos and karaoke clubs were pretty good places to meet other single people, but those who went "too often" were gossiped about.

And of course, parents were always making suggestions. "'So-and-so' has a daughter, and she's thrifty and a good housekeeper."

The village life made things much easier, as the family was in full control. Aunts or very good friends asked around in nearby villages about what appropriate matches might be coming of age (village dwellers typically married around the age of twenty-one). The "One Child" policy left rural China with a serious shortage of adult women, so each prospective bride's family was usually able to demand a new house for the couple from the prospective groom's family.

At that time, Chinese people generally matured, both physically and emotionally, very late. A friend's sixteen-year-old daughter would always hide behind her mother or father whenever I'd see her. One of my friends met his wife at an art museum. They saw each other there at the same day and time three weeks in a row before even speaking to each other.

Once, I mentioned to a friend of mine named Pan that I'd read plenty about 10,000-yuan peasants but didn't think I'd ever met one. Pan went wild, as he often did, and said, "On Saturday, I will take you to two villages with lots of them!"

At the first village, we ventured into the home of the mayor, who told us that the whole village had gone into the rabbit-breeding business. We toured the home's first floor, which is typically not given over to living space in village homes (there's usually a kitchen and a bathroom, and a large area to keep animals in times of bad weather). That was certainly the case in the mayor's home: there was no bathroom or kitchen there. The first floor was filled with rabbit cages from floor to ceiling, wall to wall.

"I own 640 rabbits!" she proudly told me, beaming. "I raise them for nine months, until the fur is right for making the linings for gloves. Each rabbit makes three pairs of gloves, and then we sell the meat at the city market."

Upstairs, there was a living room, with a sofa that converted into a bed, a small kitchen and an even smaller bedroom (the bedroom's size wasn't really a concern, as in many village homes, bedrooms were furnished with only a bed, and all the clothes and shoes were stored in a suitcase at the end of the bed or in one could slip under the bed). She showed us the bathroom had been added in the back of the second floor.

"This is better," she said, "because now we don't have to go up and down stairs."

She had three daughters living in the home with her; I'm still not sure how she got away with breaking the "One Child" policy. I guess that being the village's mayor and head of the local Communist Party meant that special rules applied.

Outside, the home had a very big garden. Her neighbor had very little land and two sons, she told me, and one of them helped her manage the garden. She went on to say that she'd adopted the young man, so her husband's family name would carry on, and that the young man's family adopted her oldest daughter—and then they married, providing each family with exactly what they wanted. Her second daughter married that same family's other son (who would then be her adoptive brother's brother, I suppose?), but that son kept his family name. That way, each family ended up with a son, and the poorer family had more land—plus they were in the rabbit business.

Curious, I asked about daughter number three.

"She is still too young," she said, "but we hope that she does well in her school tests and gets to go to college in the city. Then she can marry an educated city boy."

It was all well planned. I asked her about her mayoral responsibilities.

"I settle disputes. That's a big job, but people trust me because I'm clever and hardworking, and I've made lots of money."

In the next village Pan and I visited, most of the young people had moved to Shanghai for jobs but kept their official residence in the village, so they'd receive an allocation of land. We visited the home of a family that had taken in some sharecroppers. They weren't called that, of course, but they were poor peasants who didn't have land of their own that was arable, and they had lived too far away from a city to bring their produce to market.

The owner of the home and her family received 30 percent of everything the sharecropper family grew on the land. In return, she provided the family with a one-room house on the property and building materials to add an extra room and a kitchen.

The sharecropper family used an outhouse on the property, as their house had no indoor plumbing, but the homeowner told us, "That's better than what they had in their village, and our village also has an elementary school, so their children can be educated."

I was a little surprised after touring these villages about the size of the families—multiple children? In China? I asked Pan if the "One Child" policy wasn't enforced in villages.

He smiled. "From 1989 on, the government has depended so heavily on peasants that they've left them alone. Besides, they're clever enough to know what to say to outsiders and the authorities. Their lives are getting better and better."

In China at the time, the marriage ritual began by registering the marriage with a local government agency. Those with money then held a banquet to celebrate the occasion. May and October generally have the best weather and are lucky months, so all the better restaurants and hotel ballrooms booked up months in advance with wedding banquets.

The banquets were for show, so families would spend way too much on them. Brides would dress in three to five different outfits, including a Western-style white bridal gown (usually rented) and a *qipao* or *cheongsam*, a traditional long, tight, and red silk dress with at least one high slit to show off the legs (but also to allow her to walk). The other outfits varied, but at city weddings, a fitted business suit was usually worn at some point.

At the start of the banquet, the bride and groom would stand at the hall entrance. The groom would hand out cigarettes to each guest, and the bride would bow as she lit each one. After everyone was seated and began to eat, the bride and groom would walk from table to table and propose a toast (over shots of liquor) at each one—and everyone at the table was expected to knock back the shot each time. Not surprisingly, the bride and groom got drunk rather quickly, so the best man takes over drinking their shots (wise couples pick a best man who can hold his liquor).

In villages, weddings worked differently if there was no budget for an elaborate banquet. The groom's family would travel to the bride's home in her village with lots of food and presents, and there would be plenty of food, drink, music, and even dancers provided by the bride's family as well. After a day of celebration and perhaps a few stupid tricks to embarrass the bride and groom, the couple travels back to the groom's village—hopefully to their own new home.

Minority regions had their own marriage customs. In one area, the oldest woman in the village was responsible for making all the matches, usually from the same village but always from the same tribe. One minority group's wedding celebrations typically include a fake kidnapping of the bride: she is spirited away to the groom's home or village, and her family arrives soon after filled with false outrage, demanding a dowry and gifts. Each minority group has its own unique take on wedding garb, and it's common to see traveling shows with beautiful young women dressed up in the colorful wedding costumes of various tribes.

After 1990, things changed. It became much more common for brides and grooms to find each other without involvement by their families, and growing affluence led to many more destination weddings—sometimes for many couples at once.

Once, when I was visiting Putoushan, a mountain island just southeast of Shanghai also known as Buddha Island, I witnessed just such an event. Putoushan is home to seven Buddhist temples and is sacred in Chinese Buddhism.

From my spot near the harbor, I spied a big tour boat as it pulled up to the dock. Suddenly, a group of women wearing elaborate costumes and playing cymbals and other musical instruments and similarly costumed men dancing and playing drums began to fill the path leading from the dock to the nearest temple. (The small island only has one set of these "greeters," so mass weddings are scheduled in a staggered fashion so they can participate in all of them.)

Slowly, couples began to debark the boat in a long line and follow the path to the temple. I couldn't believe how many there were—eventually, someone involved in the event told me there were 135 couples in all. As they reached the temple, a monk blessed them, one by one. Each couple lit a candle and placed it in front of the temple's Buddha statue, and then all the newlyweds gathered in the temple's courtyard, where a group of monks chanted a blessing. Representatives from island hotels stood around holding up signs with their hotel's name in Chinese and English, and the couples lined up for their respective hotels. This particular wedding group had booked a two-night stay on the island, but some groups stayed longer.

———————————

Putoushan is special in many ways. Legend has it that the earth was born out of a giant split rock on the island where the ocean comes roaring out. In addition to its seven major Buddhist temples there, there are also several monasteries, and the island also boasts some very nice beaches. But the best of all of Putoushan's features is that it is the place the Monkey King, immortalized in Journey to the West, uses as his springboard to heaven.

Each time I visited Putoushan, I always hoped there would be a wedding going on. On another occasion, I accompanied my wife, Janet, when she took her class of ten students, plus our three children, to the island on the public ferry from Shanghai. Several other people on the ferry took note of so many foreign children with one couple, and word quickly spread that they were all ours. We were approached by countless people who gave us a thumbs up and telling us that the gods had surely blessed us, or that they gods were surely happy with us to have given us so many children. For a while, we tried to explain the situation, but eventually we gave up and went with the flow.

In the early years of the Great Modernization, most city dwellers who were newly married received housing from the husband's or the wife's *danwei*. But by the 1990s, most *danweis* got out of the housing business and sold off the units to their occupants. If no public housing was available to them, young couples moved in with the husband's parents—even if there was no room for them. One young professor friend of mine returned from getting his doctorate at the University of Michigan with his wife and baby, but neither spouse's *danwei* provided housing. His parents lived in a one-bedroom apartment, so they enclosed the apartment's balcony—a space about four feet by eight feet—to serve as a bedroom for the young couple and their baby (in the winter, they slept in the living room).

Another problem faced by most couples was the ability to

spend time together. Early on in the Great Modernization, the Chinese work week was six days long, and all businesses were operational every day of the week. Eventually the government realized that they needed their workers to spend the money they earned at work to benefit the economy, and in order for them to have time to shop, they would need more time off from work. The work week was shaved down from five and half days a week to eventually its current state of five days a week, but businesses still operate seven days a week. That means that everyone has different days off during the week, which makes it challenging to find a spouse with the same schedule.

The Tiananmen Square demonstrations were the best-known events in China in 1989 beyond its borders, but another seismic shift happened that same year that caused tremendous upheaval in Chinese society. Prior to that year, when people finished their schooling, the government assigned them to *danweis*. In 1989, that practice came to an end, and people had to find their own jobs. For those with education and skills, there were plenty of opportunities, but many others could not find employment. While the government claims there is no unemployment in China, that's simply not true. The Chinese use a different term: "waiting for work." Many people who were "waiting for work" had to take short-term jobs, like construction work, or were forced into unsanctioned, or even illegal, ventures like hawking knockoff goods or prostitution.

The Aging of China

Around the same time, China began to face a huge problem: its aging population, with fewer and fewer workers and more and more retirees. The "One Child" policy was largely to blame, so couples were then allowed to have a second child. The change began in villages, but they slowly spread to cities as well, which represented another problem for young families: their apartments were so small that making room for a second child was very difficult.

The aging problem is exacerbated by the fact that increasingly, young Chinese women see little reason to marry. The same phenomenon has plagued Singapore and Japan. A woman might wonder, "I have a good job, and I live with my parents. Why should I marry and have a child? I'll have to do all the household work and my work outside the home as well. There's such a housing shortage that half or more of our income would go to rent, and we'd only have a room or two at the most. There's nothing in this for me."

Many Chinese women think, and perhaps rightly so, that the available young men are spoiled by their parents and expect their wives to mother them along with their children. Of course, this thinking upsets their parents, who want grandchildren, but then again, it's nice having a daughter around to look after you when you get old. Young men who can't find a wife never hear the end of it from their parents. They want someone to carry on the family name, and more importantly, they want a daughter-in-law to take care of them in their old age.

Across the nation, the fallout from the "One Child" policy continues. Traditionally, there were enough children in the family to take care of the parents when they got old, but now, a single child may be responsible for two parents and four grandparents as well. So many young people who were born and raised in villages have left for the cities, leaving their parents and grandparents behind with no one to look after them.

It has long been a tradition for a son and his wife to take care of the son's parents, but who, then, would take care of the wife's parents?

Increasingly, Chinese people are growing old on their own, with no one to look after them. Even if they saved their money diligently throughout their working years, the money they made then can't compare to today's salaries. One doctor I know earned about $700 a year in 1985 and retired in 2000. Today, doctors in China make anywhere from $20,000 to $40,000 a year—and the cost of living has gone up along with those salaries. Even if my friend saved 50 percent of his annual salary, how could he possibly keep up?

In recent years, the Chinese government raised the retirement age for women from fifty-five to sixty and for men from sixty to sixty-five. Some believe it should be increased again, but younger employees want the top jobs those would-be retirees currently occupy, and they say that older people have not kept up with the computer and communication skills that are now necessary for competent work. Some older people have found low-level jobs to keep themselves afloat, but most people who have had careers as professionals would consider taking such a job as "losing face."

———————

Among my many retired and retiring friends, there is a great divide. Those who are older have been through hell and back—World War II, the Japanese occupation, the civil war between he Nationals and the Communists, the Communist purges of the middle and upper classes, the mass starvation of the Great Leap Forward, and the Cultural Revolution—so they find the peace of retirement wonderful.

For these older retirees, no matter what housing or money problems they face, retirement means peace at last. They can get up when they want and visit the nearest park for exercises and mediation. Some do tai chi, and others walk backward around and around the park, both to maintain agility. Old men bring their pet birds to the park in cages and get together in groups to chat and let their birds sing.

Each evening, after dinner, these same people return to the park, along with many younger single people, for night exercise and also for dance lessons—any kind you can imagine. In the evenings, the old men leave the birds at home and gather in smaller groups, maybe four to six people, for lively games and gambling. Young couples rent boats in the park's lake for snuggling or disappear into the bushes for a little privacy. It's a time for the old to take joy in seeing how much the lives of today's young people are in China have improved—so much better than their own younger years.

The younger retirees fear their retirement. If grandchildren live nearby, they might spend their days looking after them, but many are growing old without any family around. They aren't comfortable spending time with older retirees, as they were just children when their elders suffered through the worst of the Cultural Revolution. They have lived their adulthood in the new China, a race with no ending in which everything is changing, all the time.

They, too, have made it to their retirement. They, too, can go to the park. Some participate in activities, but many just wander the streets, looking in the colorful store windows at the things they can't afford because they no longer work. Just a few years before, they'd been the new China, and now, many feel that they are nothing.

In other Asian countries, retired people—especially women—often spend their days meditating at temples or shrines. But China has few of them, and those that do exist are intended for tourists, rather than for contemplation. Some go to malls every day to walk, because they are climate controlled. Others stay home, glued to the television day and night. Their children scold them: "Why don't you get out of the house and do something, anything!" But by the time they finally reach retirement, these people are tired. The one constant in life in China, from school age until the end of the working years, is stress. In retirement, these people quickly find their stress replaced with boredom, but their anxiety persists as they feel they are part of a world in which they do not belong.

It is easier to grow old in the villages of China, to be sure. Even if your children and grandchildren have moved away to the city, you still have your garden to look after and friends who have known you all your life. Just as in the cities, the old men gather to play cards or other games for small amounts of money. They smoke, and every now and then, they share a few beers.

More than half of my closest Chinese friends are now dead. One, a famous judge who gladly spent time with me and the groups of students or faculty I brought to China, died in his apartment because of a leaky gas line. He had served as a judge in the Tokyo and Nanjing trials, and yet there wasn't a word about him in any newspaper when he died. Another friend had been a vice president of a university and held degrees from Yale and Oxford. His wife left him during the Cultural Revolution and fled to Australia, returning many years later to divorce him. He dated several professors at his university and married one of them, but his joy was short-lived. His jilted girlfriends sued him for breach of faith, and although he won the case, he lost face and was sent to teach in Macau. He died shortly after, of what mutual friends told me was a broken heart.

As one Chinese friend summed up life in China, "It is very stressful when you are young, as you are always preparing for tests. And then there is the stress of loneliness as you grow old."

Chapter 10
The Tiananmen Year

THE TIANANMEN MASSACRE OF 1989, THE PRO-democracy events leading up to it, and the crackdown that followed it loom large in memory. After the massacre, the government's first reaction was to round up and punish those who participated. The Party hierarchy considered going to great lengths to re-educate the young people, including possibly returning all college freshmen back to villages, as was done during the Cultural Revolution. Needless to say, this was very unpopular with villagers, who hated having to deal with city people.

Regional newspapers printed photographs of people being arrested and, in a few cases, being put to death. But the printed photographs of prisoners being shot failed to identify the students, which was odd—the Chinese way would have been to identify and shame them, parade them around a bit, and then put them to death, to serve as an example to others. As a result, word quickly spread, however, that these public executions were actually of criminally insane people, rather than students.

Deng realized that Chinese troops shooting unarmed students in the streets during the Tiananmen demonstrations was a bad look on the world stage, so the leaders of the military units were punished and demoted for not being able to find a way to clear the square without loss of life.

Like everything else about Tiananmen, this topic was off-limits, even for private conversations. Many of the real student leaders were able to escape from the country; this was covered by the foreign press, but not inside China. Although the Tiananmen demonstrations took weeks to develop, after the crackdown, any word of the uprising quickly came to a halt. In China, it was if it had never happened.

What resulted from Tiananmen was strange and little known to those beyond China's borders. First, the government realized that Tiananmen would have great international ramifications—huge drops in foreign business investment and international tourism, for example—so it made adjustments right away to ensure the economy would not suffer.

Being cut off from world markets was the ultimate test of China's inherent entrepreneurial gifts. Measures were taken to turn the economy inward and offset the losses in tourism and foreign investment:

- The work week was shortened to five days, and the annual fall and spring holiday periods were lengthened to encourage Chinese citizens to shop more, travel, and spend the money they earned. Employees' paid holidays were staggered during the Chinese New Year, so there would be enough transportation available for everyone to travel. Another benefit: the change led to job increases of 10 to 20 percent, as new workers had to be added to cover the newly abbreviated shifts of existing employees.

- Chinese manufacturers refocused their production on goods designed for Chinese people (lots of red packaging and large Chinese characters in gold) and created stores in which they marketed and sold these products.
- More new jobs were created by breaking ground on large infrastructure projects, such as new highways and rail systems.

Tourist spots were redesigned to increase their appeal to Chinese visitors. For example, huge bridges were constructed over the terracotta warriors and horses of Xi'an, so ten times as many people could visit at the same time. The attraction's parking lots were moved farther away, and shops were placed between to encourage visitors to spend during their holiday. Some of the shops even rented warrior costumes in adult and child sizes for photos. Among the great temple complexes of Suzhou, one particular pagoda had little appeal to modern Chinese people, so several dozen huge (twenty to forty feet high) inflatable cartoon animals and figures were added so Chinese families would bring their kids for photographs. All the historic sites in Beijing added face-painting and costume concessions.

Guilin held out the longest, but by 2000, even it sold out to gauche tourist gimmicks. The most beautiful of all Chinese cities installed fake palm trees on the lamp posts of its main street, with purple lights wrapped around the "trunks" and green ones on the "leaves." (At least the mall that was built there was constructed underground, so it didn't mar the views of the gorgeous mountains that surrounded the city.) The length of the city's river cruise was cut in half so each boat could make two trips each day. Sidewalk shops now line every street, and boats selling tourist junk pull up next to the sightseeing boats as they glide down the river.

Suddenly, discos sprouted up everywhere, mostly to keep young people busy and their minds off protesting. Most restaurants added dance floors, and when karaoke became popular almost every night, all the discos turned into karaoke bars.

Billboards that had for years been aimed at high-end Chinese and foreign consumers, with English words, began to target the 10,000-yuan peasant in Chinese instead. They were rich by Chinese standards in 1990, so lots of products and experiences were designed to appeal to them: Why not spend a third of your annual income on a color TV or a one-night vacation in the city in which you eat half the menu at a restaurant, dance the night away at a disco, and finally get a few hours of sleep at a fancy hotel, if it meant you could tell stories about it for years back home? Billboards that had advertised Japanese electronics encouraged consumers to buy Chinese soap and shampoo instead.

(As a brief aside, I have a friend who does an inventory of Shanghai billboards each year. He's found that the "One Child" policy and "Four Modernization" billboards quickly transitioned to advertisements for Japanese electronics, and then just as quickly became ads for Coca-Cola and Sprite. Chinese people love Coke and Sprite, so the government was smart to not attack them. Diet Coke never caught on in China, as among adults, having a little weight on you is considered a good thing. One Chinese friend who'd just returned from a trip to Russia exclaimed, "They even have Coke and Sprite!")

Chinese parents helped along the government's suppression attempts, as many students told me that they'd received stern lectures about the sacrifices that had been made to get them into a good university, just to have them foolishly throw it all way. "You are there to study," they were told, "so you can have a better life."

For the parents, this "better life" meant becoming rich, just like those T-shirts had declared in the markets of Shanghai. No one needed a T-shirt to tell them what to do, as the meaning of life in the new China was readily apparent. Parental crackdowns were much more effective than any government crackdown: young people knew to respect and obey their elders, or their existences would become a living hell.

After Tiananmen, any foreign tourism was just a bonus to the economy, which depended more and more on Chinese consumers. Policy changes were made to keep those consumers happy—and shopping. For example, families living south of the Yangtze River hadn't been allowed to have heat in their homes. This restriction was lifted around 1995 in order so they could all rush out to buy heaters—which, of course, they did. It's worth noting that the Chinese market for heaters differed from that of many other nations. In winter, most Chinese people wear multiple layers of clothing to combat the cold, so room heaters were the preferred option.

Televisions, which had long been exclusively luxury items, were newly appreciated as a way to keep Chinese citizens entertained, and thus busy. They suddenly became a must in every household. The government made plenty of efforts to allow its citizens to watch only approved channels, to be sure, but it couldn't stop satellite dishes from popping up on every roof in China.

Star TV, the satellite provider, brought the world to China. Its management strategy was very shrewd: they took great care to never offend the government or display any public discord in other countries, and instead they broadcast lots and lots of

R- and X-rated French movies. Even today, most at-home dinners in Chinese households have a love scene from a French film blaring in the background.

The TV was also recognized as possibly the single greatest method for marketing Chinese products to Chinese consumers. For example, fresh air is very important in Chinese culture, and most people like to be able to open their windows year-round. Chinese companies designed air conditioning units that could be mounted below windows, thus allowing the windows to be opened easily anytime. Ads on television let the whole country know about this innovation simultaneously, and today, it's hard to find a window in China that doesn't have one of these units underneath it.

Farmers and residents of villages did not support the student movement, and nearly all enlisted men in the military hailed from rural areas, which had suffered the most from the "One Child" policy. To keep the loyalty of the villagers strong, the government began to make exceptions to the policy, including allowing all rural couples whose first child was a girl to have a second after seven years had elapsed. Soon enough, even the seven-year rule was relaxed, and villagers were allowed to have their second whenever they wanted to without objection. Both the Party and the government realized the need to keep villagers happy: after all, throughout Chinese history, peasant uprisings overthrew most dynasties.

China's history has a recurring theme of switching between rule by professionals and rule by ideology (often ideologies of emperors, of course). In the 1400s, China built mighty ships that sailed all over the world, but once control changed to an ideological bent in Beijing, the ships were all destroyed. China thinks it is the center of the world and also, as the famous rocks of Hainan Island are inscribed, the "The End of the Earth."

On the political front in the late 1980s, a schism had emerged between the Experts and the Reds. Deng had been running the government and the Party along the expert, or professional, path since the end of the Cultural Revolution. He turned the day-to-day operations over to Party Secretaries General Hu Yaobang and Zhao Ziyang, both of whom favored the expert path, but their successor, Li Ping, tended more toward the hard-line Red path.

In 1986, students at colleges and universities held some small student demonstrations about their lack of both food and freedom. Hu intervened in a way that left many, including the students, believing that he was on the side of the students. In the fallout, Hu kept his title but lost a great deal of power in the top power circles in Beijing, as they thought had demonstrated weakness and had thus lost face.

Upon Hu's death in 1989, students demanded that he have a state funeral, as was expected for someone who at least in title held the top position in the country. Beijing did nothing, so the students placed a large wreath of flowers on the front of the Great Hall of the People in Beijing. The military wouldn't allow it, so the student demonstrations began.

I don't wish to retell what dozens of books have already told about Tiananmen, but one fact is important: Zhao himself went to talk to the students in an effort to end the demonstration. This, too, was looked at as a sign of weakness. He was already in hot water with Deng, as he'd been overheard on a hot mic at the 1989 Sino-Soviet Summit telling Russian President Mikhail Gorbachev that Deng really hadn't stepped back and instead remained in full control (the Chinese call this "ruling from behind the curtain"). Deng was indeed in control, and after the local Beijing military units failed to disperse the students, he called up army units from regions south of Beijing, thus spurring the Tiananmen massacre. Zhao lost his post, and despite the fact that he was quite unpopular with the people, Li Ping stepped in and switched things back to Red. It didn't take Deng long to realize that his modernization program based on leadership by experts and professionals was being challenged by Li, so he bypassed all the Beijing leaders and brought in the mayor of Shanghai, Jiang Zemin, to lead the nation.

Jiang, who had successfully led the modernization of Shanghai, set out to use the same Shanghai model, as it was called, to continue to modernize China. The Chinese newspapers ran lots of stories about what was going to happen to the student leaders who survived the massacre, but once Jiang took control, the entire topic of Tiananmen simply disappeared, never to be discussed again. The experts and professionals ruled for another twelve to fifteen years. Among their accomplishments: the rapid transfer of markets to favor Chinese consumers, keeping the economy humming along, keeping the people happy, and encouraging development of private enterprise.

This expert rule continued until Xi Jinping came to power in 2013, but really, the power shift began in 1990. Xi and his followers, known as the "princelings" because they all had famous fathers who helped them come to power, sought to undercut Jiang's power. One move was pushing through a policy through that prevented anyone engaged in private business from joining the Communist Party. The experts, who were primarily concerned with expanding the economy and uninterested in Party politics, didn't understand how this could be used against them.

After Tiananmen happened, all members of the Communist Party were forced to resign and reapply for membership. Self-criticism is revered in Chinese culture, so much so that the Party's extensive documentation on every member includes his or her self-criticism. A study comparing the thinking and acting patterns of Chinese people who had spent their lives in Hong Kong to those who had moved to there after living most of their lives in mainland China revealed that they were amazingly alike in almost every respect except one. Those who had moved to Hong Kong from the mainland were very introspective—the results of all those years of self-criticism.

Slowly but surely, Xi turned the Communist Party, which had long been on the sidelines, back into the real seat of power. He eliminated the practice of rotation of leadership and established himself as the new permanent Red leader in 2018. Under Xi, universities and state industries are no longer run by professionals. Instead, they are all led by ideological left-wing Communist followers of Xi. The new rule is not to be correct, but instead to be ideologically correct.

Under the expert rule, presidents and all key officers of Chinese universities were professional academics with advanced degrees; there was even a law that you couldn't be a university president unless you'd first served for three years as a vice president. Even still, each university always a second chain of command run by the Party. After Deng's death, the Reds began to regain power by first taking over all the lower Party positions and then gradually moving those people into decision-making positions. It was only a matter of time before the Party members took over the top administrative spots, replacing all the key professionals with Party members with little or no experience in academia. They even made fake curriculum vitae for them.

I believe that the changes of 1990 had another significant impact on China. The men who currently lead China, including Xi, were in their forties at the time. They believed that the modern China envisioned by the experts and professionals elevated to power by Deng would simply turn China into just another developed nation. These men were the true believers in Chinese Communism, and they felt that Communism in its purer state was the answer for China. They knew that the Chinese constitution gave the Party ultimate control over the nation, and they also knew that the professionals running things were too busy and preoccupied to notice as they scaled the leadership positions of the Party. Once they secured top positions in the Party, they used their power to effortlessly take over the top decision-making roles that had been held by professionals.

In the government-run press, Tiananmen was treated as a small incident at the time it occurred, and soon it wasn't mentioned at all. Word quickly spread that it was not a topic for discussion by the populace—a sharp contrast to the Gang of Four trials of the 1970s, which the Chinese press covered heavily for months. The press did extensively cover the trial of a young woman who hid her boyfriend from the authorities, but the coverage backfired when she became a martyr.

For a couple of years, the big hotels aimed at foreign tourists had a very hard time, and many of them changed ownership. I took advantage of those low 1990 prices and took a Fulbright group to China for seven weeks at a very low cost. Some said that I was unprincipled to take a group to China during this time, but my job was to teach other professors about China as it was, not about the China I wished for.

Our group stayed at the Shanghai's White Cloud Hotel, owned by the Chinese air force, for only $15 per day per person, including two meals daily. The hotel was near the military airport, and most of the workers had relatives who were in the air force. Since the hotel was such a great deal, I had extra money to spend on group meals, speakers, and travel, and the air force hadn't killed anyone during Tiananmen.

In the square in Beijing, we began staying at the Kunlun Hotel, a five-star owned by the secret police, for less than half price. The only thing I learned there is that they put little umbrellas in all the drinks (my mother, a teetotaling Methodist, absolutely loved this, because somehow, drinks with umbrellas in them didn't count, as far as she was concerned). Most Chinese people and foreign business travelers steered clear of the hotel, because they feared it would be bugged.

If they bugged our rooms, or if they didn't, I really didn't care. I told everyone to make sure they didn't do or say anything there that they wouldn't want the Chinese secret police to know about. But a friend told me that it was probably the hotel you were least likely to be bugged in—because if you were doing anything illegal, you wouldn't stay there in the first place. Just like every other body of government, the secret police owned the hotel as a way to earn FEC and provide jobs for their relatives.

We were fortunate that our 1990 trip occurred before any major changes had taken place—well, other than the fact that China's most historic locations were being turned into theme parks. Most of the other international tourist groups we ran into were from Europe or Japan, as Americans had turned away from

China as a destination. Several Chinese speakers came in to talk to our group about the demonstrations, but I had to be sure no other Chinese people were present in each case. Otherwise, the speaker would not be able to speak freely for fear that he would get into trouble.

One of the speakers, a very distinguished college administrator, told us of his own consequences for speaking out against the Tiananmen massacre. He had been told to turn in a self-criticism report and had refused, so he was called in to meet with Party leaders. The man was an outspoken but well-respected, professional leader, and he had a reputation for not being afraid of anything.

He faced the group and said, "I was taught that good Communists look after their youth. If I had a neighbor who was beating his children, I would go down to his apartment and tell him to stop. As good Communists, we are taught to prize our youth, rather than beating them. I say the same to our nation: if we are good Communists, we must stop beating our youth."

I returned with a group in 1991, and during the entire seven-week stay, not one word was mentioned about Tiananmen. China returned to usual, as if it never happened. But even the Chinese were surprised when in 1992, it seemed that the whole world had forgotten as well.

The tourists returned, and so did the escalated prices that go along with tourism. But if you visited Tiananmen Square in 1992, you'd see a camera on every lamppost. If any sign of a protest of any kind appeared, it was whisked away immediately. The outside world didn't know, or care, about the ongoing struggle between the experts and the Reds.

The biggest change, really, was not a visible one. Throughout the Great Modernization to that point, the Chinese government's view of the United States had been that it was a land that should be emulated, and that it was a partner in China's future growth. After Tiananmen, however, it was perceived as China's enemy on several fronts. The Soviet Union was collapsing, along with the Eastern Bloc in Europe. The Middle East was in turmoil. With all this as the backdrop, the United States became a single world power in a monopole system.

The Chinese authorities perceived the Tiananmen student demonstrations as a sign of how an American-centered world challenged the Chinese way of life. Democracy was a threat to any authoritarian system, and while privatization and capitalism were good for rapid growth, they were also threats to China's government-centered united currency and its production-centered Communist system.

After 1989, the Chinese government perceived America as a growing threat with no check on its military, economic, and cultural power. Chinese students read American books in school. They listened to American music and watched American movies. Television, a more international threat, was greatly influenced by American norms. More and more young people in China were wearing Western clothes and eating Western fast food, like McDonald's and Kentucky Fried Chicken. Pizza had become the party food of choice in dormitories.

The Party leadership made an effort to discourage these tendencies and stress traditional Confucist and Maoist values. At first, these efforts were subtle, but as time passed, the government was much more open about its agenda. The message was clear: China was to follow a traditional Chinese—that is, Maoist—path in terms of its politics, society, and economy.

That places China in direct conflict with not only the U.S. government but also the large American and global companies that do business there.

Much has been written about Russia's attempts to undermine the American democratic system in recent years. The Chinese have been more subtle about it, but let me be clear: they have no interest in being a second-tier power in an American-dominated world. Xi and his fellow Communist hard-liners have taken over the economic, political, and educational systems of China, and the United States is just now waking up to this reality.

During our 1990 Fulbright trip, I finally got to see Chengdu, a major city I'd somehow had missed on my earlier trips. The city, which is in the Sichuan province, holds several lessons that are eternal to understanding the Chinese people.

The first thing that comes to mind when most people think of Chengdu is the panda. The panda eats nothing but small bamboo shoots that only grow in a very small area of China. As more and more of the pandas' habitat disappeared as the area was developed for agriculture, their population shrank to near extinction. Humans are the panda's only natural predator, but they also served as something of a savior.

In the forty years that have passed since the Great Modernization began, only two nationwide campaigns have been held to raise money for a cause. The first, a Save the Great Wall campaign, was very successful in getting money to rebuild a small part of the Wall for tourism. The second was the Save the Panda campaign. It all started with encouraging schoolchildren to donate a few pennies and get a Save the Panda button, and the effort became so successful that if you weren't wearing a button, you simply weren't fully dressed. Once the money started coming in, experts from all over China and the world gathered in Chengdu and worked together for years to find a way to raise pandas in captivity.

Chengdu is now world-famous for its panda breeding program. On that first trip, in 1990, the research station was a very scientific operation; visitors were required to keep a significant distance from the pandas. The plan was to raise the baby pandas in captivity all over the world and then return them to their native habitat in the low mountains, where there were plenty of bamboo shoots for them to eat.

Today, baby pandas are a big business, and for the right price, you can have your picture taken holding one in Chengdu. What started as a rescue mission has turned into a major tourist venture—one more example of the entrepreneurial spirit of China. And the pandas? Well, instead of being transferred back to their natural habitat, most live their lives in zoos around the world.

The Chengdu area is also the home of another great triumph of Chinese expertise in engineering. China has always been plagued with periods of too little rain, leading to famine and widespread starvation, and too much rain, leading to washed-away crops. Figuring out a way to control the nation's rivers and the best and safest way to use the water they had was necessary for survival.

In the third century BC in a town called Dujiangyan, about an hour's drive from Chengdu, an engineer named Li Bing and his son, Li Erh-Lang, noted that in places where rivers and streams took a turn, the water that ran on the outside of the bend ran much faster than the water on the inside. Thus, the water on the outside of the bend was higher. This was an aha! moment: they realized that if the rivers were channeled properly, they could control its distribution.

The two used large rocks to channel the water in such a way that when it was too high, only a little of it would flood an adjacent rice field, and when it was too low, there was still enough water on the outside of the bend to allow the fields to be irrigated. In places where no large rocks were available, they selected large bamboo shoots, drilled out the centers, and filled them with rocks and pebbles. Using this method, they created manmade barriers that substituted for the rocks. Their irrigation discovery, now known as the Dujiangyan Irrigation System, allowed rice harvests to flourish—so much so that soon, there were as many people living in Sichuan as there were in all of Europe and the Middle East combined.

The Chinese idea of divinity is not a supernatural concept. Instead, people worship men who have used their ingenuity to make concrete contributions improving the welfare of their fellow Chinese citizens. Deng Xiaoping visited the statues honoring the Lis in a Chengdu park once and remarked, "Isn't it strange that during Mao's time, people worshiped him like a god instead of the Lis, who were true gods."

––––––––––––

I took a later trip to Chengdu with three other Carolina professors. We were staying in a very nice hotel—so nice that a pianist played a grand piano twenty-four hours a day in its huge lobby. Despite the poshness of our hotel, we were intrigued by the down-market hotel across the street. Its neon sign announced that it had a "Rooftop German Beer Garden," so we ventured over for a visit.

Once there, we studied the two-page menu of the beers on offer. I ordered one, and then another, and then another, and the response was always the same: "We don't have that." Finally, I asked what they did have.

"Blue Ribbon."

Now that was the beer of our college days! To our surprise, they came in cans (Chinese beers usually come in large bottles). After several rounds, we started a beer can pyramid, just like we had in our younger days on Myrtle Beach. Before long, all the other patrons began bringing their empty cans to add to the pyramid. It grew taller and taller, and with each addition, everyone in the beer garden would laugh and clap.

It was all great fun, but eventually we wanted to leave. Too bad: everyone else kept buying us rounds. Pretty soon, the other patrons were standing on a chair to add cans to the top. One man, who was very drunk, fell off the chair, and we figured that this would be the end. But no! Everybody laughed. Then another tried, and he, too, fell. Again, everyone laughed. A member of our group stood to give it a try, but I stopped him: Chinese emergency rooms were not part of our travel plan. Chinese people of all ages love to have fun, like most people, and they think a drunk is the funniest thing of all.

Chapter 11
My Magnificent Chinese Friends

T HE FIRST PERSON WE MET AT SISU WAS YANG, A young man who would become a part of our family. When I first arrived with my family, he met us at the Russian-era Friendship Hotel, where we were to attend a meeting and luncheon with the nine other Fulbright families. He let us know that he'd been taking to our assigned home for the year in the university housing after the meeting. We had been assigned to Building 2, and all of our luggage—five large suitcases and a huge metal trunk—had been delivered there.

When we got out of our meeting and lunch with the other 9 Fulbright families, we started out for Building 2, but Yang told us we'd been moved to Building 5, about a block away.

"How will we move all our heavy luggage?" I exclaimed.

"No problem!" Yang smiled. "I've already taken everything to the new apartment."

Yang was about five foot seven, and I doubt he weighed more than 140 pounds. I was amazed.

Every afternoon, Marion and Melford attended Chinese school, which included a painting class. The class was tasked with copying old Chinese masters, as is the Chinese way, but each student added some personal touches, including poems they'd written to go along with each painting. The kids' teachers were so impressed with the paintings that they wanted to enter them in a student painting contest. We didn't think that was such a good idea, but when we showed them to Yang and asked him to write the poems in Chinese on the paintings, he eagerly accepted the challenge.

Yang noted that the paintings were in the style of the Tang era, so he insisted on using the Chinese lettering style of that era. His father taught the history of Chinese writing, so Yang took the paintings home with him to enlist his father's help. Two days later, he returned with the paintings. He and his father had drafted the calligraphy for the poems for hours to make sure everything was just right for the period, and then practiced hours more before finally transferring the writing on the paintings. We were embarrassed: they were just the paintings of high school kids.

Through a professor and student exchange I'd set up between SISU and Winthrop, Yang taught Chinese and got his master's degree in history here in the United States. To my delight, he also met a fellow student who became his wife. His parents came to the U.S. to visit him while we were out of town, and we returned to find that he had gotten married in our living room during their stay. In the end, Yang decided to stay in the U.S. and received a doctorate in history from Georgetown University.

Pan Zhe Xing

SISU had seventy foreign teachers from all around the world and 700 international students, most of whom were taking Chinese. Pan Zhe Xing, the vice chair of the foreign affairs department, had jurisdiction over them all. Luckily, he had more energy that anyone I have ever known. Like Ge Pin, Pan came to Winthrop to teach Chinese for two years, and while he was there, he organized downtown shopping trips for the other foreign students every Wednesday and a special event or trip each weekend.

During the Cultural Revolution, Pan was one of six graduate students sent by Mao to Albania, one of the two states with which China had diplomatic relations; the Soviets had to give special permission for the six students to take the train through its territory. He spent four years there, and in his spare time he wrote Chinese-Albanian dictionaries. Upon the students' return to China, three of them stayed in Beijing to serve as translators for Mao, and the others, Pan included, were sent to key universities to teach Albanian.

As the demand for Albanian translators after the Great Modernization was non-existent, Pan was reassigned to his spot at SISU. He was perfect for the job. Pan spoke six languages and knew a good bit of many others. He liked to put on a show of his skills on our trips by singing the national anthem for fourteen different countries, each in their native language.

The year my family joined me in China, we accompanied several other SISU professors and administrators on a trip to a lovely oceanside retreat on Hainan Island. It was a wonderful place, but on the second day, everybody at the resort began to check out, for some mysterious reason. We were confused and wanted to stay, so SISU's academic vice president (more about him later) and Pan worked out a deal that allowed that to happen.

From then on, we had the run of the place. For each meal, we went down to a hut on the beach and ordered food—we walked right into the kitchen and pointed out what we wanted. The food was amazing, coupled with wonderful Chinese beer, and we didn't think it could get any better until the last night, when it did.

My children had bought some fireworks and were setting them off over the water. A man in his sixties, accompanied by his young granddaughter and a younger man, walked down the beach and stood about hundred feet away to watch the fireworks. They seemed to love it. Once my kids finished the show, they left, but not before the younger man stopped by the hut where we got our meals.

As soon as they left, Pan excitedly revealed the older man's identity. He was the Secretary General of the Communist Party, one of the most powerful people in China. That was why everyone had to leave the resort: because he had decided to stay there. Pan and Ho had to pull some serious strings to get the authorities to let us stay. I visited the hut to see what the Secretary General's man wanted. The man at the hut—who had no idea who they were—shrugged and said that he'd asked how much a bottle of beer cost.

———————————

Pan was a tremendous help to me in organizing three group Fulbright tours. At a time when a group of U.S. congressmen were in Beijing demanding to see what was going on in Chinese prisons, Pan made a few calls and finagled a tour of the main Shanghai prison for two of my Fulbright groups.

The cells were almost full of very young men, and most were serving eight-year terms for the crime of sex before marriage. The maximum amount of time prisoners could get off for good behavior was 15 percent of the sentence, but as the recidivism rate in China is only around 10 percent, employers line up to hire them when they get out.

Each Chinese prison has an orchestra and singing group. During the tour, we were able to hear a performance by one of China's most famous female singers, who was serving a sentence of ten years for harboring a fugitive. She had quite a story.

Her fiancé had stolen a pistol on a foreign ship—even the police and soldiers can't have pistols in China—and used it to rob a bank and shoot a teller. She allowed him to hide in her house for two days, despite a nationwide manhunt. They finally found him, and as is the Chinese way, they paraded him around the city in the back of a truck for a few days and then shot him within a week.

During his fiancée's trial, which was broadcast live in an attempt to humiliate and shame her, she stood by her man and refused to break down. The shame attempt backfired: the singer became a much-admired ideal of womanhood and received more than 1,000 letters proposing marriage. Her would-be suitors promised to love her from afar and wait for her until her release.

The woman sang two very sad songs for our group and then stood by a window, gazing out, for the rest of the concert (Chinese jail cells have no windows, so being able to spend a little time looking out a window was a rare treat). When others heard that we had gotten to hear her perform, they wanted to hear all about it.

Pan also spent two years at Winthrop through our exchange program, but immediately before it, he participated in an exchange program with the University of Arizona. When he arrived at Winthrop, I was shocked by his appearance: he looked half-starved and had very long hair.

The explanation poured out of him: he'd been assigned to stay with a doctor and his wife. In China, families share their meals together, but the American family Pan stayed with in Arizona did not. Instead, Pan was told to just get anything he wanted, whenever he wanted, from the refrigerator.

He confessed that just couldn't bring himself to get food from the family's refrigerator. It was their refrigerator, and they never told him that he was allowed to use their kitchen. We had a long talk about how things are different in America, and afterward, he seemed to better understand our crazy ways.

And about his hair: he thought that it was impolite to ask for anything that had not been offered. The family lived two miles away from the university, but Pan walked there every day because they never offered him a ride. He couldn't bring himself to ask them to take him to a barbershop. I took him to a barber right away and told him to cut it very short, as it might be months before he got another haircut.

This was Pan's first trip to America. Americans have a hard time understanding China and Chinese culture, and the Chinese have a hard time understanding us.

Ho Wei Ru

Ho Wei Ru, who played such a pivotal role in our Hainan Island getaway with the General Secretary, was a very soft-spoken but brilliant man. He showed up at my office one afternoon shortly after my arrival to introduce himself, and instead of sitting down to chat, he invited me to join him on a tour of a world-famous exhibition of *penjing* (bonsai) trees.

The collection included more than 500 different dwarf plants, and we walked among them, quietly marveling at each one. Now and then, Ho would mention something remarkable about a plant: "This pear tree is the oldest plant in the exhibition. It's 700 years old and still produces a pear every five years." "This one has been in the same family for 500 years."

I exclaimed in awe about how families could care for a single plant for so long. I soon realized that Ho's quiet demeanor suggested that if I were to say anything at all, it should be about the emotions a plant made me experience.

Ho agreed, saying, "Sometimes, I look at one plant for an hour or so, just to feel the life of the plant."

Ho's stories helped me better understand the Chinese tradition of filial piety. When he was only twenty-four and just out of graduate school, Ho went to work for the Chinese Department of Education. His first assignment was at a new college out in the western part of China, where he was to make sure it met national standards. To give you an idea of how remote this school was, it was a two-day bus ride from the end of the rail line.

At the end of the first day of the bus ride, Ho told me, he was very tired. The weather was very hot and dry, the bus had no air conditioning, and the road was more or less one big bump after another. When the bus reached to the village where the passengers were to spend the night, there were no rooms available at the only inn. Ho summoned up every ounce of courage he had and went to the village's facility for "high coders," a term referring to high-ranking members of the Communist Party. Ho was a member of the Party, but certainly not a high coder by any stretch of the imagination.

Ho explained his situation to the desk clerk, handed her his business card with both hands, and recited his name. As is customary in China, she accepted his card with both hands and repeated his name, "Ho Wei Ru," and then delivered the bad news: she was sorry to tell him that he couldn't stay there, either.

The manager of the facility, who had overheard the conversation, came over and asked to see Ho's business card. He read Ho's name aloud again—and wrapped him in a big hug. The manager pulled out his own card and handed it to Ho: "Ho Wei Ji." Chinese custom dictates that a person's first name is his family name and his second name is the generational name, a list of which is kept in the family temple. The "Wei" in this case referred to the thirty-eighth generation, so Ho and the manager were not only from the same family, but from the same generation! Not only did Ho get a room, the manager insisted on treating him to a grand dinner.

Over dinner, Ho asked his newfound cousin how his part of the family ended up so far away. The manager replied that in the eighteenth generation, an ancestor apparently displeased the emperor to such a degree that he was dispatched west, and the rest, as they say, is history.

Ho asked me how many generations back most Americans were able to trace their lineage, and I told him perhaps somewhere between two and five, given the youth of the country and the influx of immigrants from the early nineteenth century forward. I speculated aloud that thirty-eight generations had to be the longest lineage, and Ho laughed at my naivete.

"The Minister of Education [Ho's boss], Kung, has a generation name of seventy-eight. He descends from K'ung Fu Tzu!"—better known in the West as Confucius.

During the Cultural Revolution, the Communist Party made an attempt to stamp out the tradition of giving family and generational names, mostly through destroying records, but families had copied the lists many times over and buried them in strategic locations. There are 200 names with a very long history (Ho's family being one of them), but most Chinese people are not part of the 200-family clique.

———

Ho, a scholar of Chinese literature, wrote many articles about authors. I have always avidly read Chinese novels—both the classics and modern writers—but Ho introduced me to the Chinese female writers' movement that spanned 1980 to 1990. If men had written these novels, they likely would have been thrown in jail. The women who wrote these books seemed to "get away" with more, partly because they weren't taken seriously by the men in power, and partly because their skill was so great that they managed to never directly challenge the top people in charge in their writing.

I fell in love with these novels right away, and I've now read more than one hundred of their books. At Winthrop, I once taught a Revolutionary Chinese Women course in which students read both modern novels and condensed classics. I've always believed that novels are a wonderful viewpoint into another culture, so I've also read many Indian and Japanese novels, and even a Thai one.

I once asked Ho to list the ten best modern authors in China, and both of us were delighted to see that I'd already read works by five of them. A month later, I told him I'd managed to read books by all ten, and that he'd forgotten to include the wonderful Zhang Jie from his list. (When I mentioned her novel *Love Must Not Be Forgotten* to one friend, he told me that he read it every time he felt lonely so he could have a good cry.)

He responded that if my question had been which authors foreigners should read, he would have included her. But he added that he believed that she was pushing her luck with the Chinese authorities, and that it wouldn't be long before she ran afoul of them.

———————

Ho suffered greatly during the Cultural Revolution, but he graciously found humor in the experience where he could. He told many funny stories about being sent to the countryside to work on a farm, all of them about how the city boy with an Oxford education killed all the plants.

But it was impossible to find humor in the story of Ho's family. Ho's wife was the daughter of Judge Zhang, a Supreme Court judge who had been the chief judge from China during the Nanjing trials. During the Cultural Revolution, she was heavily pressured by the authorities to report on the activities of her father and husband. Ultimately, she was told that if she did report on them, she would be able to escape China with their son and go to Australia.

So she did. She told them that her husband was propagating stories and myths about ancient China. This was, of course, absolutely forbidden, as any elements of Western or ancient Chinese culture were destroyed or suppressed during the Cultural Revolution.

Ho's wife and son were permitted to go to Australia, but Ho

was placed in a twelve-foot-deep hole in the ground that was only four feet across. For two years, through winter's cold and summer's heat, Ho never left the hole. Once a day, a bucket of rice gruel was lowered down into the hole. That was Ho's only ration, and after he was finished, he had to scoop up his body waste and put it in the same bucket. He never received a change of clothes or a blanket. Somehow, he survived.

When the Cultural Revolution ended, Ho returned to his job as academic vice president at SISU. He lived alone, as his wife, still in Australia, would not agree to a divorce. When it was his turn to become president of the university, he was voted down by his peers. If he couldn't control his wife, the leadership believed, how could he control a major university?

Ho longed to see his son, who he hadn't seen since his imprisonment. Every evening, he had dinner with his father-in-law, Judge Zhang. I told him once that I found his devotion to the judge strange, since his wife, the judge's daughter, had betrayed him. He replied, "Her father never did, and he is a wonderful and great man. It my duty to look after him in his old age."

Ho held two Western guest professorships: one at Yale and another at Oxford. While he was on these sabbaticals, he visited Winthrop a number of times to deliver lectures. They were always wonderful, and we always hosted him at our house. On one of his trips, we took him to the beach for a week, and on another, we took him to our home in the mountains. After each of his trips, he always returned to his work at SISU and his responsibilities with his wife's father, who by this time was quite elderly. But even that came to an end: one cold night, the gas line to Judge Zhang's heater broke, and he died.

Ho was a delightful man, and everyone who knew him loved him. He always made time for my groups, including holding seminars for us and taking us to hard-to-access places like Mao's private dining room.

After her father's death, Ho's wife finally returned to China and divorced him. He remarried then, to a fellow SISU professor, but some of the other women he had dated over the years believed he should have married them instead. They sued him, and although Ho won the case, SISU's president decided to send him away to start a branch of the university in Macao. He died there some time later. Many friends told me that Ho died of a broken heart, separated from the city he loved, his wonderful students, and the world of ideas he cherished.

Friends for a Lifetime

My Chinese friends are my friends for a lifetime. My Chinese students will always be my students, and I know they would do anything for me.

Earlier in this chapter, I mentioned the novelist Zhang Jie. Just as Ho had predicted, eventually, she did go too far, and one of her novels was banned: it was simply impossible to get a copy. Around the same time, I was working on a paper on Zhang for a meeting, and in a note to a former student, I mentioned my frustration at not being able to get a copy of her book. A few weeks later, a Chinese-language copy of the novel arrived in my mailbox. It was from my former student, who had stolen it from the Shanghai public library. She enclosed a note: "In sending this to you, I'm keeping someone from getting in trouble for checking it out, since it's been banned." Another of my former students who happened to be at Winthrop for the exchange program translated it for me, so I could include it in my paper.

My family was among the first group of foreigners to be allowed into an area called the Lake of a Thousand Islands. On the bus ride to our destination, we passed through village after village where the residents had never before seen a bus go through the only road in town.

Each time, it took the villagers a long time to clear the road, as due to its disuse as a roadway, it had become a storage place for building materials or, in some cases, a market of sorts. But in each of these villages, the residents were so excited to see strange people that they happily moved their stuff.

Eventually, we reached a riverbank and a barge ferry. The driver was concerned that the small ferry wouldn't be able to bear the weight of the bus, so we all got off the bus and hired local rowboats to get across the small river. Once we were off the bus, the driver, along with dozens of other men, managed to get the bus on the ferry. I was sure that it would sink, but they slowly pulled the barge and the bus to the other side. Everyone clapped and cheered when we reached the other side.

Once we arrived at the lake, we were surprised to see that the only hotel was still under construction—but they assured us that they had enough completed rooms for our group. A nice young man who spoke perfect English carried our bags to our rooms. The rooms were large, and each had a connecting bath.

I was mystified as to why the doors to the bathrooms were only four feet tall. Curious, I carefully asked our translator if he could explain why while making it clear that in no way did I wish to criticize. It was clearly a very big deal that the village was building this hotel. He took me aside later and told me that no one in the village had ever been in a hotel before, so they built the bathroom doors at the same height as the outhouse doors throughout the village.

The lake was beautiful, the color of jade, and it did indeed have more than a thousand islands, most of them covered in fruit trees. We went out on the lake for a boat ride and learned that even though the lake was high in the mountains, the water kept the air temperature warm enough to prevent freezes of the fruit trees. The village had a beautiful market, and almost all of our meals featured the lake's delicious trout.

Later, we took the bus around the lake to visit another village, where again we were the first foreigners to be allowed in. We spent many happy hours exploring the town, and the children, who had never laid eyes on a foreigner before, followed us around with rapt attention. Once we reached our hotel in the second village, I was surprised to see the same young man who'd carried our luggage to our room at the hotel by the lake the previous night.

I mentioned to the young man that I'd left my shaving kit at the last hotel, and to my great surprise, he chartered a motorboat to get it for me. To express my thanks, I invited him to join us for dinner. Over dinner, we learned that the school in his village only went through the sixth grade, but he listened to the BBC and Voice of America every day to sharpen his English skills and read anything he could find in English.

When I returned to Shanghai, I made arrangements to bring this amazing young man to SISU. In addition to paying for his expenses to travel to Shanghai, I introduced him to the dean and vice president and shared his story with them. Like me, they were so impressed with his English that we conducted the whole discussion in English. The administrators told the young man that the normal admission process to SISU required taking a national test, which was only given in the last year of high school. Since he didn't have a high school education, they provided him with copies of all of the books that entering freshman students have read and made a special exception for him, admitting him to SISU within a year's time. The young man simply couldn't believe that he would be the first college graduate from his village.

In Chinese culture, people are judged based not on what they say, but instead what they do. Later, I found out that my act of kindness for this young man opened many doors for me.

———————

This is just a sampling of the many lifelong friends I've made in China. I entered each friendship with the supposition that the person both wanted and, more importantly, needed a friend. I was trusted mostly because I was a foreigner: it is very hard for Chinese people to form trust bonds with one another, for fear that a friend might one day report what's been said to the authorities in order to save his own skin. (Look no further than the story of Ho Wei Ru for evidence of this.) Every one of these friendships has enriched my life and helped me better understand China and myself. Perhaps what I understand best is how much more I have to learn.

Chapter 12
Forbidden Magnificence:
Western China

PERMISSION FOR FOREIGNERS TO ENTER WESTERN China was sharply curtailed until the late 1990s, and now, much of it is closed to tourism once again. Western China is rich in petroleum products and mineral deposits, so only foreign oil and mining company personnel are permitted to travel there. Although minority groups represent less than 10 percent of China's overall population, they tend to live along its borders, and China's western borders are home to the Uyghurs, among the most feared minority groups of all. The Uyghurs, who are Muslim, are perceived by the government as a threat to China's security. The region where they live, Xinjiang, is bordered by states with similar populations that broke away from Russia and formed independent government. That's exactly what Xi's government fears will happen in western China.

As it did in Tibet's largest city, Lhasa, the Chinese government first moved hundreds of thousands of non-Uyghur people into Urumqi, Xinjiang's largest city. Despite this effort, they still frequently lost control of the city, and ethnic clashes became commonplace. These uprisings have been met with violence, not negotiations, and recently, Xi has gone so far as to arrest and imprison thousands of Uyghurs. They will not be released until they renounce Islam and even use of the Uyghur language. To that end, Xi is seeing to it that many of the Uyghur language schools are closed as well.

Thus, if I was to visit western China, I had to find a period of relative calm in which to do it.

As a graduate student, I once wrote a paper comparing the changes in the visages of the Buddha statues found from west to east along the Silk Road (fortunately, the Freer Gallery had slides of photos of the Buddhas). On the southern route, running south of the Taklimakan Desert, the facial features of the Buddhas changed dramatically as you moved east—initially, they appeared almost Greek, and then rather Tibetan, and finally, southern Chinese. On the north side, the Buddhas looked more central Asian than Han Chinese as the route progressed eastward. Clearly, people want their deities to look like themselves. Unfortunately, the southern route has never opened to tourists, but when the northern Silk Road route opened, I seized the opportunity and crossed it on three different occasions.

There are a number of reasons why few foreigners are allowed to travel in the Xinjiang region. First, while the area is rich in deposits of oil and minerals, none of this money goes to the local population. Grinding poverty is the norm. Second, the Chinese government does most of its weapon and rocket testing there. Third, the Uyghur minority group remains a majority of the population in the west, despite the hundreds of thousands of Han Chinese who have been relocated there by the government. On my first trip, I was allowed to go only as far west as Urumqi, which seemed quite similar to any other Han Chinese city found in the east.

———————————

Still, our Silk Road travels were wonderful. On the first, we set out from Xi'an and traveled by train to Jiayu Pass, where the Great Wall ends and the desert begins. A large old fortress known as the Jiayuguan Fort, completed in 1540, still stands there—noteworthy, as most of the other fortresses had been torn down.

The opening of this route to tourism was so new that the road was still under construction, so the conditions were quite terrible and included many detours. Some of these detours were very welcome: we passed through several ancient cities that are now United Nations World Heritage Sites. Some had been abandoned for more than a thousand years, but sadly, the desert has reclaimed them.

At first glance, the cities were just clusters of empty brown buildings. But as I walked through them, I could imagine them crowded once again with thousands of merchants and travelers from all corners of the world. Each of the dead cities were somewhat different, and I found it fascinating to try to imagine them in their bustling past a thousand years before. All of the essentials of a city were still there: the streets, houses, courtyards, markets, and even an old Christian church in one. All that was missing were the people, and in each town, I pondered why. Were they killed by invaders? Did a change in weather patterns make life impossible there? Each of the towns held its own secrets.

The deserted Christian church I entered was round and re-sembled Bethlehem's village synagogue, except that it was twice as large. I could make out about half a dozen holes in the walls, which were used to store scrolls. I wondered which books of the Bible had been stored in this particular church. In the early days of Christianity, local churches could usually afford only a few, but my money was on the books of Jude, Judas, Thomas and James, the brothers of Jesus, as they were more popular in Asia than in Europe.

There were many Christians in the Xinjiang region until the First Council of Nicaea, a council of Christian bishops con-vened in what is now Turkey by Constantine in 325 AD. The council's purpose was to reach a consensus on whether there was a single, almighty God, or three different divine beings: the Father, the Son, and the Holy Spirit, and it did, settling on the latter. This differed from the beliefs of Christians who lived in this region, who worshiped only the one true God, so they were cast out from the church.

Christianity, Islam, and even Buddhism flourished and spread here to the greatest extent during the Mongol invasion of the thirteenth century. The Mongols demanded absolute control in terms of the military, politics, and trade, but they didn't care much at all about religion. Even today, small pockets of minority Christian groups persist in Xinjiang. In my travels, I've spoken with Christian priests in western China, and they all start by asking me why I believe they have been shunned by the greater Christian religion. Some of believe that Thomas the Apostle himself brought the gospel to China, and others cite Prester John, a legendary figure who many Indian Christians credit with bringing Christianity to their land.

On each Silk Road trip west, I visited a different abandoned city in the desert. One, which was abandoned during the Mongol invasion, was perched on a cliff overlooking a pretty stream, and its original wall still stood. A second was located far from the roadway, so we rented camels to ride out to it.

The city was surrounded by giant sand dunes—and by giant, I mean hundreds of feet high—and nearby vendors rented skis and snowboards to ride down them. It looked like fun, so I tried it a few times. It was in fact fun, but not really worth having pants full of sand for the rest of the day. Riding the camel back with sandy pants was out of the question, so I walked back to the bus.

The mighty Taklimakan Desert is extremely hot and dry, which has an upside: it's a great place to find mummies buried in deep underground tombs. The first one I toured was the tomb of a man who had originally been from Hangzhou. He had missed his hometown, so he had his tomb decorated with beautiful paintings of the city—green hills and lots of lakes.

On our way to see the Hangzhou-born mummy, our bus bottomed out on a mound in the rough road, both front and rear wheels ending up suspended in midair. We all got off the bus and pushed as hard as we could, from both the back and the front, to no avail. Finally, a truck came along and tried to pull the bus off the hill, with all thirty-two of us pushing with all our might. No dice.

Then someone had a great idea: we all should get on the bus and stand in the front. Both the truck and the bus had a jack, so we used them to lift the back end as we weighted down the front of the bus. Success! The driver was afraid that bus had been damaged, so he and the truck driver checked to make sure all was well. Fortunately, I always travel with two extra cases of water. They came in handy that day, in the middle of the desert with no shade. It was a misery, but after we'd gotten back on the road for about fifteen minutes, we'd all had a chance to cool off.

In the early 1980s, coal plants were everywhere, mostly because the resource is abundant there. But coal burning fouled the air so much that the government began making huge investments in alternate energy sources, like hydroelectric dams and nuclear, wind, and solar power. The latter two are everywhere in the desert sands of western China. Any trip through the west means riding past massive solar panel farms, and every mountain pass features hundreds and hundreds of giant wind turbines.

So generating electricity isn't a problem, but distributing it, and figuring out how to price it, are the primary issues. When I first arrived in China, indoor climate control and refrigerators were rare, particularly in households. Today, every Chinese consumer wants them, and most can afford to have them. They are staples in homes in cities of all sizes, and a growing number of homes in the countryside have them as well.

In eastern China, pricing is the challenge, as complex industries and manufacturing facilities compete with individual households for power. In the west, the mining and oil industries represent most of the demand, so there, the question is who gets the power.

On my first trip west, our train mysteriously stopped in Xinjiang province during the middle of the day and sat there until darkness fell. Then, Chinese army troops went from car to car and wordlessly pulled down every window shade. Clearly, there was something we weren't meant to see.

Of course, I was dying to see what was forbidden. Our group was spread out among two cars of the train, so I walked back and forth between the two trying to peek out from the gap between the cars. Alas, I couldn't outsmart the Chinese army: ten-foot-high mounds of dirt were arranged on either side of the train tracks, completely obscuring the view of the rocket and missile testing zone we were passing through.

We arrived the next morning at a station in the middle of nowhere, but a bus was there waiting for us. As we boarded, each of us received a breakfast box containing a hardboiled egg, a bun, a box of kiwi juice, and a cup of tea.

An aside here: The Chinese believe that it's impossible to live without tea. They drink it all day and night, except at meals, when they prefer a very sweet orange drink or beer. Both the beer and the tea are great, but the orange drink is way too sweet for me. Some mix it with the beer, half and half. On occasions when I attended lunches as part of speaking tours for the State Department in China, I would order the mixed orange drink and beer, and most of my delighted lunch companions would change their orders to mirror mine. Little things like that work to break down cultural barriers.

Back to the bus: the road descended deep into the Turpan Depression, the bottom of which lies 500 feet below sea level (when it comes to dry land on this planet, only the shores of the Dead Sea and Lake Assal, in Africa's Djibouti, are lower). Aydingkol Lake, there in the midst of the depression, is a magical place, a hot, humid oasis in the middle of a desert. Grapes and melons, with high sugar concentration thanks to the hot climate, fill the fields near the lake. The sidewalks of a city there, Turpan, are covered in bougainvillea and giant grapevines; walking or riding down the street is like going through a beautiful tunnel.

Another city in Xinjiang, Hami, is particularly famous in Russia for its most common export, the Hami melon. Everywhere you go in central Eurasia, the locals think their melons are the best in the world—except when it comes to Hami melons, which all bow down to. Practically everyone can tell you in great detail about the first time they had ever had one. I've had them before, and they are excellent, but I have to say I didn't find it to be the life-changing event I'd been told about.

The Bezeklik Caves, the most extensive network of Buddhist cave grottoes in the world, are close by. One of the guidebooks I read said that there were a thousand caves, but that seems like a bit of an overstatement. Ninety of the caves have been explored; perhaps a dozen or two more remain shrouded in mystery.

Each time I've visited the area, different caves have been open to the public, so a constant human presence doesn't lead to damage of the grottoes' intricate frescoes. Each cave has a statue of Buddha and holes in the walls where Buddhist texts once rested. Many of the texts were stolen by the first Europeans who came to the area. Now found in private collections and museums around the world, the Chinese government is trying to repatriate them.

Even the frescoes have been pillaged and sold to collectors. I once visited the home of a wealthy American couple and admired their Eastern art collection. As I browsed through their impressive works, I suddenly stopped.

"That looks like a Bezeklik fresco."

The couple hurriedly explained how they'd "saved it," and how much they had paid to get it. I was a good guest, but I wanted to tell them to send it back.

On another trip to Xinjiang, we decided to skip the Taklimakan and instead cut across the Gobi Desert, which is larger and very different. Unlike the mountainous terrain of the Taklimakan, the Gobi is very flat; you can see for miles in all directions. Rocks of all sizes litter the landscape, and dust devils, miniature tornadoes that skip across the desert, are everywhere. (I worried about a few of them, that they might pose a danger to us, but the bus driver reassured me that the flatness of the vista was deceiving: the dust devils were really miles away.)

Because the Gobi never had an ice age, it is a wonderful place to look for dinosaur fossils and eggs right on the surface of the sands. I bought one once in Hong Kong—so someone else plundered it—but the one I got didn't have an embryo inside. Those without embryos were priced around a hundred dollars; those with were at least a thousand—and it's illegal to buy them.

I'll be honest: Urumqi isn't my favorite city. Most of it was built quite recently to house the influx of Han Chinese people who were moved there by the government and the employees of international oil companies. It's really the only large city in the west, so it bustles with activity, particularly because of the boom in natural resource mining and drilling. Planes arrive at its airport each day from all around the world, because if you're going anywhere in central Asia, you'll probably have to stop in Urumqi.

The Uyghurs who live in Urumqi reside in the old part of town, and friction between the groups is a constant. The Uyghur people are not happy about what they believe is the exploitation of their land by China, and they receive few, if any, of the rewards. Every few years, the city is beset by large demonstrations of Uyghurs, resulting in lots of arrests.

There are two types of schools in the area: the Chinese schools, which are taught in Chinese, of course, but whose students also learn lots of English, or the Uyghur schools, which are taught exclusively in Uyghur. Graduates of the Chinese schools have a great advantage, as all new jobs and business deals are conducted in Chinese or English. Graduates of the Uyghur schools are unqualified for either because of the language barrier.

But it is the Uyghur language that makes an Uyghur an Uyghur—you cannot look at a person and know for certain that he or she is an Uyghur, especially now that Xi's government has outlawed long beards for men and veils for women in Xinjiang. It was the language of trade throughout Mongolia, central Russia, and western China for centuries. But this year, Xi, who is threatened by the difficulties he has had in controlling the Uyghurs specifically and western China in general, has made a move to close the Uyghur schools. Teachers and students alike have been arrested and forced to speak and write Chinese instead. As locals resist, still more are arrested and forced into "re-education schools." All of the mosques have been closed as well, as Xi views religion as a threat to Chinese loyalty.

Urumqi may not be an interesting city, but it does have a few interesting spots. One mosque was built in a style that would be more at home in Afghanistan, a cylindrical shape that is larger in the middle than at the bottom and top. The city has one large souk (market), but those whose travels will take them further west in Xinjiang are wise to wait for the markets of Kashgar and Upal.

One worthwhile trip away from Urumqi is about an hour and half away in the Tianshan Mountains: Tianchi (Heavenly Lake), which is ringed with beautiful snow-capped mountains.

The nomadic people of the Tianshan Mountains live in yurts; most are happy to show off their yurt for a moderate fee.

The very old and famous city of Kashgar had opened to foreigners around the time of my second trip to Xinjiang. It is the point where the southern and northern Silk Road routes diverged; at times when conflicts led to closure of both of those routes, a third route opened that ran north of the Tianshan Mountains, and it too terminated at Kashgar.

Somewhat less known is the Gold and Silver Route, which ran between the northern tribal regions of Russia and southern India and also passed through Kashgar. In southern India, gold was highly prized because of its ability to resist the monsoons and hot, humid weather so common to the area. Those in northern Russia preferred the hardness and bright shine of silver, which gleamed on uniforms and weapons alike. In many respects, Kashgar was one of the oldest seats of trade in the world.

A true Uyghur city, Kashgar must be visited on a Sunday to see the greatest market anywhere. You can buy or sell practically anything, including all kinds of animals and lots of rugs and cloth made by local tribal people. At least a hundred different languages are spoken in the market, many of them unique to a very small minority group. People come to the Kashgar market from as far away as the high valleys of the Pamir Mountains in Tajikistan.

A special sign language is used in the market for bartering animals and goods. Both buyers and sellers wear shirts with long, baggy sleeves, and they place their hands up one another's sleeve and negotiate through finger gestures until a deal is made. The benefit: other buyers and sellers have no idea what prices are being negotiated between them, so each time, the negotiation starts fresh. In the area where camels are sold, as many as fifty buyers and sellers make deals simultaneously.

Kashgar's most famous mosque, the Id Kah, is the largest mosque in China. Completed around 1442, it can accommodate as many as 20,000 worshipers. But Xi feels threatened by this mosque, and he has threatened to close it.

By the time of my third trip to Xinjiang, western China had been open to the country's borders. I was finally able to take my group all the way to the city of Upal. Visiting Upal's Monday market is like stepping back in time: everyone travels by carts drawn by donkeys, and they move very fast. Drivers constantly shout "Peace! Peace!"—an admonition for people to get out of their way. Once a donkey starts moving fast, it doesn't stop for anything or anyone.

Upal is a small town near the Afghan border populated with beautiful people—particularly the women, who wear long skirts that resemble those worn by women in Tibet and Nepal. Most of the tourist books say that Upal isn't good for much more than a bathroom break, but I've found it to be charming. The tree-lined streets are gracious, and you can peer over the low walls of the residences to watch children play in the courtyards.

As I walked the streets of Upal, I was invited into several homes to share a cup of tea and a few sweet rolls. The homes are walled on three sides, but the southern exposures are open to allow light and warmth inside. The beds in the homes are elevated and surrounded by bricks, allowing a fire to be built underneath for warmth. While the fires warmed the beds, as is

the custom all over northern China, everyone from grandparents to grandchildren share the same bed for warmth.

Upal's big attraction is the ornate tomb of Mahmud al-Kashgari, who lived in the eleventh century. For eighty years, al-Kashgari traveled around Central Asia and created dictionaries of
the languages in use where he visited. Later, he cross-referenced
these individual dictionaries into much larger, comprehensive
dictionaries, which have been extremely valuable to scholars.
Our guide for the tour of the tomb was a direct descendant of
Mahmud al-Kashgari, and afterward, he asked if I was interested in learning more about his ancestors. I nodded eagerly.

The guide took me to an old cemetery and showed me the
tombs of al-Kashgari's father, grandfather, great-grandfathers,
and great-great grandfathers. Amazed, I stopped him and asked
which was the oldest of his ancestors to be buried in the cemetery. He bent over and cleaned off a stone.

"The numbers have changed, I believe, but I think this one
died in 830."

In the last few years, it has become very hard to get into Xinjiang, despite the fact that the mining and oil industries there are
providing lots of jobs (most of which pay around three times
the average salary for a Chinese person). The Uyghurs feel that
this wealth is being stolen from them, which has spurred massive demonstrations. Sometimes the Chinese military is called
in, and casualties are the result. As in Tibet, the areas that are
worth seeing are now off limits.

Chapter 13
Magnificent China on the World Stage

ROM THE LATE 1990S TO THE PRESENT—WITH DRA-
matic acceleration since the Shanghai World Expo in
2010—the nature of Chinese industry and business has changed
completely. When China first opened its doors, foreign investment started slowly, with joint ventures between foreign corporations and Chinese firms. These agreements usually called
for a percentage of each joint venture's ownership to be held
by each company, with the Chinese ownership level increasing
each year. After ten to twenty years—so roughly from the late
1990s to the present—the Chinese corporation would retain
full ownership of the venture.

So it is that in the last twenty years, Chinese corporations
have become critical links in the world's business and manufacturing chain, manufacturing key components for foreign
corporations. That's to say nothing of their significance within
China's borders, as much of what is manufactured is used in
Chinese industries as well. Nowhere is this more obvious than

in the realms of computers, communications equipment (including televisions), and automobiles.

This arrangement has long worked very well, and China has been a huge part of worldwide economic growth. But this interdependence has vulnerabilities, too. The COVID-19 coronavirus pandemic of 2020 greatly slowed growth in China and the rest of the world. It will take years to repair the damage that the virus has done to the worldwide supply chain.

During the years following World War II and the Communist victory over Chinese Nationalists, China became obsessed with its own security. The first move the government made to suppress any reemergence of a conflict with the Japanese or the American-backed Nationalist Chinese movement was to enter into an alliance with the Soviet Union. This was a marriage of convenience, as China had not fought its way through these wars simply to turn themselves over to the Soviets.

The Soviets never really understood China's reasoning for the alliance, but they were happy to go along: their agenda was securing an eastern front for the duration of the Cold War so they could concentrate on Europe. When I have asked Chinese people about their impressions of this Sino-Soviet period, most respond that the Soviets tried to treat China like another Poland.

One responded defiantly, "We are not, nor have we ever have been, a satellite of Russia!"

As part of the alliance, the Soviets did help China rebuild some of the destruction caused by the wars—including infrastructure—but they always maintained control over the projects, rankling their Chinese counterparts. When the Cold

War-era schism between China and the Soviets came to a head, around 1959, the Soviets left and took with them important know-how about running the systems they'd helped set up.

Many Americans believed that the two Communist powers were fully unified and that the friction between the two was just for show, but for both China and the Soviets, the dispute was real. Look no further for confirmation than the Vietnam War; China did nothing to help Vietnam and refused to allow Soviet aid bound for Vietnam to pass through its borders. It seems that Chinese people never tire of talking about all the "hateful" things the Soviets did during this time of supposed cooperation.

Soviet leadership did not conduct a state visit to China until 1989, right in the middle of the Tiananmen demonstrations. The government was embarrassed, of course, but it didn't crack down on the demonstrators until the Soviets had returned home. By 1989, conflicts of interest, security, and prestige had replaced the Russians on China's list of things to worry about.

The history of the rancor between China and Russia extends for centuries before Communism. As a Russian told once me, "Russian children have nightmares of hordes of Chinese people attacking and killing them in their beds." Many Chinese people likewise consider Russians to be "barbarians." Each looks down on the other. Russia has a vast amount of land and relatively few people, and China is exactly the opposite. Thus, when the Russians pondered who to partner with to balance out the population differential, they courted India.

That's how India ended up with a Chinese-backed Communist party, a Soviet-backed Communist party, and an

independent Indian Communist party. During its 1960 elec-
tions, I visited the Indian state of Kerala, where all three Communist groups were competing for control of the state government. I moved from island to island, each with more flowers
and beautiful, lush vegetation than I'd ever seen before, and
some of the friendliest people I'd ever met. But they weren't the
idyllic Edens that they seemed, as each village bore signs and
flags signifying one of the three Communist parties. At each,
the locals—all of whom supported the same party—would tell
me that their party was the honest one, and the others were
corrupt. In all, I visited fifteen villages on that trip, each on
a different island, and not one person could identify a single
ideological difference between the parties or why they were
each called "Communist." There was one thing everyone agreed
about: none of them liked the currently ruling Congress Party.

Today, India and China have a great deal of friction between them. Both want control over their mutual borders and
the Indian Ocean. Both have vast armies, air forces, and nuclear
weapons. The Chinese economy has grown faster than India's
and is more export oriented; the Indian economy has grown
steadily, but not in as showy a manner. In both nations, millions
and millions of citizens are moving to the cities.

India has a mixed economy, with the government involved
in the service sector and most businesses are in the private sector. The Chinese government owns a much larger percentage of
its manufacturing base. Each thinks its political system is better
than the other, and they couldn't be more different. India has an
independent court system and local, provincial, and national
elected bodies that really govern. At every level, China's government and judiciary are run by the Communist Party, and there
are few human rights. The Chinese population is a bit larger

now, but India's will soon surpass it. Trade goes on between the two nations, but neither likes to talk about it. Other than a few border-related skirmishes, the conflict has remained relatively peaceful.

———————

For some time now, mainland China has been focused on re-placing Taiwan—or Nationalist China, as it terms the island—as the "real China" in the eyes of the world. The United Nations has been useful to that end. After a long struggle, China finally gained recognition by the body and a permanent seat on its Se-curity Council by currying favor among the UN's Third-World membership.

Africa proved to be particularly fertile ground. In the early 1970s, China agreed to build an extensive railroad system in Tanzania; dozens of other infrastructure projects soon followed. Today, China has major ongoing infrastructure projects in six-ty-one African nations. Most of these projects, of course, have been designed to make extraction of natural resources easier, mostly for the benefit of China. And China's government didn't mind making sure the nations' leaders were well paid for their trouble.

For about twenty years, China maintained a rather good standing among the people of African nations, but of late, some friction has developed. For one, the nations had hoped that their own people would be involved at a high level in the infra-structure projects, but for the most part, plum jobs have gone to Chinese people instead. In other cases, nations that entered into joint ventures with China were later unable to pay for their part of the deal. Thus, full ownership of the projects, and in some cases, full access to ports, reverted to China.

Recently, I had coffee with a few friends on the Winthrop faculty. Two from Nigeria and Vietnam had recently visited their home nations for a brief visit. Both told the same story: "The Chinese own everything."

Other nations came to understand the role China would play on the world stage much more quickly than the United States. Several times, sometimes for periods lasting longer than a year, the United States didn't even have a Chinese ambassador. It was a slight that was not ignored.

For a ten-year period during the Cultural Revolution, China's only diplomatic relations were with Albania and North Korea. But China opened its doors during the Great Modernization and began its path to power, the world came to China. Between 1985 and 1986 alone, more than forty heads of state visited to China by my count, and according to China, more than sixty-one visited in 1988. These leaders came to China to pay their respects and clamor for Chinese investment. The government always made sure they went home satisfied, but their investments were shrewd and always benefited China.

When the professionals or experts took over from the Reds in 1979, China wasn't even among the top twenty trading nations in the world. In fact, it didn't rank in any statistical category except population size. Today, China is a major international actor—arguably the largest in terms of trade—and Chinese businesspeople are active in almost every nation in the world. China manufactures everything from iPhones to computers to textiles to rockets, and in 2018, the size of its navy surpassed that of the U.S. China had always had the largest military force, but now the army is fully modernized.

Over a forty-year period, more than eight hundred million Chinese people have been taught to read English. In large part, the purpose for this endeavor was so they could access the best and most up-to-date sources (even they admit that the best books and journals are all written in English). To facilitate this, China hired nearly one hundred thousand English teachers, including two of my children and my daughter-in-law. Each year, China has sent and continues to send more than a million people abroad to learn how industry, markets, and education worked in the English-speaking developed world. Hundreds of thousands of what the Chinese call "foreign experts" (that is, people like me) were brought into to China to teach its young people everything—except ideology. And except for a show at the beginning of the 2008 Beijing Olympics (which, by the way, was run by professionals), very little has ever been said or shown to the outside world about China's ideology or its Communist Party.

None of this would have been possible without professional management and a focus on educating the populace. Under the Reds, the transformation never would have occurred.

During the early years of the Great Modernization, the government feared that students who were sent abroad wouldn't return. This fear intensified immediately following the Tiananmen massacre. But by 2000, 1 million Chinese people were studying abroad, and according to officials, 85 percent returned to China within five years. Most who worked abroad sent money home to help their families get by.

My Chinese friends who chose to return after studying abroad gave me a variety of reasons why.

- First, they missed their families, as many had spouses and children at home, and all had close ties to their parents and extended families. One confided, "My parents really missed me, and I missed them. We are very close."
- Others returned so they could find another Chinese person to marry. "My family wanted me to come home and marry a Chinese woman so I could keep the family name going. Our family is very old." One friend of mine made a good living finding Chinese brides for Chinese men working and living in Canada.
- Moving back home also had its financial rewards. An international education and a strong command of English can be the keys to landing the very best jobs in the new Chinese economy.
- Right after saying that they missed their families, many friends mentioned how much they missed the foods they grew up with. I can't tell you how many times I've heard this one: "Heaven is an American bathroom, a Japanese wife, and a Chinese cook."

Most Americans who study in China do so for only a year or so. Few foreigners are fluent in Chinese, and fewer still can read it. In contrast, Chinese people have studied English all their lives, and many come to America for their degrees. Large multinational companies doing business in China often hire lots of foreign workers; some say that they fear the possibility that Chinese employees will pass their intellectual property secrets to the government. Some do exactly that. As a general rule, when expats working in China return to their home countries, a Chinese person who has studied in the United States takes over his or her job.

It took time for China to ready itself for a huge influx of foreigners. In the 1980s, only a handful of large cities—think Beijing and Shanghai—had international or American schools. Now, all the large cities do, and very large cities may have a dozen or more, including German and Japanese schools. American universities, such as Johns Hopkins and Duke, have opened branch campuses in China. The Johns Hopkins program specializes in graduate study, but Duke has an undergraduate program that is open to both American and Chinese students. In the Duke program, undergraduates spend their freshman, sophomore, and senior years in China and their junior year at the Durham campus.

China is one of the largest markets in the world, so naturally, foreign companies integrate their programs and modify their production styles especially for it. At first, foreign investment consisted of mostly Americans coming to China to help set up joint ventures. These days, it's commonplace to find top jobs at American-owned facilities in China filled by Chinese people. Of late, there's been quite a bit of nonsense rhetoric about economic independence from certain leaders, but American and Chinese companies depend on each other for vital components of their products. These joint ventures between Chinese and American companies are major actors in the world economy.

By 2000, China felt ready for the world's center stage. When Beijing was awarded the 2008 summer Olympic games, China erupted in celebration, and the government decided to totally transform Beijing. First, much of old Beijing was torn down: blocks and blocks of the oldest section around the Forbidden City were destroyed. Most of the 200- to 300-year-old homes and inns that had stood there had been built without using nails (the idea being that the buildings could better withstand earthquakes).

Beijing was one big stage, showing off the new China under the motto: "One World, One Dream." Even the people of Beijing were transformed, with campaigns to stop public spitting and campaigns to dress with national pride. The city's legendary smog and traffic problems were mitigated by allowing residents to drive only on odd or even days depending on their license plate numbers, and by closing manufacturing plants and industries that surrounded Beijing during the Games. Subway lines were extended by twice their original length, and eighty new stations were added. The size of the airport was doubled. Roads were widened and parking lots expanded to handle the anticipated 3.3 million cars that the Games would bring. New railroad lines were built and old ones were rebuilt, and fast trains were added to reach venues outside Beijing.

Worldwide, 4.7 billion people watched the opening ceremonies of the Games—the largest audience to watch any event ever in the world. By any standard, the 2008 Olympic Games in Beijing were a success.; the International Olympic Committee was so impressed that it awarded Beijing the 2022 Winter Olympics, making the city the first to host both a summer and a winter Games. Chinese people are right to be proud of this accomplishment.

While China did put on a wonderful show for the world, there was plenty of evidence of what hadn't changed. For the duration of the Games, censorship was tightened all over China, and minority areas were strictly off limits. Foreigners who had hoped that the Games would change Chinese politics were disappointed. If anything, the country's strict government control was spotlighted: some said they hadn't seen such strict control since the Mao era.

Shanghai and Beijing share a very competitive relationship. Just two years after the Beijing summer Games, Shanghai hosted the Expo 2010, a world's fair-type exhibition that drew more than 73 million attendees. But despite the rivalry, Shanghai made no attempts to outdo the show put on by Beijing. Beijing wants to be a major political center, and Shanghai intends to be the key financial, industrial, technical, and trade center for both Asia and the world. While Beijing is primarily occupied by bureaucrats, Shanghai is a true city of immigrants who have come to China from all around the world to make their own success.

The 2010 Expo had a $48 billion budget, and Shanghai's financial might ensured that it was completed with a $152 million surplus. The fair was held in the region near the Nanpu and Lupu bridges across the Huangpu River, which connect Shanghai's central financial districts on either side of the river. The world's fastest train, the MAG, crossed under the Huangpu to take passengers from the heart of the Expo directly to a new space-age airport. On the edge of the financial district, the top of the Opal Tower gave Expo visitors a panoramic view of the world's largest city. The land used for the fair had primarily been home to old warehouses and dry docks; in all, 18,000 warehouses and 270 factories were destroyed or moved to accommodate the new construction. The buildings intended for the fair were built in such a way that they could either be easily taken down or repurposed for another use once the Expo was over. Some slums were torn down, but none in the historic areas of the city.

Landlocked Beijing has lots of land surrounding it, but Shanghai's site on the river and sea limits its capacity for expansion. Beyond the site of the Expo, Shanghai underwent quite a bit more sprucing up. Four thousand older taxis were taken off the streets and replaced with twice that number of brand-new models. Shanghai's first ring road was built in 1990, and by the time of the fair, there were five going not only around the city but also over the city, so houses and businesses did not have to be moved. These elevated beltway roads also contain tracks for rapid rail, making it easy to get from anywhere in the city to anywhere else in the city.

As extensive as Shanghai's transportation network is, there are still traffic backups during rush hour in the world's largest city. The rapid rail lines also extend miles out into adjacent provinces, mitigating some car traffic into the city. Trucks are allowed on Shanghai's roads only between 10 p.m. and 6 a.m., which aids the flow of traffic but also means Shanghai is alive with activity twenty-four hours a day.

The Shanghai Stock Exchange put on quite a show for the Expo as well. By 2010, it was mostly operated by computer, with just a dozen or so traders on the exchange floor at any given time. The leadership of the exchange, which is located in a beautiful building, knew that lots of visitors would want to see it in full operation—so it filled the floor with traders.

During my visit to the Expo, I noted with admiration that the city had taken down all of its old cinder-block walls and replaced them with beautiful rock walls. A few days later, I leaned against one and realized that vinyl wall covering had been placed over the walls.

Of course! Why waste money on something that will be up for just a few months? It occurred to me that the vinyl wallcovering was a good analogue to a lot of what I witnessed in China. If you really want to understand China, you can't take things at face value.

China's GDP is now roughly equal to that of the United States. China leads the world in rocket launches, and they even handle transport of many American satellites. Its military is the largest in the world and now very well equipped. I can't say for sure how battle-ready the troops are, but most come from rural areas, and in the aftermath of Tiananmen, rules changed to ensure that soldiers' allegiances were clear.

During the first days of Tiananmen, the Beijing-based troops refused to move against the demonstrators, which could have included their families and friends. The government had to bring in troops from south central China to get the demonstrators out of the Square. Today's troops are intentionally stationed far away from their hometowns. They aren't allowed to date local girls and don't get time off to go to city nightspots.

It's true that Shanghai mints a new millionaire every day, and farmers who live near cities have greatly increased their annual income. But there is another China. Like many rapidly developing nations, China has a few very rich citizens and a lot of poor ones. But even they have running water and indoor toilets, so they're not considered poor by Third World standards.

Building a true middle class remains a problem. In 1995, the average annual income was $1,000, and now it's ten times that—still a long way from the $40,000 to $50,000 annual salaries common to most Western nations. Retirement and medical care are covered by the state, so paychecks don't have those deductions, and take-home pay is subsidized for those with previous military service, extra work, and even many years on the job.

To be sure, not all of China is modernized. As I traveled through villages on my way to and from the Yunnan province in north central China recently, I saw many of the older people still wearing the blue uniforms of the Cultural Revolution. When I asked one villager about it, I was told that Chinese women are skilled at patching clothes, and many of the residents had never been to a town, much less a city.

These people are not forgotten. It's just that in China, like many of the "mini-dragons" (for example, South Korea, Taiwan, Hong Kong, Singapore, and Malaysia) that underwent rapid modernizations, it's very hard to elevate a middle class. The mini-dragons also struggle to develop a strong middle class to this day, but none of them face the additional challenges of such a massive population.

During a talk I gave on China's magnificent growth, I was asked by an attendee to sum up the main reasons for the country's rapid success. It wasn't an easy question, and I confess that I wandered all over the place trying to answer it. I'll try to do better here.

First of all, the Chinese population is well educated, and its culture prizes hard work. Knowledge of English opens up the world, so Deng's resolve to ensure that his people learned it was key to success. The Chinese people firmly believe in the value of education and have for thousands of years. I had never before, nor have I since, taught students who were so serious about learning. I've never known people who were more dedicated to seeing that their children received the best education possible. Obtaining an education takes a lot of hard work, and figuring out what to do with that education and succeeding at your job doesn't just happen either.

When I tell my Chinese friends "just relax," they stare at me and tell me with confidence that that's simply not the Chinese way. My Chinese friends are all business, and it seems that buying and selling just comes naturally to them. When I ask them about professionals or experts they respect, they talk not about how smart they are but instead about how hard they work.

China's willingness to innovate continues to be important. Deng worried about opening China's rigid social and political systems to the outside world at a fast pace, so he used Special Economic Zones (SEZs) to curtail the process and limit it to specific cities and areas. Most developed nations use SEZs to spur growth by limiting taxation on manufactured goods, but Deng used them like quarantine areas for capitalism, to see what elements of it would work for China without disrupting Chinese society and Communist principles.

Some were great successes. Shenzhen is a model example of a small village that transformed into an economic powerhouse. But there were also failures: on Hainan Island, the SEZ was used to circumvent taxes on imported cars and vans and then sell them at inflated prices on the open market. Another example is the use of residence cards in SEZs. It was thought that cities would develop faster if the residents who already lived there received training and education, so nonresidents were kept out and denied these privileges. Exactly the opposite occurred. As hard as the city's residents worked, the nonresidents worked even harder because they were focused on the goal of obtaining residency, if not for themselves then for their children. Once residence cards were eliminated, the cities' growth and development exploded.

Certainly the fact that experts were in charge of Chinese businesses, industries, education, and government for a forty-year period helped set the stage for the nation's stratospheric growth. But now, under Xi's leadership, the Party has taken over all of the key administrative positions. I doubt that the rapid development will continue, and what does continue will certainly occur at a slower pace. To Xi, ideology is much more important than development.

China still faces many other problems, most notably its location. China borders fourteen very different nations, and it shares two borders with Russia—something no country would wish for. North Korea is a constant danger, and China doesn't seem to a handle on keeping the nation from either collapsing or creating open conflicts—internally or externally. A Chinese official once told me, "It's like having a crazy person living in the next apartment."

On China's eastern and western borders, Russia looms large. But China doesn't consider it to be a great threat. I have never met a Chinese person who doesn't look down on Russia as a failed state. Russia, on the other hand, fears problems with the West and China alike.

Presently, Russia's obsession is the West, as it fears the open nature of its societies much more than a powerful China. The Russian government's main problem is maintaining control over a vast nation; it was been on the verge of serious civil conflict several times during the forty years of the Great Modernization of China. I happened to be in Russia in October 1993, when its president Boris Yeltsin ordered his army to shell and storm the country's legislature (known as the White House). The family I was staying with felt torn by the conflict: its members included personnel in the Russian army and officers in the nationalized police, which sided with the legislators rebelling against Yeltsin. When I traveled to China shortly afterward, everyone was very curious about the Russian conflict—so clearly, the Chinese press covered it in great detail.

As I've mentioned previously, China has plenty of trouble at home with its Muslim population. The country borders many Islamic nations, including Pakistan, Afghanistan, Kazakhstan, Kyrgyzstan, and Tajikistan to the west and Mongolia to the north, and the Chinese government simply doesn't understand religion. Unlike failed ideologies, they don't just go away.

Currently, Xi's China has imprisoned nearly one million Uyghurs in a massive re-education and forced labor program intended to transform these Muslims into Chinese Communists. It's not working, and the government's solution is to apply even more force. Neighboring Islamic nations are beginning to speak out about the mistreatment of their brothers and sisters in China, and that means even more trouble. Much of China's ambitious 2025 strategic plan, which I'll discuss later, is dependent on good relations and cooperation with the nations on its western border

China's Islamic problems are not unique. So far, Xi has managed to more or less get away with his anti-Muslim domestic policies and still side with Muslim nations on the world stage. How long he'll be able to maintain this balancing act is unknown.

––––––––––––

Southeastern China was long devoted to rice production, but a shift began some years ago. All of a sudden, factories dedicated to manufacturing giant trucks and excavation machines began to pop up, particularly along the border with Vietnam. It seemed odd to me, all these factories in the middle of nowhere, until I realized the true purpose. Land and labor were cheap there, and

China was engaged in countless major construction projects in Vietnam. If the excavation machines were built nearby, they could be placed on the giant trucks built in the same factories and driven right across the border. At the time, some Vietnamese feared that China sought to annex the country, but China had other plans. Becoming the world's largest trading country means doing business in and with any nation where a profit can be made, regardless of how its government is run.

A Vietnamese friend just back from a visit home with his family told me, "We beat the Japanese, the French, and the Americans, just to have China come in and buy our country." He added, "These days, you have a choice: either grow rice or get a job working for the Chinese."

India is looked down on by most Chinese people, but in fact, India is competitive with China in almost every respect, and the Chinese know it. Currently the second most populous nation in the world, it will soon be number one. Each thinks its ideology and government is superior, and each thinks its own modernization process far surpasses the other. China also resents the close relationships that exist among India, Nepal, and Tibet, including the fact that India is the home of the exiled Dalai Lama.

Pakistan represents an entirely different problem for China that intensifies its challenges with India. India and Pakistan face off regularly—especially when it comes to the disputed region of Kashmir—and China always sides with Pakistan. But Pakistan is an Islamic state, and Xi's treatment of the Uyghurs is a sticking point.

Pakistan plays a vital role in Xi's Belt and Road Initiative, which he aims to implement on a global scale in 152 countries.

The initiative involves building roads, railroads, bridges, and ports around the world to better facilitate trade. Currently, China is engaged in building roads leading south from Kashgar over and around the Himalayas to a new port under construction in Gwadar, Pakistan. China's intent is to use Gwadar as an entry point to the Arabian Sea and on to the Middle East.

Hambantota, a port in Sri Lanka, and several other ports in southeast Asia are already in use as part of the initiative, providing China's naval ships with refueling stations—and surrounding India with the Chinese navy. Like the African nations I mentioned earlier, Sri Lanka has not been able to pay its share of the costs to construct Hambantota, so China has taken it over. I doubt that Pakistan will be able to pay for its portion of the Gwadar construction. If so, China will have another strategic port, but this one will be special because of its road and bridge connections to western China.

Why bridges? Everywhere you go in China, there are bridges. While other nations build tunnels, China prefers bridges. They've long been used to span China's great rivers, but they are now used to go around mountains and across vast spaces between them. Many of these bridges are double deckers, with trains on one level and cars and trucks on the other.

All this infrastructure construction provides money, investment, and skilled jobs for Chinese people around the world. Many joke now that the "sun never sets on the Chinese flag."

———————

Then there is the problem of the United States. For years, America invested heavily in development in China, because we believed a developed China would become a good trading partner and that communism would fall once the nation had a taste of capitalism. The United States is just now awakening to the reality of the new China and is unsure of how to deal with it. We could end up coexisting peacefully as competitors, but it's a fine line between this and animosity.

This is a time when great leadership is needed to keep the world peaceful, and neither China nor the United States have it. Press reports in both countries lead one to believe that China and America are engaged in constant conflict, but the nations are very interdependent on many issues. We are major trading partners. We cooperate on worldwide health issues. China depends on American markets for many of its goods, and vice versa. China is a major investor in American debt.

Trade wars generate a lot of headlines, but most are minor and could and should be solved easily through market diplomacy. But every time America raises tariffs China returns with its own on tariffs on American agriculture. If the world is to prosper, both nations must cooperate.

They're known worldwide for their strength as builders, but the Chinese are great planners, too. One of my favorite places to visit in Shanghai is its planning office. There, you'll find countless maps showing enterprises all over the world that China has planned for the next five, ten, and twenty years. Every time I've asked a question of the staff, I've found that they've already thought through all the options and scenarios, but they're always on the lookout for suggestions.

The latest is China's controversial 2025 strategic plan. A significant portion of it is devoted to tackling China's middle-class problem. At present, less than 40 percent of all purchased equipment and materials in China are produced domestically.

The 2025 plan's goal is to increase this to 70 percent, creating lots of middle-income jobs in the process. China presently imports most of its medical supplies and pharmaceuticals (as was evident with its lack of medical supplies and personnel in the wake of the 2020 COVID-19 coronavirus pandemic throughout China and, later, the world), so beefing up production in those areas is a cornerstone of the plan.

The plan also calls for a dramatic increase in production of components and products that are high on the mechanical and electronic value chains. Chinese-made cell phones are already giving Samsung and Apple serious competition on the domestic front, and they'll soon be making waves in the U.S. market.

The 2025 plan has plenty of other targets: increasing the volume of international component shipping by 80 percent; increasing trade with the "mini-dragon" nations; and producing a higher percentage of domestically consumed computer chips, automobiles, robotics, and aerospace technology.

This represents a fraction of the 2025 plan's many objectives. Some have expressed concern that the plan's stated objective of dramatically increasing middle-income jobs may end up eliminating a similar number of low-wage jobs and spiking unemployment overall.

Deng's realization that China needed professional leadership was the key to the successes of the forty-year Great Modernization. If you look at any area of China that has been transformed—public and private sectors alike—you'll see that well-trained professionals led the transformation.

Chinese businesspeople often speak of the many roads China has taken to achieve its success. The professionals noted that the United States had well-established brands, so they quickly made a strategic decision to make and market components to these brands rather than directly compete with them. They figured out what would sell well in the Chinese market versus what would be best to export, and then determined how best to manufacture those products.

Next, they realized that there was a tremendous space in the U.S. market below the well-known American brands for lower-priced alternatives. Pick up a product in any American discount store and you'll likely find a "made in China" label on it.

The professionals also saw an opportunity to offshore production of many of these items to other, less-developed nations. Increasingly, low-end products are manufactured in Chinese plants in these countries. The outer package of a three-pack of name-brand underwear I bought at an American discount store clearly stated that it was made in China, but each pair of the underwear inside had a different country of manufacture: one in Thailand, another in Sri Lanka, and the third in Bangladesh.

China doesn't mind taking on name brands in Third World countries, and if the market is large enough, they'll find a way to manufacture the product in the nation itself or manufacture it in a neighboring country and transport it to the market. China also doesn't shy away from going head to head against high-end products in developed nations, but they generally stay away from marketing them in the brand's home country.

As it is the world's largest market for cars, American and European automotive manufacturers design cars specifically for China. Low-end imported cars never caught on because the Chinese found them expensive for what you get, and most had features they weren't interested in. A friend once remarked, "I don't mind manually rolling up my windows, and what's the purpose of a big back seat? The only people who ever ride in it are my mother and my daughter, and they're used to riding on the back of my bicycle."

Speaking of bikes, the latest Chinese fad is the motorized bicycle, which sells for around $200, or you can buy a motor and convert a standard bike. Many of my friends have replaced their cars with these bikes.

One friend told me, "Why get stuck in traffic jams or worry about parking? Every little bump on your car costs thousands to fix. With the bike, I can go anywhere and park for five cents a day—and if I ever have a problem, there's a man on every corner who can fix it."

Now that Xi is stressing ideological purity over professional leadership, many of the ambitious ideas laid out in the 2025 strategic plan may change. The highest priority of Xi and his followers is to spread Chinese Communist purity throughout China. Most Chinese people are apolitical, so by and large, the government gets away with whatever it likes. Business owners will continue to submit to whatever political charades are necessary as long as doing so will keep their businesses free from government control.

So far, Xi's agenda of total ideological purity extends only as far as China's borders. Increasingly, China's neighbors fear that it will again try to export its ideology, just as it did in the 1950s and 1960s. They know it will be much harder to resist this time because of China's deep investments and entrenchment in their countries.

Chapter 14
Life in Magnificent China,
Forty Years Later

URING A 1980 TRIP TO PUTUOSHAN (BUDDHA ISLAND), I
saw seven old ladies with bound feet sitting on a stone wall
in front of the Puji Temple. Three of them were wearing the blue
uniforms of the Cultural Revolution, and none could walk without assistance. The women were engaged in lively conversations;
while they frequently talked over another, they all seemed to be
really listening, too. On the side of the temple, another group
of women were washing clothes—really beating the devil out of
each garment—and they, too, were having a loud discussion. I
was told that these sorts of conversations were the Chinese way.

By my next trip, in 1986, the old women with the bound
feet were long gone. In all likelihood, they were dead, as foot
binding had been illegal since 1911. Instead, a family with two
children—probably the second one born just before the "One
Child" policy came into effect—were sitting on the wall having a picnic. There was still a group of women washing clothes
nearby, but this time, the only thing you could hear other than

the sound of them beating the clothes was a small portable radio playing Chinese pop songs.

When I visited in 1995, a group of schoolchildren sat on the wall having loads of fun—all laughing and talking at once. Suddenly, their teacher got them up and made them stand at attention, like little soldiers, in front of the main temple for a group photo. I was so surprised: not a single child made a funny face or held up fingers behind the head of the child in front of her. It worried me. Are these kids or little soldiers?

But then the kids started messing up each other's hair and tickling each other. The teacher tried to get them to pose for another picture but soon gave up. Kids were kids, and since none of them had sisters or brothers, their friends were even more special to them. Surely they all knew that Sun Wukong, the Monkey King, used a rock just a few thousand feet up the beach to jump into heaven and receive advice from the Buddha. The women doing the laundry were still there, listening to what sounded to me like the same song they'd been listening to nine years before.

On my last visit, in 2014, that same wall was crowded with a dozen teenagers and a couple of women in their thirties. They were all engrossed in the same thing: staring into their cell phones and ignoring the beauty of the sea in front of them and the temple behind them. None of them made a sound. It is such a beautiful place that you'd think that at least one of them would take some pictures. After a long while, one got up and took a selfie, but it was an up-close shot that could have been taken in a shopping mall, for all anyone who saw it would know. The silence was overwhelming. Eventually it dawned on me that no one was washing clothes. Everyone has machines to do that now.

Until 2000, the only way to get to Putuoshan was an overnight boat ride. The distinguishing feature of the boat was that it was completely infested with what must have been the largest roaches in the world. Each time, I'd book a private room, and each time, the roaches would beat me to it. They were so big that they feared nothing—they made no effort to hide when you turned on the light.

But in 2000, a road from Shanghai to Putuoshan opened. It involved traveling bridge after bridge, island-hopping from Ningbo all the way to beautiful Buddha Island, and what had been an overnight journey could now be completed in only two hours.

I made the trip that year in a friend's new and completely roach-free Volvo. As I drove through each of the islands—about a dozen in all—it struck me that each of them seemed to have its own mission. One was full of fishermen's houses. The next was a storage place for old submarines.

But the greatest wonder of all was the manmade steel island encircled by a dozen container ships. It was possible to dock six of them at once (the other six were waiting their turn), and giant cranes hovered over the ships, sorting containers at amazing speeds. The ships were destined for Shanghai and other ports all around the world, and performing the sorting process here, off site, meant that the ship could be unloaded in port in a tenth of the time. Sorting in port takes up valuable money, time, and space; sorting at sea saves all of those things. It's just another example of the modernity and efficiency of the new China.

I have traveled to China fifty-eight times in thirty-eight of the last forty years, and every trip was full of surprises. The China of today is vastly different from the China of 1979; nearly every physical element of the country was different. China leads the world in infrastructure development. Every major city is connected by new airports, by elevated roads, and by fast trains to every other city.

A good illustration of the rapid infrastructure development can be found in the town of Qufu. In 1985, I first visited the city, which is the birthplace of Confucius, who was born in 551 BC as K'ung Fu Tzu. My train arrived in the middle of the night in a town some distance from my destination. I had to wake up a cab driver to take me the rest of the way on a road that had been paved at some point in the past but was so full with potholes, the twenty-mile drive took well over an hour.

Qufu is one of my favorite places to visit. The school Confucius established is still there, probably because the town is so far off the beaten track. The school has a large courtyard, with trees that are centuries old, and a family cemetery with generations and generations of the K'ung family buried there. During the Cultural Revolution, the Red Guard dug up the entire area where Confucius' grave and monument are located, but they never found his body. If they'd read Confucius' work more and the Little Red Book less, they would have known that Confucius always took the clever route and never the obvious road.

When I returned to Qufu ten years later, the train still arrived at three in the morning, but a nice bus was there waiting to take me the rest of the way on a freshly paved road. Again in 2012, I returned for the third time, this time via an air-conditioned bus (with a bathroom!) on an elevated four-lane highway that runs from Nanjing to Jinan.

I missed the Tiananmen year, as foreigners were not welcomed then. I missed 2019 because of the chill of Xi's programs. I didn't see the shift from expert rule to Party rule coming, and I certainly didn't realize what a big change it would be for China. Xi's rise to power clearly represented a movement away from expert control, but I remained so fixed on studying the development and positive changes that went along with China's modernization that I completely missed it, for the most part. I was judging the new China by a different standard than the one the Party was using.

The Party had been watching its power slip away, year after year. The new China I liked so much was a challenge to the Party's importance. When Xi took over and published his own little two-volume set, The Governance of China, it read like something from the past. The Party doesn't want China to be modern first and foremost. They want a Chinese Communist nation. In their opinion, China was becoming less Chinese— and certainly less Communist.

I should have known something was wrong when the time for my international relations textbook to be updated came and went. Just a few years earlier, I'd been urged to get started on an update, but suddenly there were lots of reasons to just leave it as it was. I became concerned when I realized that the focus of China's military had been changed from coastal protection to Asian dominance but missed its shift toward world dominance. I knew something was amiss when many of my friends became reluctant to talk about anything substantive besides social chitchat. Then several of my friends began to move away from China, to New Zealand, to Hong Kong, and even to the United States.

But I was shocked when Xi declared himself Chairman of the Party for life and assumed control of the government and the military. There had been so many signs, of course, of the coming chill, but I'd been so impressed and entranced with how far China had come in so few years that I just couldn't, or wouldn't, believe it would return to an authoritarian-controlled system run by nonprofessionals. That had been tried and had failed so many times before! Clearly, I misjudged China's movements. I thought of the moves in purely economic terms, that it was creating new markets to ensure a constant stream of natural resources and an abundance of food for its people.

But as I look back, I can remember how my friends knew all along that China could shift back, how easy it could be to revert to a Party-controlled, ideological nation. My children often remarked about how "uptight" our Chinese friends seemed. I had long ago written that off to the stresses they faced that were obvious: coping with major changes, figuring out how to come to terms with a rush of success. I'd never experienced China while it remained under tight ideological control, but everyone who was older than forty knew all too well what it was like to live in a dictatorial system, and to fear the secret police. To know that the only truth was whatever the Party said it was. To know that laws don't matter. If the Party wanted a new leader of their own to take over an industry, it didn't matter that all the laws clearly stated that only people who were well trained, educated, and experienced could have the job. That didn't matter in the 1950s, during the Great Leap Forward. It didn't matter during the Cultural Revolution. Sadly, it doesn't matter now. All that matters is that the chosen person has the right connections to the top Party people.

Once this realization dawned on me, I began to fear that my very presence could endanger my friends. For that reason, I chose not to return in 2019. Many were forced into retirement or demoted; all were replaced by Xi's Party people. Physically,

China has completely transformed from a backward Third World nation into a modern, industrialized one. But the same cell phones that liberated the youth of China allow the Party to listen in on every verbal or text conversation—another instrument of control.

———————

In 1979, everyone rode bicycles, walked, or took the bus. At every intersection, hundreds of bikes would cluster together. A lone policeman stood on a small, three-foot-high platform in the middle of the intersection, and the moment turned his sign over from red to green, mass chaos would ensue, just like the beginning of a stock-car race. The first few would get across, but then those who wanted to turn left began weaving among the sea of bikes coming the other way. A few would bump into each other, and by the tail end of the cluster, most would get off their bikes and push them in front of the crowd coming in the other direction. and most got off their bikes and just pushed then in front of the crowd coming the other way. When the sign would turn red, in an instant, chaos would turn to calm. How in the hell do they do this, I thought, without having a crash at every intersection? Every city sidewalk was the same story: hundreds of people going in each direction, but no one would ever collide.

At each bus stop, people would fight to get off the bus and more still would fight to get on. There would be people on the bus yelling that it was full, but no one would listen. They'd just keep cramming more and more people on. Sometimes, the result of all that shouting and pushing was a full-blown fight. (A friend told me once that bus fighting is the national sport of China.) Sometimes, a policeman would get on the bus and pull somebody off for fighting. I can't imagine how he could be sure he got the right person, but it didn't seem to matter. As soon as the policeman showed up, the packed bus was silent as a tomb. Nobody wanted to be the one who got pulled off.

By 2018, the city landscape was completely transformed. At those same intersections, there were very few bikes, but lots of cars (in some cases, the "old roads" are now exclusively pedestrian malls). The real traffic, however, was running overhead on an elevated road four stories in the sky. Just under the elevated road, fast trains whooshed past. If you miss one train, you can just wait a few minutes for the next one. There was no need for pedestrians to cross at the intersection, because an elevated roundabout allowed for easy foot traffic. They never set foot on the road below. All of this is even more amazing given that the population of most of these cities has more than doubled in the years since 1979.

I know that the Chinese people are much better off than they were during the horrible days of the Cultural Revolution. They have apartments, cars, running water. They have university degrees and plump little children with red cheeks. But to me, Xi's changes are a step firmly in the wrong direction: an ideologically centered state is a repressive state.

Perhaps I'm overreacting and judging these developments through my own prism. For me, there will be no more travel to areas like western China and other minority regions, where people are being forced into hard labor and losing their identities. There will be no more speaking tours, and certainly no more years of teaching classes for university professors and writing textbooks.

When I visit my old friends, I can sense their anxiety. They have no freedom to talk about and evaluate the changes that are going on. They lead modern lives, but deep down, I can feel their fear. I'll never be able to truly understand their fear, because I've never lived with a shadow hanging over my head like they do.

———————

Gone, too, is my dream that the twenty-first century would be a time of peaceful cooperation between America and China. The ongoing trade war is felt even by the Chinese people who live in America. They care about China's welfare and are open in their questioning of why we would pursue a policy that hurts the poorest Americans and Chinese alike. If America is supposed to be a beacon of freedom for the world, they say, then why is the American dream being destroyed from the inside out?

The trade war has only heightened my personal concerns. It seems to me that the negotiators on both sides don't understand that trade wars are the absolute worst way to settle trade differences. Neither side wins, but each side continually escalates the war in an effort to appear as the "winner." Both sides end up hurting their own industries. Across America, farmers have been hurt badly, and the American taxpayers are bailing them out. The steel industry and both the automotive and airline industries have taken serious hits as well. Both sides have lost much more revenue from lost employment than either will ever gain from making a shift in the trade balance equal to less than one-tenth of one percent. The worst thing imaginable is to take steps that hurt us in the long run due to our fear of the world.

The Americans want to talk about an even trade balance, with no notion that trade balance is among the least of China's

problems. Many Chinese intellectuals have told me of their desire for China to attach itself so tightly to America that it would
never experience another downward turn.

But the Obama administration gave few signs of acceding
to these wishes, and now the Trump administration continues
to pull America away from not only China, but the rest of the
world as well. (Many say that Xi and Trump are cut from the
same cloth.) The likely result will be the decline of American influence and the rise of Chinese influence throughout the world.
I am much more concerned about the conflict itself than I am
about whether we win the trade war. Neither nation can rely on
skilled leaders who understand the world we all live in.

The trade war makes no sense at all, and it illustrates how
little the leaders of either nation know about trade. Each nation certainly has trade problems, but trade problems must be
settled by experts. Yes, China steals the intellectual property
of American companies, but for years now, we simply haven't
made any sort of investment to secure it. The best way to secure our intellectual property is to let it be known that we know
what is going on, and to take our own measures to stop it. My
many years of working and studying there have taught me that
the best way to deal with China is to treat them with respect,
but also to let them know as soon as you realize they are not
playing fair.

Every element of the negotiations must be done in private,
so neither side loses face or prestige. (Another benefit: each
leader can say whatever he likes and portray the negotiation
as a win for his side.) Trade conflicts can and should be solved
away from the spotlight, and fair, open trade between these
two superpowers is an absolute must for a peaceful, prosperous
world. America must understand its adversary and control its

own worst impulses. China is very status conscious, and economic war games are viewed as a symbol of weakness.

My friends also point to other recent moves here in the United States, such as restrictions on reproductive choice, health care and education budget slashing, starting conflicts with smaller nations, allowing the Russian government to interfere in American politics with impunity, and deserting our longtime allies, and ask, "What good are your freedoms if you can't use them?" To them, in so many respects, China seems very progressive compared to America. Thus, more and more of them are returning to China.

China is modernized, but now what? The economy continues to rise, but at a much slower pace than just a few years ago. Its new leaders are making so many new demands and placing so many rules and restrictions on its people. Failing to follow them, even out of ignorance, can ruin your life and the lives of your family forever.

What, exactly, do China's leaders want? To me, the answer is clear: thought control. No more foreign textbooks for universities. No free conversations about world affairs. Certainly no more lecture tours about "Understanding American Foreign Policy," with thousands in attendance. Part of the fault lies with America's own leadership. Our unpredictability makes not only China nervous but also the other major nations of the world. In the area of international relations and foreign policy, unpredictability is perhaps the great danger. So the Chinese Communist Party wants to ensure predictability, and total control of the thoughts and behavior of the Chinese people is the best way to get it.

Increasingly, Xi imagines the new China as the sole world power. His navy, with its new state-of-the-art technology, goes on "world peace tours" not to fight anyone but to show off its power. His ships sail to Chinese-owned ports around the world, including in western Europe. Much has been written about Xi's Belt and Road Initiative and 2025 strategic plan. The details change from year to year, but the main message remains the same: China is taking control of ports, railroads, roads, railroads, and mines in nation after nation, and those nations are worried. They've finally come to realize that their future is dependent on going along with what China wants.

China will be a world power, and it will use its connections to all or most of the world via the modern technology and infrastructure it has built elsewhere. Consider China's ninety-nine-year lease of Hong Kong to the United Kingdom. When the lease ran out, China took it back.

When China took over, back in 1997, Hong Kong was to be ruled under a policy known as "one country, two systems." The banking system, currency, local government, and judiciary that had been developed in Hong Kong would be allowed to continue, in the name of progress. But now Xi is stressing his "One China" dogma and trying to bring Hong Kong under the control of China's central government. Chinese students—and most other Hong Kong residents—want more autonomy, not less, leading to mass demonstrations and clashes with Chinese military and police. These demonstrations are now common-place, and many have led to violence from both sides. The demonstrations and the attempts to quash them have hurt Xi's image abroad and at home, hampering his desire to project an image of China as one big happy family with him in absolute control as its leader.

Deng wanted to do the same in Taiwan but couldn't pull it off because of American influence. That influence has waned enough to place their end goal in sight. As soon as the time is right and America turns its back, China will seize Taiwan.

All these plans for world domination place the Party leadership and the expert leaders at odds. Xi and the Party want to transform China ideologically and to increase its power and status in the world. Reaching these goals requires professional and expert knowledge, and that's exactly what Xi has spent the last few years expunging from leadership roles.

The Party advocates that ideology under lifetime control of one man: Xi Jinping. The main criteria governing decision-making at all levels of business, education, and government must be based on the Communist Party line he creates. The Party has always retained ideological control in the sense that it has controlled the press. For most of the years of the Great Modernization, the Party played a supporting role while Deng Xiaoping's professionals controlled the realms of education, business, and industry. The professionals succeeded because they were allowed to lead and dominate. During the forty years of the Great Modernization, this dominance has been asserted in three stages.

- The first five years were focused on training the professionals. The brightest minds in China were allowed to travel and study the world and bring back what they'd learned to serve China.
- For the next thirty years, the newly trained professionals turned China's Third World agricultural-based economy into a modern industrial state.
- In the most recent five years, the Party has reemerged in control.

Since Xi announced that he will be the head of the military, the government, and the Party for life, growth has slowed. The Party is good at making plans but has trouble turning them into action. For that, you need professionals.

The Party has always maintained control of the judicial system. The new China may be modernized, but human rights do not exist there. China has not and does not want to become a free democracy. The Party uses the police and the courts to control dissent. Even when the experts controlled most sectors, there was never a free press—another key to democracy.

The Chinese missile program is very advanced. In 2017, the United States announced its new class of aircraft carriers, the Gerald R. Ford Class, and shortly after, the Chinese began to claim that it had a new missile able to sink any ship. To prove the point, it sent an older ship out to sea and filmed the missile destroying it. The United States had become dependent on Chinese missiles to carry our satellites into orbit and supply the space station, but now we are at work on modernizing our missile program so we will become less dependent.

Few of the most ambitious goals of the 2025 strategic plan and Belt and Road Initiative have reached fruition, but they haven't been abandoned. Now, Xi judges success only by assessing the Party's level of ideological control, rather than whether a goal is achieved. The one area that remains on schedule is the buildup of China's military.

While the military's propaganda stresses that it is leading the Chinese people to great heights, it seems to me that every move it makes is an effort to increase Xi's power and spread fear. The military's budget has increased at a rate much faster than the growth of the economy.

The increased spending, it seems, is spent on strengthening China's offensive capabilities rather than the defensive power stressed by Deng and Mao. In my opinion, that's because the Party realizes it will need its military to control its people. Soldiers are easy to indoctrinate. People are more problematic. The Party doesn't trust its civilian population and spends much of its time and money on control measures. In my opinion, the military would rather stay out of domestic and ideological issues, but they have been forced by Xi to punish and police their own countrymen—for example, rounding up the Uyghurs and supervising them in forced labor camps. So maybe this is wishful thinking on my part.

The Party has long made it seem that they have retained control over the military. But up through the Tiananmen year and on through the years that followed, Deng and the experts really controlled the military, and it was their efforts that turned China into a modern fighting force. Now the Party takes credit for these changes.

The military still revered Mao during the first years of my China trips. I'd occasionally spot a group of soldiers sitting by the side of a road with Mao's Little Red Book, reading aloud and reciting Mao's sayings. By the mid-1980s, this came to an end, but that was long after Mao's book had fallen into disuse by the civilian sector.

Xi took over the military in 2014 and required his book The Governance of China to be studied at its daily meetings throughout China. Any military leaders who were not in favor of his changes were either demoted or forced into retirement. The new military leaders were handpicked by Xi, so they follow the Party line. Despite this, they continue to call themselves the "vanguard of revolution."

Xi's military has also been very aggressive in dealing with Chinese minority groups, like the Uyghurs. Under Mao and Deng, all minorities other than Tibetans were elevated. In the propaganda film The East Is Red, as the Red Army took over each minority region, its residents were depicted as welcoming the Communists with open arms, dancing, and singing. Until recently, every minority group had its own school system, taught in its native language, alongside the traditional Chinese schools. But Xi wants to force minority groups into giving up their identities, so he is closing the traditional language schools and making all children learn exclusively in Chinese.

During the years when the experts had the upper hand, disputes for control of Asian waterways were relatively rare. The few flare-ups that occurred were treated as local issues and settled quickly. With the ascendance of Xi, military conflicts are on the rise, and a battle of words between the U.S. and China is as well. Xi likes to describe the United States as a warmongering nation, pointing out that since the Second World War, we have engaged in twenty-two wars and China has been in none. (Interesting that he doesn't count any of the wars and skirmishes China has entered—and there have been plenty—but he counts every little scrimmage America has gotten into.) But he does have a point: America has been in a number of conflicts with other nations since World War II.

Xi exerts power over not only the military, but also education, government, industry, minority affairs, and even the everyday life of the average Chinese citizen. But if Chinese power and the standard of living among Chinese people continues to stagnate, and in some respects, slide, as they have during the last two years, change may occur. Even during Mao's rule, after the Great Leap Forward, power shifted to the more practical wing of the Communist Party. After the failure of the Cultural Revolution, Deng emerged to place China on a less ideological and more realistic path.

The Party is in control now, but that doesn't mean it will be five or ten years in the future. The Chinese way to stay in power is to have rivals disappear. Xi doesn't seem to mind having prominent people vanish, generally justifying it by saying that they were corrupt. He doesn't bother with trials. Everyone knows that if you cross Xi, you will be charged with some crime and simply disappear. The Chinese people have long been accustomed to arbitrary control by the government, but they have also become accustomed to modern life. If Party decisions lead to recessions or even depressions, I do not think the Chinese will stand for it.

I was slow to understand the significance of Xi's takeover of control "for life." Now, his secret informers are everywhere; reportedly, there are six officers of the secret police to every thousand Chinese citizens, and the Party has installed its members strategically. No one knows who to trust, so it's safer to not trust anyone.

On a recent trip to a Chinese university, I met the new president and four vice presidents—all of whom were Party loyalists with no academic background. But an article about them in China Daily reported that they all had a great deal of experience and training at the university. The university's previous leaders had been members of the Communist Party, but they weren't Xi's people. Just being a Party member does not make you safe.

Every time a Party leader replaces a well-trained professional leader, the realistic worry that work will be rewarded based on its ideological purity rather than quantifiable accomplishments rears its ugly head. From 1995 to 2015, every Chinese person I knew worked hard and strived to get ahead in his or her occupation. The Party was not much of a concern—you merely tipped your hat to it as you went about your business. Everyone knew that China's goal was a modern economy and not a democratic state, but as long as the quality of life and standard of living kept rising among the Chinese people, most of them didn't care. "Become rich" was all everyone could think about.

In my judgment, a return to the terrible days of the pre-professional period is not just a possibility. It is likely to happen. No one talks about it, or much of anything else. My friends used to freely recount their harrowing experiences of life under Mao during the Great Leap Forward and the Cultural Revolution, but now they are silent on even that, for fear that Xi's observers will take it as a statement against Xi and his ideology. The hardest lesson the Chinese people have learned from their history is to keep their heads down, work hard, and never mention what goes on in Beijing.

But Xi is hard to ignore. His picture is everywhere, just as Mao's once was. His visage graces the front page of every newspaper. His picture is painted on the sides of mosques and plastered over images of Jesus Christ on churches. Many houses of worship are being destroyed, and those that remain—I think they're only there to show off to tourists—don't allow children to attend.

For years, the Party ignored the practice of religion, unless someone dared to proselytize a faith by openly inviting others to attend home worship services or by giving out Bibles or religious tracts. Now Xi is cracking down on all religions, saying that the people who practice them are against Chinese Communism.

Pollution remains a major problem in China. There are many hydroelectric dams, quite a few nuclear plants, miles of wind turbines, and acres of solar panels. China is keenly aware of the realities of global warming and its role in accelerating climate change. But lots of coal-fired power plants still stand, and while electric cars are popular, most of China's cars run on gasoline.

And then there is the question of waste. As new innovations arrive in the country, a tide of garbage comes along with them. China's modern families have adopted disposable diapers, a departure from the split pants babies used to wear. The new fast-food restaurants produce lots of waste, just as they do in other developed nations. Most items purchased in the supermarkets and department stores of China are wrapped or bagged. Most of China's land is already in use for agriculture or housing. There's nowhere for the trash to go.

The current dilemma of China's massive population will be an even greater problem in the future. Right now in China, there are 115 males to every 100 females, a legacy of the "One Child" policy. A surplus of single men creates all sorts of social and economic problems, and as they grow old, who will look after them? Chinese people on the whole are living longer, and the percentage of retirees is increasing at an alarming rate. In coming years, China will suffer a labor shortage, and a smaller number of workers will have to support a larger number of retirees.

China's most dangerous neighbor is North Korea. Xi simply doesn't know what to do about it. He fears the rebel state will drag China into a conflict that could escalate to a worldwide scale; at the same time, he also fears that it will collapse and that China will have to bail it out, setting back his aggressive plans elsewhere for years.

The minority regions of south China worry Xi as well. Minority groups in southern China have networks of relatives in Vietnam, Laos, Thailand, and Myanmar, and they're able to get across the borders as easily as crossing the street. As a result, the south has a booming black market of drugs, weapons, and pretty much any other illicit thing you can imagine.

For years, China looked on America as a model—even if it wasn't something that was talked about. The Chinese people made major sacrifices to send millions of their young people to study at American universities—mostly for very specific majors, like business, computer science, physics, and medicine. (The Chinese students who studied in other fields generally planned to stay in the United States, and of course plenty of the first group also hoped to stay. It seemed to me that the women were particularly interested in staying, as they felt opportunities were much better for them here. My female undergraduate students always wanted to talk about life in America, and the male students rarely did. (In fact, the return rate was pretty evenly split between the genders.) My undergraduate students have done extremely well in American business and medicine, and many of my graduate students have gone on to work for think tanks, have created their own businesses, or have done very well in the field of computer science here.

While America and its culture remains very popular among the Chinese public, we are viewed by the Party as a competitor and a threat. Xi has banned many foreign films and blocked many TV programs—especially those that have appeal to young people. The internet is closely monitored, and if a user gives any signs of not following the Party line, he or she is disconnected.

Foreign fashions are being replaced with traditional Chinese dress. If you have tattoos, they must be covered, and athletes must wear long-sleeved shirts. Pop music has largely been replaced with traditional Chinese music. Young students must wear uniforms to school, and this rule is increasingly being applied at universities as well. Haircuts for both men and women must meet certain standards; the streaks of purple or green that young Chinese girls often liked to put in their hair are now forbidden.

The message behind all of these rules is consistent: you are Chinese, and you are not an individual. You are to look, speak, and act as one. In the spring of 2019, it seemed that the Party was publishing a new set of rules every week. Failure to obey was met with swift punishment.

Throughout this book, I've noted how tense Chinese people always seem to be. We speak about this often in my family. I long ascribed this tension to the stresses of doing well in school, of finding a good job, of marrying, of having a child, and of being successful in their chosen professions. I now know the truth: the Chinese view history as a circle. During the professional period, the line drawing the circle was always going up, and doing so at a rapid pace. Chinese people know, from thousands of years of experience, that what goes up will go down. The tension was a result of constant vigilance, of watching for the signs that would determine the next direction of history.

The reemergence of the Communist Party, Xi declaring himself an emperor for life, and even the Party going after minorities—these were all signs of the other shoe dropping. A university president being replaced with a Party operative with little or no educational background: another sign. The head of a business or industry disappearing and being replaced by someone interested in Party loyalty over profit and growth: yet another. The people who are the last to recognize the signs suffer the most. Before the Cultural Revolution, Western classical music was celebrated in China. But some time after the Revolution began, a world-class pianist who had been a good friend of mine was beaten to death by the Red Guard with the legs of her piano bench. The Party is making a comeback, to be sure, and the professionals are ill equipped to deal with it.

On the domestic front, the drawbacks of greater personal wealth seem to preoccupy the Chinese much more than issues on the world stage. As more people have moved to the cities and have become wealthy, everything has become more expensive, and in some cases, a lot more expensive. For example, the price of fish has skyrocketed, as the rivers and ocean waters simply don't have enough fish to meet the demand of a newly wealthy nation.

The Chinese are clever, however, and it seems that every waterway is home to a fish farm these days. I once took a group on a tour of a leather jacket factory with a large moat around it. The moat was so full of fish that dozens jumped out of the water at any given moment. Curious, I asked the director of the factory about the moat.

"The factory was built on low, wet ground," he said. "Originally, they dug a moat to drain the site, but the water just wouldn't go away. Someone had the bright idea to add some fish to the water and keep them fed.

"Before long, the moat was full of fish, and our workers had plenty to take home with them. One of our workers had an unemployed wife, so she started taking some of the fish to market. Now we employ three people full-time to look after the fish and sell them at the market."

I mentioned earlier in the book that the Chinese are masters of self-criticism. I've picked up the habit myself. Of late, I've become obsessed with the modernization of China, and anything that poses a threat to it throws me into a panic. A few of my Chinese friends shared my panic, but really, only a few. Most are concerned about the shift, but far from panicked.

One friend told me, "Dr. Wilson, you understand lot about China, but you are not Chinese. Chinese view history as a circle. The circle has now changed, and it will change again. Ideology has been a central part of being Chinese since Confucius' time. We are accustomed to having set rules by which you govern and are governed. The leaders of business, government, industry, and education have always had to deal with some Party official. They've always known that someday, the circle would turn and that official would be placed in charge. Modernism won't go away. It'll just be demoted for a while. Yes, some people will suffer, but in any system, there are those who suffer and those who rule. We certainly hope that we will never have another Cultural Revolution, but you must remember that the Party leadership stopped the horrors of that period."

I didn't say what I was thinking: that the Party leaders had started it.

He continued, "Xi may have all the votes in the Party Congress, but no emperor can live forever. China will live forever. You use modernity and lack of conflict to judge where China is, but to us, ideological correctness is also important. Our ideology never went away when we were allowed to travel abroad. We still had to have Party approval and often had to bring a Party official along.

"Chinese Communism gave us peace after years of war. You have said many times that no one can understand China without understanding Confucius. In truth, you can't understand China without understanding how important our central ideology is in determining what we should and shouldn't do. What ideas are correct and which ones aren't. In the West, your religions, democracies, and philosophical history are intertwined from the Greeks forward. But the opinions of the people or of some God have never meant much to Chinese people. Lots of Chinese people left China to get an education, and those who stayed abroad accepted your system. Those who returned didn't bring your system here. Instead, they accepted the present system."

I know that he spoke the truth, but what he described was not the system I had dreamed of for China. The reality is that most Chinese people are satisfied with what they have after having so little for so long: an apartment with running water and electricity and a bathroom, for example. Climate control, to keep them cool in the summer and warm in the winter. Most have color TVs and cell phones. Many have cars, and those who don't have access to excellent public transportation. There are plenty of jobs. There are schools and universities. So what if they lose a few freedoms? They certainly didn't have any of these things forty years ago, including the freedom.

I was made to feel at home in China for forty years because I had knowledge the country needed. I'm glad that I helped fulfill a need, but I know I am no longer welcome there. I love China. Now that I am eighty, I must slowly come around to the notion that the best thing I can do to help the country I love is to help my fellow Americans better understand China.

Chapter 15
The Magnificent Wonders of
Ancient and New China

T HE THREE GREAT WONDERS OF ANCIENT CHINA—
the Great Wall, the Silk Road, and the Grand Canal—are
the pride of the Chinese people. In my opinion, the fourth great
wonder of ancient China is the most amazing of them all. But
more about that later.

The Great Wall was constructed to protect China from
its primary perceived threat: the nomadic tribes of the north.
The Wall was built and rebuilt, dynasty after dynasty, for more
than two thousand years. Some of my friends in China like to
kid that empires don't need a wall (they find our current wall
controversy very amusing), but all Chinese people are proud
of their magnificent Great Wall. Millions have contributed to
rebuild the parts that are currently open to tourists, and visiting
dignitaries always make a stop to get their picture taken on the
Great Wall.

The Silk Road was China's connection to the rest of the
world and the key to the riches of the silk trade. The harsh

climate of the Taklimakan Desert had long blocked land travel, but the Chinese cleverly overcame this obstacle. Thousands of miles of underground tunnels had been constructed to connect the glaciers of the Tianshan Mountains to manmade stops along the Silk Road, effectively creating oases that could sustain travelers along the way. The tunnels often caved in and had to be rerouted, but they have been maintained for over a thousand years. To this day, the old Silk Road oases remain as little green patches in the desert that produce wonderful vegetables.

The tunnels are best viewed from the air, with dozens of entry holes covered in thatch lined up for miles from the mountains to the edges of the desert. Even today, nomads still pitch their yurts over the holes to access a form of air conditioning— cool air rising from the cold mountain water streaming below them.

These regularly spaced oases made trade possible for Chinese merchants and resulted in tremendous wealth in various kingdoms across the desert. In effect, the Silk Road was the world's east-west highway, and its existence enabled China to be informed about the rest of the world. It's interesting that throughout that time, China remained a great mystery to the West, but Chinese scholars were knowledgeable about events elsewhere.

The third wonder of ancient China, the Grand Canal, has been and still is the north-south connection that unites the great west-to-east flowing rivers of China. A substantial portion of the canal was constructed before the birth of Christ.

The canal's construction created a navigable mode of transport from the north to the south of China (think of it as a manmade Mississippi River). No other nation has ever embarked upon such a massive project; many of the canal's channels required digging through mountains. Today, some of the ancient locks of the Grand Canal are still operable and keep the waterway in regular use.

One of my favorite pastimes is to sit on a bridge or the bank of the Grand Canal and watch a seemingly unbroken line of barges full of goods sail past. At the rear of each barge, a small hut houses the family that operates the ship. Often, I'll see a child flying a kite or dangling a fishing line off the stern. Watching the ships is akin to watching the world go by, and I find it amazing that these practices have gone on for thousands of years.

To me, the fourth and most significant ancient wonder of China is its common written language. No other great ancient civilization in the world had a standardized language uniting the entire country. Spoken language differed from region to region, but a shared Chinese script has been in continuous use for more than two thousand years.

The practical benefits of this shared written language cannot be overstated: everything from simple communications to government edicts could travel simply and easily from the capital to any other location in the country. Rubbings of art and poetry carved into stones called steles were also easily copied and spread across the country, unifying the Chinese culture.

Today, a "stele forest" stands on the grounds of a museum in Xi'an, its thousands of messages and pictures relaying the history of each dynasty and other critical pieces of Chinese culture (for example, the sayings of Confucius). Because of the steles, these are literally carved into stone for eternity.

In modernized China, four great new wonders have arisen: urbanization; agriculture industrialization; modernized science and industry; and the nation's role as a world power. During my forty years of living in and exploring most of China on fifty-eight separate trips, I've gotten to see each of these amazing transformations occur.

Nearly one billion Chinese people have left their villages and moved to the cities in the past forty years. No greater migration of people in such a short time has taken place in the history of the world. Amazingly enough, this migration occurred in an orderly and peaceful manner—another first.

Today, more than 100 Chinese cities have populations of over one million people. Forty years ago, it was a daunting ordeal to travel from one city to another, but now connections are easy and fast via air, rail, or highway. connected with the others by air, rail and roads. The dirt-road journey from Beijing to its port city, Tianjin, took five hours in 1979. On the modern superhighways, it takes as little as an hour by car, and the high-speed train can make it in half the time.

Some of the cities have shown magnificent growth. In 1979, the small town of Shenzhen had a population of two thousand people, one small hotel, two paved streets, and one taxicab. It's now a futuristic city that's home to more than twelve million people, offices of most Fortune 500 companies, and a host of glitzy new hotels. The gridded streets range from four to eight lanes, with elevated walkways and crosswalks. Most Shenzhen residents have university degrees. The skyline is presently studded with high-rise cranes that continue to literally build out the city in two directions, toward its megacity neighbors Hong Kong and West Guangzhou. Today, more than forty-four million people live in the metropolitan area of Guangzhou.

The largest city-limits population belongs to Shanghai, with more than twenty-six million residents (another ten million reside within its metropolitan area). Many say it is the world's largest city. Some fascinating facts about Shanghai include:

- The east bank of the Huangpu River has been transformed from a village of boat repair shops and vegetable farms—reachable only by ferry even as late as 1986—into superclusters of some of the tallest structures in the world. Six of the twelve tallest buildings in China tower over this Pudong district, and numerous tunnels and bridges connect the two banks of the river.

- Back in 1986, Shanghai's apartment buildings were all ugly four- or five-story cinderblock affairs in the Soviet style. While a few of these still remain in industrial areas, most have been replaced with gleaming twenty- to thirty-story towers.

- Shanghai claims to be not just the most significant trade city in China—it professes number one status in the world. As I mentioned earlier, the port is so massive that manmade islands have been constructed offshore to sort the cargo of the endless stream of container ships waiting to unload.

- Twelve of Shanghai's largest universities have moved their undergraduate campuses to a separate "university city" connected by elevated rapid rail to the main city. While the separate city was a good idea, the founders failed to plan for one thing: parking for the thousands of students who now own cars.

Shanghai served as my personal headquarters for each of my trips to China, and each time I arrived there, I felt as though I had come to a completely different city. One year, I was shocked to find that every single building that previously had a flat roof had been renovated and now boasted V-shaped a tile roof. Puzzled, I stopped in at the city planning office to ask why such a massive project had been done.

The planner I spoke with told me, "It was the only sensible thing to do. The tile roofs keep buildings cooler in the summer and warmer in the winter, thus saving the city millions of dollars. This alone allowed the new roofs to pay for themselves in a little over one year."

He paused and then continued. "On top of that, the new roofs improved the overall appearance of the city. Many residents used to dry their clothes on bamboo poles that stuck out of their windows. If it rained, the clothes got wet all over again and dripped on the heads of pedestrians passing below. Now, every building has an attic space to hang up clothes under the tile roofs. The clothes dry faster, and people never have to worry about rain."

Several aspects of Chinese village life made the adjustment to city life much easier. For one, villagers always lived in close contact with their neighbors, so sharing space in an apartment complex wasn't really much of a change. And while using paper money might not seem like a major transition to Americans, it is a major hurdle in other nations. Rural people in most developing countries still use barter systems for most goods or services, but Chinese villagers have been using money for thousands of years.

City jobs most often require collective work, which Chinese villagers were quite accustomed to. For example, water management, which is the most critical part of agriculture in China, has always required collective efforts like terracing fields or channeling rivers.

Very good government-run health care is available in rural areas, and the government is the major provider in cities as well—plus more advanced care is widely available there. (The cities also offer private specialty health care to their rich and upper-middle class residents who can afford it.) When people become sick, they are able to receive excellent treatment at little or no cost, no matter where they live. Needless to say, this has greatly increased life expectancy, but that too has a downside: an aging population.

While most elderly villagers continue to live in the villages of their birth, more and more are moving to the cities to live with their adult children. While this makes apartment living even more crowded than before, grandparents make themselves useful, helping to raise their grandchildren, grocery shop, and cook for the family. To most Chinese people, "private space" is an unknown commodity.

One of Deng's primary goals for the Great Modernizations was industrialization of China's agriculture—the second new great wonder. The 1.4 billion people living in China today are fed using far less arable land, as city sprawl has overtaken thousands of acres of farmland. At the same time, far fewer people are engaged in agricultural work.

Throughout China's history, the nation has suffered through many famines, revolutions, and plagues. Those days are almost forgotten. Grants of private plots to farmers multiplied production, as people tend to take much better care of their own land allocations than communal lands. Better seeds, lots of fertilizer, and even greater amounts of manual labor alongside mechanical plows and harvesters have magnified crop yields.

The production of Chinese farms has mostly kept up with the country's rapid population growth and movement of people from rural areas to cities. On occasions when reduced harvests occur, the cause is usually a financial one. Farmers are tempted to plant crops that sell for higher prices, but the government attempts to reduce this risk by requiring them to produce a certain amount of grain and turn it over in order to keep their personal land allotment. Savvy farmers get around this rule by planting the more lucrative crops, using the proceeds to buy grain from government stores, and turning the newly purchased grain over to the government yet again to fulfill the requirement. Some joke that a good bit of China's wheat and rice travels back and forth from the country to city dozens of times before it is consumed.

That said, China does have to import grain products from every grain-producing area of the world to feed its booming population. When the United States tried to limit its soybean exports as part of the ongoing trade war, China found new suppliers within a month's time. While demand was met with a supply, this constituted a considerable hardship for Chinese consumers and American farmers alike, as it takes time to develop crops. This has been an object lesson for China: its leaders will be much more wary of becoming dependent on a single nation for a critical resource in the future.

The third of China's four new wonders is the modernization of its science and industry. This has transformed not only China, but the world as well. In a very short period of time, China has been transformed from a poor, agrarian nation that had to import almost everything it consumed to the number-one trading nation in the world, ranking at the top in almost every industrial arena.

One of China's dams, the massive Three Gorges, produces more electricity than any other in the world. Chinese cities once were lit only by candles, the moon, and stars at night, but now they gleam continuously. In fact, China's demand for electricity is so great that a new nuclear power plant comes online nearly every year. As you travel west, hundreds of thousands of wind turbines and vast solar farms serve as alternate sources. Unfortunately, this still doesn't meet demand, so hundreds of coal-fired plants continue to pollute the air.

All of this development—infrastructure, dams, railroads, and skyscrapers—would not be possible without vast amounts of Chinese steel, aluminum, and concrete. China has some of the largest and most modern plants in the world, producing so much of these commodities that they are able to meet domestic demand and also supply the rest of the world. Because most other industrialized nations have not invested as heavily in new technologies that allow for increased production, these Chinese exports tend to undercut prices in world markets—a major source of friction in foreign relations.

In 1985, the first private Chinese citizen bought a car. It was such a sensation that it made the front page of newspapers all over China. Today, the Chinese are the number-one consumers of new cars in the world. While all major international automakers have factories in China (and of course, there are unique Chinese automakers as well), domestic production is not sufficient to meet domestic demand.

China is also the number-one importer of foreign cars. The American automobile industry is particularly dependent on China. In Charleston, South Carolina, where I live, container ships full of locally produced BMWs, Mercedes, and Volvos set sail for China every day.

Back in 1985, only a few Chinese container ships arrived in Charleston's harbor each month, and those that did contained mostly soybeans. Today, countless ships unload Chinese-man-ufactured goods in that same harbor every day.

The China I visited in 1979 was much the same as other Third World countries I've lived and worked in, such as India and Pakistan. For the most part, power was generated by hu-man and animal effort. The planes, trains, cars, and trucks in use were all imported, and most were decrepit leftovers from China's warm relationship with the Soviets in the 1950s. There were few manufacturing plants with industrial machines, and the ones that were in operation had second-hand textile ma-chinery imported from places like my hometown, Rock Hill, South Carolina. The rest were factories that made products by hand.

So now, on to China's fourth new wonder: its role as a world power.

During the first thirty-five of my forty years in China, I watched in amazement as a mostly agrarian nation transformed into one of the leading countries in the world—and in many aspects, the leader. China now produces beyond the limits of its own do-mestic demand and is a major world exporter of all things me-chanical. Its entry into world markets has impacted the price of almost everything.

This pattern also exists in most areas of commercial goods. Chinese businesses first work to meet their domestic demand and then use that production capacity to become a major par-ticipant on the world market. I've heard many Chinese people remark that while it took more than two hundred years for the West to transform from an agrarian to an industrial society, China did it in only thirty-five.

During the Cultural Revolution, few foreign ships came and went from China's harbors except some containing Canadian grain, and most of the country's mills and plants were often destroyed. Today, China's harbors are so crowded that offshore stations have been built to load and unload container ships and get them back out to sea in hours, rather than days. Under its 152-country Belt and Road Initiative, China is building ports all over the world and rail and road connections all over Asia and Europe.

———————

Chinese children begin their English instruction in preschool. They are proficient by the time they are ready for university, whether they study in China or elsewhere in the world. Today, more than one million Chinese students are studying abroad, with the largest group in America. As soon as they return to China, they go right to work, and many have two jobs upon their return. For example, a woman might have a first job as an engineer and a second as an on-site instructor for other engineers.

———————

Early on in the Great Modernization, joint ventures with foreign multinational corporations (MNCs) were very popular. Many started as 100 percent foreign owned, but with each year, the percentage of its Chinese ownership increased. The benefits were obvious: foreign companies had access to huge pools of good workers at a fraction of what they would cost in developed nations, and that workforce was hungry to learn and willing to work hard. China was open to all types of ownership configurations. Some businesses began as with partial domestic ownership, with profit sharing, and those few that were totally foreign owned were taxed at higher rates.

Many workers were sent to developed nations to learn how to use and maintain machinery, and in some cases, to copy them. Many businesses purchased machines with the express intent of disassembling them and figuring out how to duplicate the machinery, piece by piece, in China. MNCs often complain about stolen technology, but few of them win their disputes.

Many nations in southern and southeastern Asia have been referred to of late as "mini dragons." They've also developed at remarkable rates, but China is the largest dragon of them all. It has transformed into a developed country full of well-educated people, which has shifted China from a position as a minor act on the world stage to one of the two largest economic actors on earth.

Given this change, nations in the region must resist needless trade wars. So far, cooperation has been good, due in large part to China's major investments in other countries. China has also avoided major military engagements, but its increasing naval power has made many of its neighbors nervous. These nations have long counted on the United States and its allies to maintain a balance of military power in the region, but America's gradual withdrawal from the area has left them feeling very vulnerable. The U.S. government's recent willingness to start trade wars and underestimate how quickly they can escalate hasn't helped.

The danger has increased dramatically with China's new leadership, which stresses ideology over development. Throughout the Great Modernization, the message was "cooperate and prosper." Now, it's "cooperate or else." China's international interests are moving above and beyond the economic power it exerts on other nations in its region, and that makes the whole world nervous.

China has always judged its importance, and the importance of other nations, by its own standards. For years, America has been number one, but developments that have occurred over the last two years have changed the Chinese view of America. They now see us as standing alone, while before they viewed America as the leader of a large group of developed nations.

And status is important in China. The Chinese are amazed, for example, that the United States has begun to treat Russia as an equal and has even appeared to give deference to Russia. Recent events in which Saudi Arabia and North Korea have gotten the better of America have led to more shock and consternation. The Chinese consider all three of these countries to be failed nation-states unworthy of the attention or concern of a major state. I've been asked time and again why the U.S. would even think of considering these nations as being important.

For example, the Chinese were in disbelief when the United States picked China's historic enemy and—increasingly so— puppet state of Vietnam as the location for a major meeting with North Korea's leader. In China, the opinion goes that small states should always pay deference to more powerful states, who are expected to host the lesser states. To them, nations like Russia, Saudi Arabia, North Korea, and Vietnam should come to America and pay homage, and not the other way around.

A full discussion of the strengths and weaknesses of the modern Chinese economy would require another book, but one significant issue is worth noting here. China has based its economy on a world with lots of free trade, and many of its products are dependent on components made in other nations. As a result, increases in regulation or duties can pose great danger to China's supply chain. Thinking and planning on a long-run timetable has served China well up until recently, but it has also rendered China vulnerable in times of rapid economic change.

The country relies on imports for most of its basic food needs, for example. A long-term dependence on America for some of its agricultural products has made it very hard for China to quickly find new suppliers in this time of tariffs, as planting and harvesting crops takes time. Nations like Canada and Brazil can step in to fill these needs, but not overnight.

Adjustment to rapid change requires expertise, so under its new leadership, China is very vulnerable to rapid international change. The country's large and well-educated population is a great source of strength, of course, but a population numbered in excess of a billion also makes responding to rapid change a challenge.

While China may be left confused about America's future role on the world stage, they know with certainty that they are one of the two most powerful states in the world, and increasingly, many Chinese have come to believe that China is the number one nation in the world. Those who think otherwise do so not because of what America has or hasn't done, but instead because of recent changes in China.

I wish I could stop right here, but major developments in China as well as the United States over the last few years have made things quite a bit more worrisome. Forty years ago, when the practical group under Deng Xiaoping gained control, the professionals who ran every element of Chinese society were cross-trained in every area—even the Chinese government was run by professionals, and the Communist Party itself ended up relegated to a small role in China's development. Clearly, through all that time, the important people were the professional managers, rather than the Party people. But ignoring the Party all those years had a cost: it left the door wide open for Xi Jinping to rise to power.

Few people cared about the Party until Xi and his people took over. The Party leadership was set up to change every ten years, and after the first five years of the leadership term, the Party picked the person who would rule after the current chairman's term was over. After Deng and the professionals Deng had hand-picked had finished their terms, the Party people came back under the leadership of Hu Jintao. Hu was followed by Xi—a firm believer in absolute Party control. Xi got the Party Congress to name him Chairman of the Party, head of the government, and head of the military for life. Xi thinks of himself as the new Mao, and he believes that his ideology should rule all areas of life in China.

So far, the results of this change have been mixed. Xi wants all Chinese to not only to be alike but also to think the same way. The Party has aggressive, forward-looking plans with names like "2025" and "Belt and Road Initiative" that have caused conflicts in minority areas. The fallout from these conflicts has been the arrest and forced labor of more than 100,000 people. Xi has removed books by foreign authors from colleges and universities, considering them to be nothing more than "intellectual pollution." He has also collected his sayings into a little book, just as Mao did.

Xi has surrounded himself with yes-people who back him 100 percent. These people are often referred to as "princelings" because they all have powerful and rich fathers. He also relies on a large team of spies—about sixty of them among every thousand Chinese citizens—to root out any pro-Deng loyalists.

Leadership roles in business, industry, government, and education that were previously filled by trained professionals are now staffed with Party officials trained only in the Party line, with little knowledge of the institutions they've taken over (even going so far as to make up fake curricula vitae for the officials and publish them in the newspapers). The experts were unilaterally removed and replaced with Party officials with no training or practical experience. Those skilled professionals who do still remain in place must now answer to Party officials in top decision-making positions.

Most observers have credited China's current business slump to natural market cycles. They may be right, but I believe that running a country based on an ideology is quite impractical. Every sector of Chinese society needs well-trained, experienced people at the top, and without them, business will suffer.

Add to this the trade war between China and the United States, which should never have happened. Most Chinese blame America, maybe because they have to, but it seems to me that the actions both nations have taken reveal how little the present leaders know about each other and about the world. It's very dangerous for leaders of two superpowers to ignore practical advice and make judgments based on their own myopic and limited ideologies. Doing so may work for manipulating their own populations, but it's a recipe for failure on the world stage.

In early 2020, the COVID-19 coronavirus pandemic shined a light on new and complicating aspects of China's integration into the global economic system. The resulting quarantines stopped production and shipment worldwide of high-tech products, including iPhones, as vital components of most electronic devices are made in China. Because China is the major producer of surgical face masks, the pandemic spurred a worldwide shortage. During the early months of the pandemic, China itself became the consumer of most of these products, leaving none to be exported.

This reveals another weakness in China's political system: leaving major problems to be solved by Party decision makers—problems that are best left to professionals—will ultimately lead to disaster. My friends have told me that Dr. Li Wenliang, the doctor who discovered the virus and later died from it, probably succumbed because he was under arrest for alerting others about the illness. Xi himself went into hiding for two weeks during the height of the crisis—leading many to believe that he disappeared because of his own fears of the virus.

I firmly believe that ideologies are merely simplified concepts of reality that are suitable only for manipulating ignorant people. They're a terrible way to run a country, and a worse and even dangerous way to run a nation's foreign policy. Neither the United States nor China came this far and developed this much as a result of having untrained leaders with no understanding of or interest in learning how their nations reached their levels of power and economic strength.

Several recent books focused on the new Chinese super-state have foretold of its coming ascension to world domination. Still others claim the so-called American Era will continue to be the status quo in the future. But unless educated, experienced leadership emerges in both countries, I fear that their intertwined futures will be of full of danger—to themselves, each other, and the world.

Acknowledgments

I THANK MY LATE WIFE JANET, MY DAUGHTER MARION, and my sons Melford III and John Lytle for being good sports while I traveled and worked in China. They were adventurous enough to accompany me to Shanghai in 1985 to live, work, and study for the academic year; later, my children worked for years in China on their own. No one could have a better family.

My gratitude goes to my late aunt and uncle Mary O. and Ed Rice who lived in China in the 1920s and 1930s building girls' schools and hospitals. They shared their experiences and their love for China with me when I lived with them in Pakistan in 1960—thus sparking my lifelong interest in China.

As an undergraduate at Wofford College, I was privileged to study Confucius under Vincent Miller, an Ezra Pound expert, and Chinese art specialist Constance Armitage, one of the first people to explore the Buddhist caves in Western China.

At American University, I was fortunate to study with Lord and Lady Lindsay, who lived for eight years with Mao in Yan'an, and with Carl C. Taylor, an expert on Third World village development.

I also extend my thanks to the Fulbright Program and to Indira Gandhi, for supporting my study of village development in India.

Joe Lanford in Rock Hill was the brains behind two development corporations I chaired, and he deserves most of the credit for their success.

I am thankful to the administration and faculty of Shanghai International Studies University for making SISU my second home during my years in China, and also for welcoming my family in 1985 and the other years they spent teaching there. My life is richer for all of my relationships with friends and colleagues at SISU, including my graduate students who were faculty at twenty separate universities in China. They helped me better understand China's diversity.

I thank the Ministry of Education and SISU International Press for publishing my three university textbooks.

I could not have accomplished what I did without awards from the Fulbright Program to teach and study in Shanghai and to lead four Fulbright groups of university professors to study various developmental subjects in China. I am also indebted to the United States Departments of State and Education for supporting my lecture tours.

I thank Winthrop University, my academic home for fifty years, for granting me the time I needed to support my interest and love of China.

Last, but not least, I thank my wife, Pat Wolman, for putting up with me while I wrote this book.

About the Author

Dr. Melford Wilson holds a B.A. from Wofford College, a M.A. in Asian Studies, and a Ph.D. in International Relations from the American University. A Distinguished Professor and Vice President at Winthrop University, he also holds a Key to the City of Shanghai.

Dr. Wilson is an Honorary Distinguished Professor at Shanghai International Studies University. He has been a visiting lecturer for the State Department, and he has authored four books.

Dr. Wilson is also the recipient of five Fulbright awards. He has worked in the U.S., India, U.A.E., China, Pakistan, and Japan, and he now lives in Charleston and Rock Hill, South Carolina.

Made in the USA
Columbia, SC
28 October 2020